P. Grunding / M. Bachmann

WORLD ANABOLIC REVIEW

1996

M. B. MUSCLE BOOKS

Important Notice:

This book is not intended to be a guideline for the taking of anabolic/androgenic steroids or other drugs. Neither the publisher nor the authors advocates, encourages or endorses the use of anabolic/androgenic steroids or other pharmaceuticals in sports. All subjects discussed in this book serve as general information only. The descriptions made are not medical recommendations but, for the most part, are based on empirical values. We explicitly disapprove of the illegal purchase and possession of (foreign) prescription drugs. Improper and unqualified use of these drugs can cause harmful side effects. Every athlete who intends to take them should always consult a qualified physician. Principally, we disapprove of the administration of pharmaceuticals to minors to improve their athletic performance. WE DO NOT ASSUME LIABILITY FOR THE APPLICATION OF THE INFORMATION INCLUDED IN THIS BOOK.

CONTENT

PREFACE

The present work is in clear contrast to previously published books on the subject of "Anabolic Steroids." It tries to address all athletes, from the curious up to the ambitious athletes in competition, who already have some experience with steroids. To provide this group with necessary and interesting information, completely unconventional methods have been used.

The reader will get a current and almost complete overall view of the steroid compounds that are used in sports and are commercially available. Detailed configurations of these drugs help one to understand their different characteristics and effects. To cope with the problem of the black market and its numerous fake steroids, this book includes more than 500 photos depicting current, original steroids and their fakes. The clinically-oriented features are integrated with other important factors such as workout and nutrition. The book concludes by conveying a general and basic knowledge of steroids. In order to contribute to the understanding of this treatise, the use of technical and medical-academic language has been avoided, since it would only confuse the reader.

The objective of this book is to analytically present the current situation of steroids in bodybuilding, and attempt to make the entire subject of anabolics understandable. On one hand, educated athletes will be able to make the right choices; and, on the other hand, the treatise will contribute to solving the undoubtedly existing problem of anabolics. The publisher and authors, at this time, would like to emphasize once again that anabolic/androgenic steroids must never be taken without the supervision of a physician.

THE SIGNIFICANCE AND FUNCTION OF TESTOSTERONE

Although we tried hard not to give this book too theoretical or scientific an appearance so that it would avoid looking like a biology textbook but rather be a useful source of information for the intake of pharmaceutical compounds, we would like to begin with an exception. Since testosterone is the basis of almost all anabolic/androgenic steroids every athlete should have a certain basic knowledge of this hormone. Most of the information on testosterone given in this chapter, even in a more or less altered form, is also valid for anabolic/androgenic steroids. Those of you who carefully read this short, introductory chapter will better understand the many characteristics of the steroids discussed further on in this book.

Testosterone is the most important representative of the male sex hormones, also called androgens. The body uses cholesterol as a basis for the development of this hormone group. The androgens are produced by the Leydig's cells in the male gonads (testes). The final product is testosterone which fulfills three functions in the organism:

1.) The development of secondary male sex characteristics (increased growth of body hair, beard growth, deep voice, increased production of sebaceous glands, development of the penis, aggressiveness, sexual behavior, libido, etc.) and the maturation of sperm. These aspects are also called the androgenic functions of testosterone. Men distinguish themselves from women by the amount of testosterone produced daily. Men produce between 4 and10 mg of testosterone daily while women produce only 0.15 - 0.4 mg/day (only about 1/25th of the male's).

2.) Promotion of the protein biosynthesis: Responsible for this process are the highly anabolic characteristics of testosterone. Accelerated muscle buildup, increased formation of red blood cells, faster regeneration, and a shorter recovery time after injuries or illness are achieved. The entire metabolism is stimulated, and the burning of bodyfat is activated.

3.) Inhibition of the gonadal regulating cycle: This includes the hypothalamohypophysial testicular axis which regulates the amount of testosterone produced in the organism. If the testosterone concentration in the blood is high, the testes will signal the hypothalamus to release less LHRH (leutenizing hormone releasing hormone). Thus the hypophysis releases less gonadotropin LH (leutenizing hormone) and FSH (follic stimulating hormone). Consequently, the Leydig's cells in the testes reduce the production of testosterone.

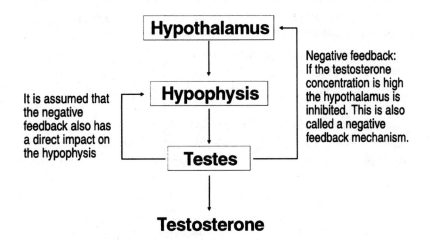

It is interesting to note that the female sex hormone estradiol also has a distinct effect on the gonadal regulating cycle. Small amounts of this hormone already have an inhibiting effect on the hypothalamus which, as we have seen, results in a reduced testosterone production by the testes. This characteristic becomes particulary important when bodybuilders use steroids that easily convert into estrogen. In 1935, researchers for the first time isolated testosterone from the testes of bulls and manufactured it in crystalline form. During the 1940's, injectable testosterone was produced in larger quantities in Europe to accelerate the regenerating process of the undernourished, particularly the prisoners of war. During this time testosterone was probably also administered to German soldiers to increase their aggressiveness. By the end of that decade Russian weightlifters discovered the performance-enhancing characteristics of exogenous testosterone, which could be seen by continuously broken world records of that time.

GENERAL INFORMATION ON STEROIDS

Based on the current situation, almost everyone connects the word "steroids" with anabolic steroids, which to the layman is better known under the name of "anabolics." It is often forgotten, however, that the name "steroids" is only the generic term for various steroid hormones. Their representatives are the suprarenal cortical hormones (gluco- and mineralcorticoids), the female sex hormones (estrogen and gestagen), as well as the male sex hormones (androgens). In this book we will look exclusively at the last version of the hormones, of which testosterone is the most important representative. The reader has already been introduced to it in the previous chapter. When the term "steroids" is used on the following pages, we will be referring to the group of anabolic/androgenic steroids.

Anabolic/androgenic steroids are synthetically manufactured compounds which are similar to the natural male androgen, testosterone. They are therefore defined as synthetic derivatives of testosterone. The main reason for their original development was the intention to produce a product which would include the highly anabolic effect of testosterone while, at the same time, exclude the negative aspects of the pronounced androgenic components. "Great efforts were made to develop a pure anabolic without androgenic 'side effects' " (Kochakian 1976; Krüskemper 1965). (Quotation from *Doping - verbotene Arzneimittel im Sport*, page 51, Dirk Clasing, Manfred Donike, u.a.). To achieve this goal various changes to the steroid molecule were made. The newly- developed steroids distinguished themselves through either a decreased effect with a weaker anabolic and androgenic effect or with an increased effectiveness, after both the anabolic and androgenic components had been increased. Structural changes in some steroids resulted in an even higher androgyny but reduced the anabolic activity. This partly explains the considerable differences in effect, effectiveness, and side effects of common steroids. Manufacturing a pure anabolic, i.e. complete separation of anabolic and androgenic effect, however, was not achieved. A so-called anabolic steroid (anabolic), therefore, also has a certain androgenic effect and, correspondingly, an androgenic steroid (androgen) also has anabolic characteristics.

One would therefore assume that for a fast buildup of strength and muscle mass a predominantly anabolic steroid with only minimal androgyny should be selected, correct? Unfortunately not, because the name "anabolic steroid" does not tell us about the strength of the anabolic effect but only indicates that the anabolic/androgenic relationship in the original steroid, testosterone, was shifted. In order to determine this relationship and thus be able to classify a steroid as an anabolic or an androgenic, testosterone serves as a parameter. Steroids which are less androgenic are called anabolic steroids, while steroids which are equally or even more androgenic, are called androgenic steroids. Where then lies the problem? Very simple: The reduction of the androgenic effect goes hand in hand with a reduction of anabolic activity so that an anabolic, no doubt, is less androgenic than testosterone but also much less anabolic, thus causing a loss in effect. When reading the following chapters the reader will notice that the so-called "mass steroids" come exclusively from the group of androgenic steroids and are both highly androgenic and highly anabolic. "...the best androgen, namely testosterone, is again the most important anabolic in a man." (from *Doping - verbotene Arzneimittel im Sport*, Dirk Clasing, Manfred Donike et al). The athlete is in a dilemma now, since the androgenic steroids are not only more effective but unfortunately also more harmful. From this we can derive a certain rule: the more effective a steroid, the more androgenic its substance and the more harmful it is for the organism.

The often-heard and widely-read reproach that anabolic steroids cause very severe and, in part, irreparable damage can therefore not be fully accepted. It is true that mainly androgenic steroids are responsible for most side effects. A generalization such as, for example, "steroids cause liver damage" is nonsense since there are different types of steroids.

The first anabolic/androgenic steroids were officially available during the 1950's. Only a decade later, most of today's available compounds were already on the market. In the meantime, only few new steroids have been developed, so these compounds can be called relatively old drugs. There were certainly various movements and changes in the field of steroids, however. Many steroids were removed from the market; some were later reintroduced in other countries under a generic name; a few new steroids were added during the 1980's but the great, pioneering developments did not take place. Nevertheless steroids are still the most effective method of improving athletic performance. During the 1950's steroids were still being introduced to the sports world. An important role in the developing interaction between steroids and sports was played by the introduction of Dianabol, an oral steroid developed in 1956 by the team physician of the American weightlifters, Dr. John Ziegler, in collaboration with the pharmaceutical manufacturer CIBA. "This compound and its successor were first extremely popular among heavy-weight athletes during the late 1950's and later used in many other sports disciplines. An almost inflationary increase was brought about by the bodybuilding movement of the 1960's and 1970's. To an increased extent these substances were used by female athletes as well. In 1974 the IOC (International Olympic Committee) passed a resolution to add anabolics to the doping list. The Olympic Games in Montreal in 1976 were the first that tested for anabolics." (from *Doping im Sport*, by Sehling, Pollert, Hackfort). Today's situation is marked by an enormous diffusion of these drugs, as Melvin H. Williams confirms in his book *Records through Doping*: "In the meantime, anabolic steroids are a group of drugs whose consumption by athletes has reached epidemic proportions. There are estimates that more than one million Americans are taking anabolic steroids including many male and female athletes of all age groups, from the mature professional athlete to the student in puberty. Since steroids must be prescribed by a physician, a flourishing black market has developed with sales of more than 100 million dollars per year." The estimated sales for the U.S. are certainly much too low and therefore this figure more likely reflects sales in a European country such as Germany. One of the reasons for the increased use of anabolic/androgenic steroids is the increasing popularity of bodybuilding. "Steroid use has increased in direct proportion to the popularity of bodybuilding. As bodybuilding came out of an obscure subculture in the 1970's, so did steroids. In the 1980's, as bodybuilding entered the mainstream, so did steroids. Later that decade, as bodybuilding became popular in the high schools, so did steroid use." (*Anabolic Reference Guide*, 6th Issue, 1991, W.N. Phillips). As long as a muscular body is portrayed as desirable and no effective "natural substitute" is found to replace anabolic/androgenic steroids, it is impossible to dissuade athletes from taking pharmaceutical products. The recent popularity of Clenbuterol shows that athletes prefer products which help them achieve their goals faster. If growth hormones were available at a reasonable price they would be as widespread as steroids.

Nevertheless, steroids are not a wonder drug since their effectiveness depends on external factors such as workout, nutrition, attitude, and the genetic predisposition of the individual. This last point, in particular, will determine how the individual responds to the intake of anabolic/androgenic steroids and how the organism copes with their side effects.

THE EFFECT OF STEROIDS

The physiology of anabolic/androgenic steroids is a very complex subject. It is almost impossible to give exact configurations of all biochemical processes which take place in the body during the intake of steroids. Still, we would like to give the reader a general, simplified overview of these processes since a certain prior knowledge and understanding is of fundamental importance. Since athletes are exclusively interested in the performance-enhancing characteristics of steroids, this chapter will stress their effects on the muscle cell.

Steroids are either injected intramuscularly or taken orally. When injected, the substance directly enters the bloodstream while tablets, taken orally, reach the liver through the gastrointestinal tract. Here the substance is either completely or partially destroyed or sent into the bloodstream in its original form. The administered steroid is now present in the blood in the form of numerous steroid molecules which, through blood circulation, move around the entire body. Each steroid molecule contains a certain message or certain information which it tries to transmit to specific body cells. The cells designated for this purpose possess various receptor types on their membranes. One of these is the steroid receptor which, for example, is present in large amounts at the muscle cell. The form and size of these steroid receptors match those of the steroid molecules. Receptor and molecule show a high affinity, comparable to a key that fits the right lock. The steroid receptor absorbs the matching molecule while rejecting thousands of other molecules which do not fit in size and shape. The same is also true for the many other receptor types which cannot work with the steroid molecule since they are waiting for different molecules. Only when the steroid receptor and the steroid molecule have formed a complex can the molecule transmit its message to the muscle cell. During this process it must be observed that the steroid molecules in the bloodstream, to a large extent, should have already previously bonded with binding proteins (SHBG = sex hormone binding globulin). Simplified, this means that usually close to 98% of the steroid molecules in the blood are bonded with binding proteins while only 2% of the steroid molecules are present in a free and unbonded state. The latter form is also called the active steroid molecules since only these can form the steroid receptor complex. The steroid molecules bonded to SHBG are called the passive steroid molecules since, at this time and in this condition, they cannot be absorbed by the muscle cell, and are therefore ineffective. It should be mentioned that the SHBG bonding behavior of some steroids is slightly different, so that the percentage figures can slightly differ.

The formed steroid receptor complex now travels to the cell nucleus where it bonds to certain sequences on the nucleic acid sections of DNA (desoxy ribonuclein acid). Now a transcription takes place, where a template of the DNA is made. The resulting MRNA (messenger ribonuclein acid) leaves the cell nucleus and bonds with the RNA in the cytoplasm (liquid cell part) where, through translation, an increased protein synthesis takes place. When combined with an intense weightlifting workout, an increase in the diameter of the muscle cell occurs (muscular hypertrophy). Although the increased protein synthesis is considered to be the most important effect of steroids on the muscle cell, the steroid molecules also forward other information which is important for athletes. There is increased evidence that steroids have a high anticatabolic effect. Thus, the rate at which protein in the muscle cell is broken down, is reduced. The steroid molecules occupy the cortisone receptors on the membrane of the muscle cell and block them. Therefore, the cortisone produced by the body, a highly catabolic (reducing) hormone, cannot become effective and the muscle cell does not release protein.

Another advantage of steroids is that they increase the phosphocreatine synthesis (CP) in the muscle cell. CP is of crucial importance during the restoration of ATP (adenosine triphosphate). ATP is required for all muscle contractions since it is the fuel the muscle needs to enable it to work. ATP is stored in the muscle cell and is changed into ADP (adenosine diphosphate) when needed. This process releases energy, allowing the muscle to contract. To change ADP back to ATP, phosphocreatine (CP) is needed. The more CP that is available, the faster ADP can be reconverted and the more ATP is thus available to the muscle. In practice, this means that the muscle becomes stronger but not larger. Those of you who have already tried the steroid oxandrolone will have noticed that this compound, for the most part results in a strength gain. This is made possible since oxandrolone highly increases the phosphocreatine synthesis in the muscle cell. Another factor which benefits the athlete is that steroids store more carbohydrates in the muscle cell in form of glycogen. This process, together with a higher liquid retention which takes place simultaneously, results in a higher muscle volume, improved endurance, and more strength. Steroids also reduce the release of endogenous insulin since the steroids allow the muscle cell to absorb nutrients (carbohydrates in the form of glucose and protein in the form of amino-acids) by depending less on the insulin. This helps the athlete in lowering the bodyfat content and hardening the muscles since insulin, in addition to being a highly anabolic hormone, also converts glucose into glycerol and then into triglyceride, thus stimulating the growth of fat cells.

Those of you who have already taken steroids know that during training, a considerably improved pump effect in the respective muscles takes place, which by insiders is called "steroid pump." The reason for this is that steroids increase the blood volume and the amount of red blood cells in the body. The muscle has a larger appearance and becomes more vascular. In addition to these advantages, the increased blood flow allows for a greater transport of nutrients to the muscle cells. In particular, the highly androgenic steroids such as Dianabol, Testosterone, and most of all, Anadrol, cause a significant increase in the blood volume which sometimes results in an extreme, even painful, pump effect during workout. The improved oxygen supply which results at the same time is often turned into an advantage by medium and long distance runners.

After the steroid receptor complex has done its job in the cell nucleus, the steroid molecule returns to the blood system and can either be reused briefly for the same purpose or changed into a weaker, ineffective molecule, which is then excreted through the urine. Not all steroid molecules in the plasma (fluid portion of the blood) are, after exogenous administration, either directly bound to SHBG or present as free, active molecules. A certain portion can be immediately metabolized and eliminated by the body. Another part, however, can be converted into the female sex hormone estrogen. This is an aromatizing process and the term, at first, seems difficult to understand. When taking a closer look at the structure of the male sex hormone testosterone and the female hormone estradiol it is noticed that both structures are quite similar. The body can easily make the necessary structural changes on the molecule by using certain enzymes. Some steroid molecules, like parts of endogenous and exogenous testosterone, convert into dihydrotestosterone (DHT). Although DHT shows a higher affinity to the receptors of the muscle cell than testosterone does —leading some experts believe that DHT is more effective than testosterone— it also has a higher bonding potential with the receptors of sebaceous glands and hair follicles. It is interesting to note that DHT cannot be converted into estrogen. In the end, all these molecules are excreted in the urine.

We are aware that, while reading this chapter, some questions will remain unanswered and, due to the large amount of complex information, some of it might not be immediately clear and understandable. The athlete should, however, have gained a certain insight into the processes occurring in the body when steroids are taken so that the different characteristics and effects of the steroid compounds described in the following pages can be more easily understood.

DESCRIPTION OF THE INDIVIDUAL DRUGS

With this chapter we begin the practical guide section of this book. We have tried to make the following subject as complete as possible. Special attention has been paid to extensive and detailed descriptions of the anabolic/androgenic steroids and other pharmaceutical compounds used by athletes.

The drugs are listed in alphabetical order. Since every substance is readily available in various compounds we have selected the brand name for the heading. In a few instances the substance itself is classified alphabetically. The second line always gives the substance of the drug listed in the heading. Under the title "trade name" a variety of worldwide available compounds are given, each of which also contains the substance listed under the heading. In addition, in the following order are listed the quantity of the substance, the type of administration, the manufacturer's name, and the manufacturing country. Following, these compounds are discussed in detail. In order to complete the respective description, in most cases, the reader will find several photos of the described drugs. These are photos of original drugs only. Fake compounds will be discussed separately in one of the following chapters. The medications are not shown in actual size.

Explanations:

(o.c.)	Out of commerce/off the market
Tab.	Tablet
Cap.	Capsule
Amp.	Ampule
Inj.	Injection
Drg.	Dragee
100mg/ml	100 mg substance contained in one milliliter of injection liquid
I.U.	International Units
mcg	Microgram (1/1,000 milligram; 1/1,000,000 gram)
A	Austria
AUS	Australia
B	Belgium
BG	Bulgaria
CH	Switzerland
CZ	(Former) Czech Republic
G	Germany
DK	Denmark
ES	Spain
FI	Finland
FR	France
GB	Great Britain
GR	Greece
HU	Hungary
I	Italy
NL	Netherlands
NO	Norway
PL	Poland
PT	Portugal
S	Sweden
TK	Turkey
YU	(Former) Yugoslavia
U.S.	United States of America

Indications concerning trade names and prices are current as of August 1995. Due to various factors changes in the future cannot be excluded.

ALDACTONE

Substance: spironolactone

Trade names

Aldactacine 40 comp	25 mg tab.;	Searle ES
Aldactone	25, 50, 100 mg tab;	Searle S, PT, FI, DK, ES, FR, CH, NL, U.S. Mexico, Panama, Guatemala,El Salvador, Honduras, Dom. Rep., Costa Rica Lepetit I, Galencia CZ Vianex GR
Aldactone	25, 50 mg drg.;	Boehringer G, A
Aldactone	100 mg cap.;	Boehringer G, A
Aldactone	100 mg tab.;	Searle GR, ES
Aldopur	50, 100 mg drg.;	Hormosan G
Aquareduct (o.c.)	50, 100 mg tab.;	Azupharma G
Deverol	50 mg tab.;	Waldheim A
Duraspiron	50, 100 mg tab.;	Durachemie G
Jenaspiron	50, 100 mg tab.;	Jenapharm G
Osyrol	50, 100 mg tab;	Hoechst G
Spiractone	25, 100 mg tab.;	Elvipi GR
Spiresis	25, 50, 100 mg tab.;	Lkefarmos FI
Spiridon	25, 100 mg tab.;	Orion FI
Spirix	25, 50, 100 mg tab.;	Benzon FI, NO; Nycomed DK
Spiroctan	25, 50 mg drg.;	Boehringer CH
Spiroctan	100 mg cap.;	Boehringer CH
Spirohexal	100 mg tab.;	Hexal Pharma A
Spirolang	25, 50, 100 mg cap.;	Sit I
Spirolone	25 mg tab.;	Berk CZ
Spiron	25, 100 mg tab.;	Ercopharm DK
Spirono-ISIS 50/100	50, 100 mg tab.;	ISIS Pharma G
Spironolacton dumex	50, 100 mg tab.;	Dumex NL
Spironolacton Heumann	50, 100 mg tab.;	Heumann G

Spironolacton mp	25, 50 mg, tab.;	MP NO
Spironolacton Stada	50, 100 mg tab.;	Stadapharm G (o.c.)
Spironolacton-ratiopharm(o.c.)	50, 100 mg. tab.;	ratiopharm G
Spironolactone scher	50, 75 mg tab.;	Scher FR
Spironolactone (o.c.)	50, 100 mg tab.;	Lederle U.S.
Spironolactone (o.c.)	50, 100 mg tab.;	Geneva U.S.
Spironolactone (o.c.)	50, 100 mg tab.;	Warner Chilcott U.S.
Spironolactone	25 mg tab.;	Mylan U.S.
Spironolactonum gf	25, 50, 100 mg tab.;	Gf NL
Spironolactonum pharbita	25, 50, 100 mg tab.;	Pharbita NL
Spironolakton Bota	25, 50, 100 mg tab.;	Bota S
Spironolakton Fermenta	50, 100 mg tab.;	Fermenta S
Spironolakton NM Parma	25, 50, 100 mg tab.;	NM Pharma S
Spiro-Tablinen (o.c.)	100 mg tab.;	Sanorana G
Spiro-Tablinen-Tabletten	100 mg tab.;	Wenig A
Verospiron	25 mg tab.;	Hormosan G
Verospiron	50, 100 mg cap.	Hormosan G
Verospiron	25 mg tab.;	Gedeon Richter HU, CZ

Remark: Internationally, numerous other compounds containing the substance spironolactone are available. Due to limited space they are not listed here.

Aldactone is a diuretic and belongs to the subgroup of potassium-sparing diuretics. Aldactone is an aldosterone antagonist. It influences the body's own hormone, aldosterone, which accelerates the excretion of potassium and reduces the excretion of sodium and water. Simplified, aldosterone regulates the endogenous water household. The higher the aldosterone level, the more water is stored in the body. The use of Aldactone results in a significant reduction in the aldosterone level so that an increased excretion of sodium and water occurs while, at the same time, potassium is reabsorbed. This also explains why Aldactone is called a potassium-sparing diuretic since it does not cause a loss of potassium like thiazides and furosemides (lasix) do. Athletes must strictly observe that during the use of Aldactone no additional potassium is taken since this would cause a life-threatening increase in the serum potassium level. Potassium-sparing diuretics have relatively low diuretic effects so that Aldactone can be called a mild diuretic. It is interesting to note that Aldactone is also an antiandrogen since it reduces the androgen level. Female athletes take advantage of this characteristic by using it to mini-mize the virilization symptoms during steroid treatment or the symptoms after treatment. For this purpose Aldactone is normally taken daily for 10 to14 days, usually in a dose of 50 mg/day. In men this could cause problems since the relationship of the andro-gen level to the estrogen level changes in favor of the latter. Thus, common side effects in men include pain in the nipples and breast swelling (gynecomastia).

Bodybuilders use Aldactone almost exclusively during the last week before a competition. Since this causes neither a dramatic nor an immediately noticeable draining effect, it is usually taken over 5-6 days in a dosage of 2 tablets of 50 mg daily. Aldactone should not be used to expediently drain water at the last minute. Both male and female athletes take it. The side effects of potassium-saving diuret-ics are relatively low compared to thiazides and furosemides. The main problems in men consist of gynecomastia and possible impo-tence. Other side effects can be low blood pressure, muscle spasms, dizziness, gastrointestinal pain, vomiting, irregular pulse rate, and fatigue. It is important to note that there is no significant increase in the serum potassium level (see above).

Aldactone is a prescription drug availabe in American pharmacies. Aldactone by Boehringer Mannheim of Germany is often found on the black market. A package contains 50 dragees of 50 mg each and costs approx. $30. on the black market. The Mexican Aldactone by Searle can also frequently be found on the black market. The 25 mg tablets are of light-brown color, indented, and have a SEARLE im-print. The original package contains three strips, each with 10 tab-lets. There are currently no Aldactone fakes available.

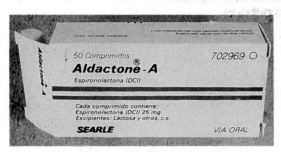

Aldactone–A with blister from Spain

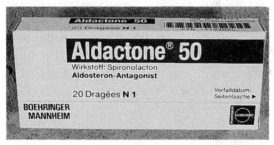

Aldactone 50 with blister from Germany

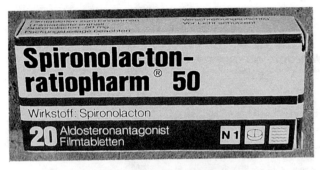

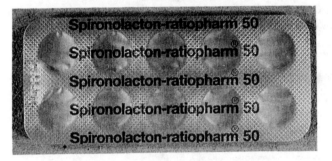

Spironolacton by ratiopharm/Germany

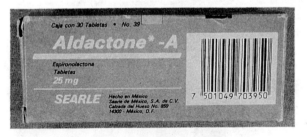

Aldactone-A with blister by Searle/Mexico

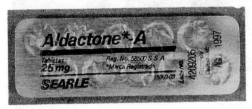

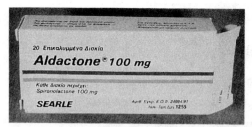

Aldactone 100mg from Greece

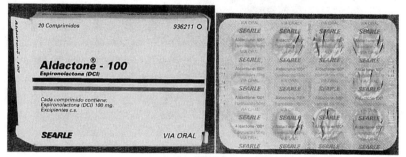

Aldactone-100 from Spain

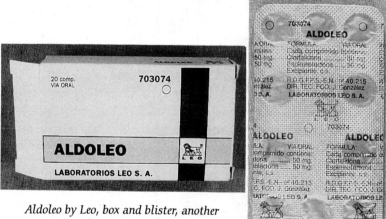

*Aldoleo by Leo, box and blister, another
spironolactone from Spain.*

ANABOLICUM VISTER

Substance: quinbolone

Trade names

Anabolicum Vister	10 mg cap.;	Parke Davis Italy
Anabolicum Vister	drops;	Parke Davis Italy

Anabolicum Vister is an oral steroid produced only in Italy. It is administered in an unusual form since it is either taken as a capsule or in drops. The latter type of administration is not used by athletes. In schools of medicine Anabolicum Vister is used primarily in treating of the elderly, in particular women after menopause, and for the treatment of general diseases and symptoms of old age. This is due to the fact that Anabolicum Vister is a very weak androgenic steroid which is well-tolerated. It has mainly an anabolic effect which stimulates the protein synthesis and has the welcome characteristic that it does not aromatize. It also causes only a low retention of water and salt. In addition, the substance is not 17-alpha alkalifying and consequently, not liver-toxic. However, all these positive characteristics make Anabolicum Vister a very weak steroid which does not help athletes achieve significant improvements. Women, older athletes, and steroid novices may gain some advantages while the more advanced will be disappointed by its effect. Men usually need very high doses in the range of 80-120 mg/day to feel anything at all, while some women react with a small muscle gain and a nice strength gain by taking only 30-40 mg/day. As mentioned earlier, the side effects are minimal and usually occur in persons taking high doses and showing a sensitivity to the androgenic residual effect. Thirty capsules come in a glass bottle with a screw cap, packaged in a matching box. Anabolicum Vister is rarely found on the black market since there are very few requests from athletes.

ANADROL 50

Substance: oxymetholone

Trade names

Anadrol 50	50 mg tab.;	Syntex U.S.
Anapolon 50	50 mg tab.;	Syntex GB
Anapolon	50 mg tab.;	Syntex BG
Anapolon (o.c.)	2.5 mg tab.;	Ibrahim TK
Anapolon	5 mg tab.;	Ibrahim TK
Anapolon	50 mg tab.;	Ibrahim TK
Anasteron (o.c.)	50 mg tab.;	Syntex GR, S
Dynasten (o.c.)	50 mg tab.;	Cilag PT
Hemogenin	50 mg tab.;	Syntex Brazil
Oxitosona 50 (o.c.)	50 mg tab.;	Syntex ES
Plenastril (o.c.)	50 mg tab.;	Grünenthal A; Proto-chemie CH
Roboral	50 mg tab.;	Abic Israel; Ramat-Gan Israel
Synasteron	50 mg tab.;	Sarva B

"Anadrol is the most effective oral steroid commercially available." (Daniel Duchaine, Underground Steroid Handbook 2)

"A diabolically strong drug. I find Anadrol too strong. If a person weighed more than 250 pounds he would probably know how to deal with it but I would not give it to anyone smaller who is interested in it." (From Vitasport no. 13, March 1988).

"It (Anadrol) was the most popular oral steroid used by American athletes in 1990." (W.N. Phillips, Anabolic Reference Guide, 6th Issue, 1992).

"Take Anadrol and gain 40 pounds of muscle in 8 weeks, then drop dead." (Cambridge Ergogenic Institute, Ultimate Steroid Manual).

The substance oxymetholone was introduced on the market by Syntex Company in 1960. It was produced by various manufacturers in different countries until the early 1990's and was easily available under its respective trade names (see list). In the meantime, however, the situation changed greatly and between 1991 and 1993 various compounds were taken off the market. Especially painful was the phase-out of Plenastril, which had been manufactured in Austria and Switzerland. It was very popular with athletes due to its good effect. Since a continued supply of the Spanish Oxitosona 50 was plentiful on the black market, this gap could be filled. When Syntex Latino, however, phased out Oxitosona 50 at the beginning of 1993, the situation aggravated. Hoarding by dealers and drastic price increases were the consequences. Currently, the original Oxitosona 50 is rarely found on the black market and consequently, it is expensive. The only original compounds which are still available in Europe are Anapolon 50 by Syntex England, Anapolon by Syntex Bulgaria, Anapolon by Ibrahim Turkey and Synasteron by Sarva Belgium. It is quite impossible to find an original American Anadrol 50. On the black market one almost exclusively finds the English Anapolon 50 and the Brasilian Hemogenin.

One hundred Anapolon tablets are sold in a small, grey plastic container with a white tear-off top. This container has the exact same size as a 35 mm photo-film case. The manufacturer supplies the plastic container in a matching box (see photo). Please note that this compound is sold without a package insert, so its absense is no reason to worry about the drug's authenticity. In England the user information is in the hands of the physician and is not enclosed with the product, as is usually the custom. The Anapolon tablets are indented on the bottom, and on the left of each breakage line the number "50" is imprinted. On the back, the manufacturer's name, Syntex, is imprinted. The price on the black market is approx. $150 - 250 for 100 tablets. Those who can still receive some of the remaining Spanish Oxitosona 50 pay $350 - 400 for a box with ten push-through strips of 10 tablets each. The tablets are indented on one side but have no imprint. Since there are many "Oxy"-fakes availabe the athlete must be very cautious and pay close attention that his product, especially the push-through strip, looks exactly like the one on the photo in this book. The original "Oxys" have their expiration date stamped into the box; fakes only have the expiration date printed on the box. Such fakes can be easily identified since there is a line code on the side of the box which cannot be torn off from the paper carton. With the originals there is usually a perforation punched around the line card, allowing it to be torn off. The Brasilian Hemogenin can be found more frequently on the American market. There are ten tablets in a push-through strip with the product name and the manufacturer printed in green on the back of the strip. Conspicuous are the diagonal print going from the lower left to the upper right and the intense reflection of the aluminum foil. The tablets are white, indented, and have no imprint. The Brasilian Sarsa-Syntex Company has packed each push-through strip individually in a green/white/red box fitting perfectly in form and size. Reference number, manufacturing information, and expiration date are visibly stamped on the lateral side of the box. Several fakes of this compound also exist.

Anadrol 50 is the strongest and, at the same time, also the most effective oral steroid. The compound has an extremely high androgenic effect which goes hand in hand with an extremely intense anabolic component. For this reason, dramatic gains in strength and muscle mass can be achieved in a very short time. An increase in body weight of 10 -15 pounds or more in only 14 days is not unusual. Water retention is considerable, so that the muscle diameter quickly increases and the user gets a massive appearance within record time. Since the muscle cell draws a lot of water, the entire muscle system of most athletes looks smooth, in part even puffy. Anadrol does not cause a qualitative muscle gain but rather a quantitative one which in the off-season is quite welcome. Anadrol "lubricates" the joints since water is stored there as well. On the one hand this is a factor in the enormous increase of strength and, on the other hand, it allows athletes with joint problems a painless workout. Powerlifters in the higher weight classes are sold on Anadrol. A strict diet, together with the simultaneous intake of Nolvadex and Proviron, can significantly reduce water retention so that a distinct increase in the solid muscles is possible. By taking Anadrol the athlete experiences an enormous "pump effect" during the workout in the exercised muscles. The blood volume in the body is significantly elevated causing a higher blood supply to the muscles during workout. Anadrol increases the number of red blood cells, allowing the muscle to absorb more oxygen. The muscle thus has a higher endurance and performance level. Consequently, the athlete can rely on great power and high strength even after several sets. Some bodybuilders report such an enormous and in part painful "pump" that they end their workout after only a few sets or work on another muscle. The often-mentioned "steroid pump" manifests itself to an extreme by the intake of Anadrol and during workout it gives the athlete a fantastic and satisfying sensation. The highly androgenic effect of Anadrol stimulates the regeneration of the body so that the often-feared "overtraining" is unlikely. The athlete often feels that only hours after a strenuous workout he is ready for more. Even if he works out six days a week he makes continued progress. Although Anadrol is not a steroid used in preparation for a competition, it does help more than any other steroid during dieting to maintain the muscle mass and to allow an intense workout. Many bodybuilders therefore use it up to about one week before a competition, solving the problem of water retention by taking antiestrogens and diuretics so that they will apppear bulky and hard when in the limelight.

As for the dosage, opinions differ. The manufacturer of the former Spanish Oxitosona 50 tablets, Syntex Latino, recommends a daily dosage of 0,5 - 2,5 mg per pounds of body weight. A bodybuilder weighing 200 pounds could therefore take up to 500 mg per day which corresponds to 10 tablets. These indications, however, are completely unrealistic, much too high, and could cause severe side effects. A dosage sufficient for any athlete would be 0,5 - 0,8 mg per pound of body weight/day. This corresponds to 1-4 tablets; i.e. 50-200 mg/day. Under no circumstances should an athlete take more than four tablets in any given day. We are of the opinion that a daily intake of three tablets should not be exceeded. Those of you who would like to try Anadrol 50 for the first time should begin with an intake of only one 50 mg tablet. After a few days or even better, after one week, the daily dosage can be increased to two tablets, one tablet each in the morning and evening, taken with meals. Athletes who are more advanced or weigh more than 220 pounds can increase the dosage to 150 mg/day in the third week. This dosage, however, should not be taken for periods longer than two to three weeks. Following, the dose should be reduced by one tablet every week. Since Anadrol 50 quickly saturates the receptors, its intake should not exceed six weeks. The dramatic mass buildup which often occurs shortly after administration rapidly decreases, so that either the dosage must be increased (which the athlete should avoid due to the considerable side effects) or, even better, another product should be used. Those who take Anadrol 50 for more than 5-6 weeks should be able to gain 20 - 25 pounds. These should be satisfying results and thus encourage the athlete to discontinue using the compound. After discontinuing Anadrol, it is important to continue steroid treatment with another compound since, otherwise, a drastic reduction takes place and the user, as is often observed, within a short period looks the same as before the treatment. No other anabolic/androgenic steroid causes such a fast and drastic loss in strength and mass as does Anadrol 50. A famous powerlifter once said: "When you urinate three times after discontinuing the product, you'll weigh 10 pounds less and lift 25 pounds less." For this reason far-sighted athletes continue their treatment with injectable testosterone such as Sustanon 250 or Testosterone enanthate for several weeks. Bodybuilders often combine Anadrol with Deca-Durabolin or Testosterone to build up strength and mass. A very effective stack which is also favored by professionals consists of Anadrol 100 mg+/day, Parabolon 228 mg+/week, and Sustanon 500 mg+/week. This stack quickly improves strength and mass but it is not suitable for and steroid novices. Anadrol 50 is not a steroid for novices and should only be used after the athlete has achieved a certain development or has had experience with various "weaker" compounds. Stories that the elite bodybuilder uses 8-10 or more Anadrol tablets daily belongs to the realm of fairy tales. It is rare that any ambitous competing bodybuilder can do without the support of 50 mg Oxymetholon tablets; however, taking 8, 10 or 12 tablets daily is more than the organism can handle. Anadrol 50 is to be taken seriously and the prevailing bodybuilder mentality "more is better" is out of place; that will be pointed out very clearly in the following paragraphs.

Anadrol 50 is unfortunately also the most harmful oral steroid. Its intake can cause many considerable side effects. Since it is 17-alpha alkylated it is very liver-toxic. Most users can expect certain pathological changes in their liver values after approximately one week. An increase in liver values of both the enzymes GOT and GPT, also called transaminases, often cannot be avoided. Elevated GOT and GPT values are indications of hepatitis, i.e. a liver infection. Those who discontinue oxymetholone will usually show normal values within two months. Longer intake and/or higher doses can cause a yellow discoloration of fingernails, eyes, or skin (jaundice). This is because oxymetholone induces an increase of biliburin in the liver, producing a bile pigment which causes the yellow discoloring of the skin. The liver enzyme gamma-GT also reacts sensitively to the oxymetholone, causing it to elevate. If high dosages of Anadrol 50 are taken over a long period, there is an increased risk that the described liver changes could end up damaging the liver. During the intake of Anadrol 50, the liver values, GOT, GPT, bilirubin, gamma-GT, and alkaline phosphatase (AP), as well as the LDH/HBDH quotient, should always be checked by a competent physician. Anadrol 50 (representing all oxymetholone-containing steroid products) is the only anabolic/androgenic steroid which was linked with liver cancer (see translation of package insert on Spanish Oxitosona 50).

The compound oxymetholone easily converts into estrogen. This causes signs of feminization (e.g. gynecomastia) and the already-mentioned water retention which in turn requires the intake of antiestrogens (e.g. Nolvadex and Proviron) and an increased use of diuretics (e.g. Lasix) before a competition. The increased water retention, in addition to the aesthetical problems, can be further detrimental since it may cause high blood pressure. In extreme cases the intake of an anti-hypertensive drug, e.g. Catapresan, may be necessary. Since a substantial amount of the compound converts into dihydrotestosterone (DHT) in the body, it is possible that, with a given disposition, severe acne and an increased hair loss can occur. Bodybuilders who experience a severe steroid acne caused by Anadrol can get this problem under control by using the prescription drug Accutane.

Other possible side effects may include headaches, nausea, vomiting, stomach aches, lack of appetite, insomnia, and diarrhea. The athlete can expect a feeling of "general indisposition" with the intake of Anadrol which is completely in contrast to Dianabol which conveys a "sense of well-being". This often creates a paradoxical situation since the athlete continues to become stronger and bulkier while, at the same time, he does not feel well. The increased aggressiveness is caused by the resulting high level of androgen and occurs mostly when large quantities of testosterone are "shot" simultaneously with the Anadrol. Anadrol is not a steroid for older athletes since they react more sensitively to possible side effects, and the risk of liver damage and prostate cancer increases. Since the drug is usually taken with a diet rich in calories and fat needed to build up mass, the cholesterol level and the LDL values might increase while the HDL values decrease. The body's own production of testosterone is considerably reduced since Anadrol has an inhibiting effect on the hypothalamus, which in turn completely reduces or stops the release of GnRH (gonadotropin releasing hormone). For this reason the intake of testosterone-stimulating compounds such as HCG and Clomid (see relative characteristics) is absolutely necessary to maintain the hormone production in the testes. When first taking Anadrol, many athletes report a considerable increase in their sexual desire which, however, decreases after a few weeks. Some athletes also report problems with the prostate gland during the use of Anadrol 50. A prostate hypertrophy is possible, in which the enlarged prostate complicates the release of urine through the urethra. A complete emptying of the bladder becomes more complicated, i.e. after urinating some urine still remains in the bladder, causing the athlete to feel a greater than usual urge to urinate, especially at night. When in the restroom, however, he has difficulty "releasing water." Those of you who take Anadol 50 regularly and/or over longer periods should, from time to time, have a physician examine the size of the prostate in order to be sure that there is no abnormal growth in the gland.

Anadrol 50 is not recommended for women since it causes many and, in part, irreversible virilizing symptoms such as acne, clitorial hypertrophy, deep voice, increased hair growth on the legs, beard growth, missed periods, increased libido, and hair loss. Anadrol is simply too strong for the female organism and accordingly, it is poorly tolerated. Some national and international competing female athletes, however, do take Anadol 50 during their "massbuilding phase" and achieve enormous progress. Women who do not want to give up the distinct performance-enhancing effect of Anadrol 50 but, at the same time, would like to reduce possible side effects caused by androgen, could consider taking half a tablet (25 mg) every two days, combined with a "mild" injectable anabolic steroid such as Primobolan Depot or Durabolin. Ultimately, the use of Anadrol 50 and its dosage are an expression of the female athlete's personal willingness to take risks. In schools of medicine Anadrol 50 is used in the treatment of bone marrow disorders and anemia with abnormal blood formation. (For further information on the substance oxymetholone please refer to the American translation of the original instructions of the Spanish Oxitosona 50 compound; see illustration).

OXITOSONA® - 50 — Oxymetholone Tablets

Characteristics
Oxymetholone is a steroid with very strong anabolic and androgenic effects. On patients with anemia it stimulates the production and urinary excretion of eritropoyetin due to the insufficiency of the bone marrow and in the case of anemia, it stimulates, in regular intervals, the eritopoyesis due to insufficient production of hemoglobin.

Composition
Each tablet contains:
50 mg Oxymetholone (D.C.I.), lactose, and other agents, c.s.

Application
Osteomyelitis, anemia with hematosis and mielofibrosis, bone marrow insufficiency due to intoxication (chlorbenzol, fenibutazon, D.D.T., chloramfenicol.)
Oxitosona-50 cannot replace any necessary additional treatment such as transfusions, adjustment of iron deficiency, folic acid, vitamin B12, or piridoxin therapies with antibiotics and the appropriate use of corticosteroids.

Dosage Instruction
Only to be taken under the supervision of a physician.
The recommended dosage for children and adults is between 1 and 5 mg per kg of body weight and per day and it can be reduced accordingly, depending on the development of the bone structure.
The result of treatment may not be immediate since the time of intake may be prolonged due to developments and characteristics of the recovery process. Generally, it is taken for 3-6 months unless discontinued earlier.
Some patients need the integration of therapy after discontinuing the product or even during the discontinuation process, in particular, if they suffer from innate transferable anemia.

Counterindications
(Oxitosona-50 must not be used in the following cases:)
Prostate cancer or breast cancer in men;
Pregnancy;
The effects of anabolic steroids on newborns are unknown and their use is therefore not recommended; nephritis; hypersensitivity to drugs; liver disease.

Precautions
Due to possible damaging effects of oxymetholone it is recommended that liver values be checked periodically.
In older women menstrual cycles might be missed. In this case treatment with high doses of progesterone is recommended to normalize the menstrual cycle. In some patients iron deficiency was noticed. A regular check of the blood's iron level is therefore recommended. In case of iron deficiency this mineral should be taken as a supplement. This drug should be used with caution on patients with heart, liver, or kidney disease. In cases of edemas they can usually be controlled by taking diuretics and/or by manual treatment. Treatment must be discontinued when symptoms of hypercalcemia appear.
Anabolic steroids can alter the blood sugar values. For this reason, diabetics should check their blood sugar and change the insulin and tablet dosage accordingly.
Treatment should be made with caution on patients with prostate dysfunction or hypertrophy.
This drug can also alter the cholesterol level. Administration of the drug should be done with caution on patients with vessel disorders, who have suffered a myocardial infarct, or who suffer from coronary artery disease. Therapy should be adjusted to the cholesterol level.
In rare cases long-term treatment can result in permanent liver damage and even death.
There is suspicion that long-term treatment whit this drug can cause liver cancer, liver peliosis, leukemia, and virilization in women.
This medicine contains lactose. In certain cases signs of incompatibility in children and young adults have been observed. The low amount of lactose is probably not sufficient to cause such incompatibilities. In case of diarrhea see your physician.

Warning
Do not use in sports.

Incompatibility
Anabolic steroids can increase the sensitivity to anticoagulants; in this case the dosage is to be reduced.

Side Effects
The already known side effects of anabolic hormones are accompanied by a high degree of effectiveness. Occasionally jaundice and an elevation of bilirubin, alcaliphosphate, and transaminase levels were noticed. These values go back to normal when treatment is discontinued. Virilization was noticed in children when an overdose of 1-2 mg per kg of body weight per day was administered. In men a reduction in the testes function was noticed.
Women can experience masculinization symptoms, deep voice, change in libido, and irregular menstrual cycles. Other side effects of the anabolic therapy include nausea, diarrhea, agitation, insomnia, trembling, cramps, and epiphysis in children. In rare cases liver intoxication, cholestasis in the liver, and hepatic coma may occur.
Changes in diagnosis may appear as well, e.g. changes in the metopion and thyroid function, electrolytical changes, changes in cholesterol level, coagulation changes, and an increased creatine excretion.

Intoxication and Treatment
The intentional or unintentional overdose could result in hydroelectrolytical dysfunctions and liver intoxication in sensitive patients. Treatment consists of pumping the stomach while simultaneously engaging in a symptomatic therapy.

Packaging
Packages of 100 tablets of 50 mg Oxymetholone.

MUST BE PRESCRIBED BY A PHYSICIAN
Drugs must be kept out of reach of children.
SYNTEX LATINO, S.A.
C/, Severo Ochoa, 13-Polig.Ind.Leganes (Madrid)

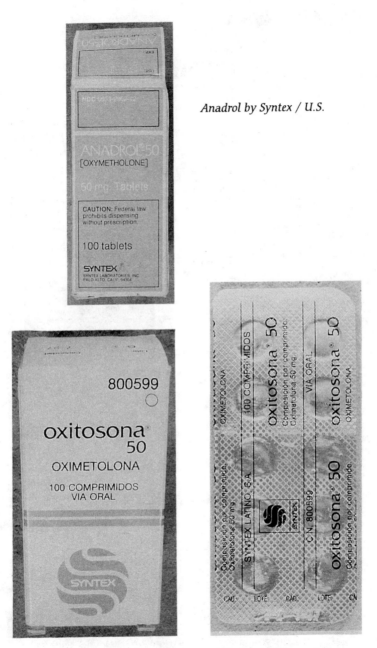

Anadrol by Syntex / U.S.

Oxitosona with blister by Syntex / Spain, out of commerce

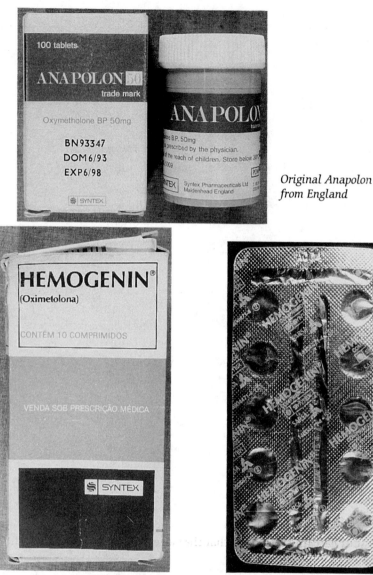

Original Anapolon from England

Hemogenin with blister, Oxymetholone from Brazil

Anapolon by Syntex / Turkey!

ANADUR

Substance: nandrolone hexyloxyphenylpropionate

Trade names

Anador	50 mg/ml;	Pharmacia FR
Anadur	50 mg/ml;	Kabi Pharmacia G, A, CH,O;
		Pharmacia B, NL, FI, CZ
Anadur	50 mg/2ml;	Eczacibasi TK
Anadur	25 mg/ml;	Lundbeck DK
Anadur	25 mg/ml;	Lundbeck DK
Anadur (o.c.)	25 mg/ml;	Leo ES
Anadurin	50 mg/ml;	Xponei GR

Anadur is one of many steroids which contains the compound nandrolone. Although available in many countries athletes do not use it often. Since its effect is similar to Deca-Durabolin's most people see no reason to take Anadur. This product does, however, have a few characteristics which make it different from "Deca" and therefore an interesting drug. Anadur is the longest lasting nandrolone. After only one injection the substance remains active in the body for four weeks. Anadur, above all, has an anabolic effect which stimulates the protein synthesis and, as with all nandrolones, requires a high protein intake. Although almost everyone knows that during the intake of steroids more protein is needed, the effect of nandrolone depends on this requirement more than any other steroid. Although this is generally uncommon with steroid products, the consumer information on Anadur points out this fact: "During treatment with Anadur care must be taken that the patient eats a fully balanced diet with adequate protein." In practice, it has been shown that a daily minimum amount of 1 - 1.5 mg/pound of body weight is required. Anadur is not a steroid to be used to achieve rapid gains in weight and strength but is a classic, basic anabolic steroid which can be stored in the body, allowing a slow but solid muscle gain and an even strength gain. Athletes using Anadur report less water retention than with Deca. For this reason some bodybuilders prefer Anadur when preparing for a competition. It must be observed, however, that in this phase usage of Anadur should be combined with stronger androgenic steroids such as Parabolan or Testosterone propionate, since the androgenic effect of Anadur is too low to protect against the loss of muscle from overtraining during a diet. Because of its slow, even, and compatible effect it is mostly used during steroid treatments which last for several months. For the most part, progress made during this period usually remains after discontinuing the product. Anadur is also a suitable compound for steroid novices and female athletes. When taking 50-100 mg every 10 days women normally show no virilization symptoms and they like to combine Anadur with Winstrol tablets, Primobolan S-tablets, or Oxandrolone. Men do not have to take antiestrogens since Anadur aromatizes only lightly and only in rare cases does it lead to gynecomastia.

The side effects of Anadur are even less than those of Deca-Durabolin. Liver damage can be excluded so that it can even be taken by people with liver disease. Virilization symptoms such as acne, hoarseness, deep voice, hirsutism, and increase in libido only occur, if at all, in very sensitive women. A higher blood pressure, due to a low water and salt retention, cannot be excluded but rarely occurs. The use of testosterone-stimulating compounds such as HCG or Clomid is not necessary since Anadur influences the hypothalamohypophysial testicular axis only slightly so that the endogenous testosterone production is not significantly reduced and the risk of a spermatogenic inhibition is minimal. Anadur is a very compatible steroid which improves the general condition and well-being of its user. Some athletes mention an improved psychological well being. As for the dosage, good results can be obtained with 200 mg every 10 days. Contrary to Deca, which athletes usually inject weekly, Anadur produces extremely long effects, allowing large intervals between injections. It is inconvenient for athletes that most of them must fall back on the German or Belgian Anadur, or French Anador which requires the purchase and injection of four 50 mg ampules. Athletes who are not afraid of larger injections therefore use one large 4 ml injection every 10 days. The high price of Anadur can really frighten the athlete. On the U.S. black market, one large ampule costs approx. $13 to $15. A U.S pharmaceutical product does not exist. The Belgian and Turkish Anadur, the French Anador, and the Greek version Anadurin are individually packed and costs approx. $10-15 per 50 mg/ampule on the black market. Insufficient availability on the black market forces athletes to use the more readily available Deca-Durabolin. Unlike Deca, there are no fakes of Anadur.

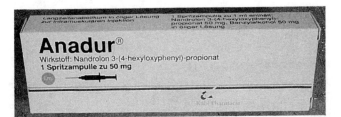

Anadur with rediject syring from Germany

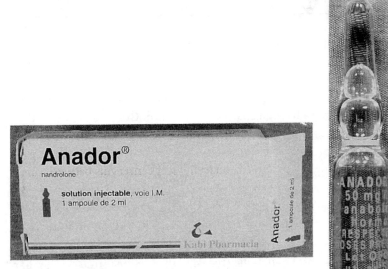

Anador with ampule by Kabi Pharmacia / France

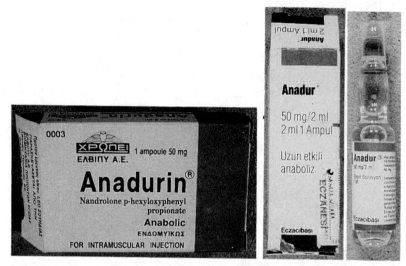

Anadurin from Greece   Anadur with ampule from Turkey

ANDRIOL

Substance: testosterone undecanoate

Trade names

Andriol	40 mg caps.;	Organon CH, NL, PL, G, A, PT, HU, Thailand; Ravasini I
Androxon	40 mg caps.;	Organon NO, Brazil
Panteston	40 mg caps.;	Organon FI, FR
Restandol	40 mg caps.;	Organon DK, GB, GR
Undestor	40 mg caps.;	Organon B, S, BG, CZ
Virigen	40 mg caps.;	Organon TK

Andriol is one of the few new steroids developed during the last few years. Unlike most anabolic steroids which were found on the market during the 1950's and 1960's (and which in part, have disappeared) Andriol has only been available since the early 1980's. This fact probably explains why Andriol holds a special place among the steroids. Andriol is a revolutionary steroid because, besides methyltestosterone, it is the only effective oral testosterone compound. Testosterone itself, if taken orally, is ineffective since it is reabsorbed through the portal vein (1) and immediately deactivated by the liver. The substance testosterone undecanoate contained in Andriol, however, is reabsorbed from the intestine through the lymphatic system, thus bypassing the liver and becoming effective. The liver function is not affected by this. Testosterone undecanoate is a fatty acid ester of the natural androgen, testosterone, and in the body is for the most part transformed into dihydrotestosterone, a metabolite of testosterone. For this reason Andriol aromatizes only minimally, meaning that only a very small part of the substance can be converted into estrogen, since the dihydrotestosterone does not aromatize. The users of Andriol therefore do not experience feminization symptoms such as gynecomastia or increased body fat. This makes it a welcome alternative for athletes who have problems with the common injectable testosterone compounds. Due to this, Andriol is also suitable for precompetition workouts. An additional advantage of Andriol's non-aromatizing quality consists of the fact that the body's own hormone production is only affected after a long-term administration of very high dosages. Andriol has only a low inhibitive effect on the hypothalamus so that the release of LHRH (luteinizing hormone releasing hormone) is rarely influenced. This is very important since—as we know—LHRH stimulates the hypophysis to release gonadotropine which causes the Ledig's cells in the testes to produce testosterone. Consequently, Andriol should be the perfect steroid; however, this is not the case.

The disadvantage of Andriol is that it only becomes effective if taken in high doses. Even if a dose of 200 mg of Andriol/day is taken, the testosterone level in the blood is still too low for a bodybuilder to gain strength and muscle growth. The need for such a high daily dosage can be explained by its extremely short half-life time since the substance testosterone undecanoate is excreted very quickly by the body through the urine. The capsules, therefore, are effective for only a few hours so that 6-7 capsules, that is 240-280 mg (minimum), must be taken daily to achieve good results comparable to those of injectable compounds. This, however, puts the athlete in a dosage range which begins to influence the hormone production and the compound now more readily converts into estrogen. Such a dose can also manifest itself in a higher retention of sodium and water. This is one factor which competing athletes must consider. Another disadvantage is Andriol's high price. A package with 60 capsules costs approximately $80. and the minimum daily dose of 6-7 capsules thus costs almost $8. For those athletes who would like to try Andriol 8 capsules (320 mg daily) should be taken. The capsules should be taken three times daily (approximately every 8 hours) after meals so that the substance can be properly reabsorbed. However, even this high dosage does not guarantee satisfactory results. Those of you who believe that you need even higher doses should then consider that it might be more sensible to switch to the injectable testosterone. Andriol is often combined with oxandrolone since oxandrolone also does not suppress the production of testosterone and, in addition, does not aromatize. The Andriol/Oxandrolone stack gives athletes who do not yet have much experience with steroids a fairly large strength increase and also often substantial muscle growth. For athletes over forty this combination is also of interest. Those working out for competitions and wanting to avoid injections on a regular basis can substitute Testosterone propionate with Andriol. Since Andriol is quickly eliminated by the body it should also be considered for use before competitions requiring doping tests. Women should avoid Andriol since the androgenic component—common with testosterone—is also strongly developed in this compound. Andriol intake can occasionally lead to high blood pressure, retention of fluids, acne, sexual overstimulation, and, in women, the well-known virilization symptoms.

Andriol should be stored in a cool place (6 - 15 °C), preferably in the refrigerator. Since the capsules are extremely sensitive to heat they can easily melt into an undefinable shape if left in direct sunlight, e.g. in a car. Because of its unusual administration, Andriol cannot be easily faked. The original Testosterone undeconoate comes in a small, oval-shaped red capsule with "DV 3" imprinted on the top while the name "ORG" is printed on the bottom. The inscription cannot be removed by scratching it with your fingernails. Although Andriol is usually not faked, it is, however, possible that someone could be selling you common wheat oil capsules. Buyers should therefore always check the imprint on the capsule. In Thailand, Andriol by Organon-Holland is freely available in pharmacies without prescription. It has a very competitive price and is offered in packaging which is quite unusual for this compound. Ten capsules are welded into a double-layered strip of aluminum foil with a relatively large blue imprint. Ten of these strips are packed into one box (see photo). The package insert is both in Thailandian and English.

Andriol has reached a sort of cult status in the U.S. and is often too highly praised (Anabolic Reference Guide, 6th Issue: "If it were around in the United States, its popularity would be comparable to the old oral Dianabol"; or Daniel Duchaine, Underground Steroid Handbook 2: "Andriol would be above Dianabol in preference if it were readily available at a decent price in the states." Also Anabolic Reference Update, March 1988: "We give Androxon our best rating.") We, however, do not share this opinion. Since Testosterone undecanoate is rarely available in the States, a mythos seems to have developed which unfortunately fails to see reality. (Insiders probably still remember the "Bolasterone mythos" during the early 1980's.) In our opinion Andriol is mainly a compound for the cautious steroid user, for the athlete who experiences too many side effects from the injectable testosterone, and for older athletes. Those who take Andriol in doses of less than 240-280 mg/day will be disappointed by its effect. The greatest advantage of Andriol lies in its good compatibility. It can, for example, be used with Deca-Durabolin in long-term therapy and, in this combination and for health-conscientious athletes, it is an alternative to the famous Dianabol/Deca-Durabolin stack. Theoretically, Andriol should build up muscle and mass, in combination with noticeable water retention, in a fast and reliable way, similar to the tested injectable Testosterone Sustanon 250 and Testosterone enanthate. Unfortunately, this is not the case. Some athletes who work out for a competition store too much water due to their use of the injectable testosterone, resulting in smooth muscles. However, if they still do not want to give up Testo, they should at least not have the estrogen-linked complications caused by taking up to 240 mg Andriol/day and be able to reduce the water retention. In this phase, the estrogen level must be kept as low as possible, otherwise the best diet will be useless. The intake of Andriol makes sense in this case and usually brings acceptable results. Otherwise, Andriol is a drug better used by hobby-bodybuilders.

(1) Portal vein: also called porta hepatis is a vessel in the blood system of human beings which collects the blood from the organs of the stomach and leads it to the liver.

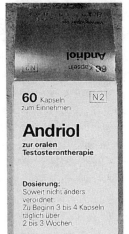
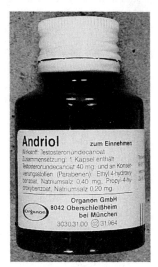

German Andriol by Organon

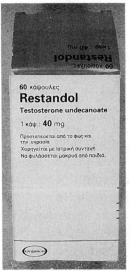
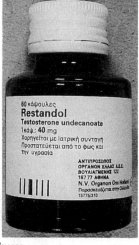

Restandol by Organon / Greece

42

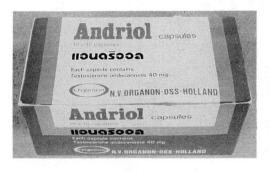

Andriol from Thailand, unusual package

Virigen from Turkey

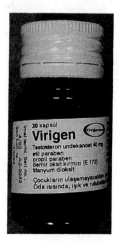

Androxon from Brazil

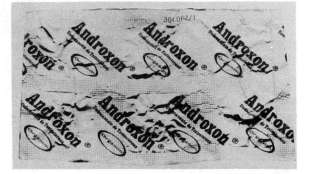

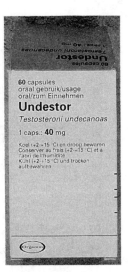

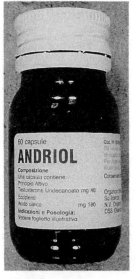

Undestor from Belgium   *Andriol from Italy*

ANDROSTANOLONE

Substance: androstanolone

Trade names

Andractim	2.5% gel	Besins-Iscovesco FR; Piette B
Apeton	5 mg, 25 mg tab.;	Fujisawa Japan
Apeton Depot	2%, 5% inj. solution;	Fujisawa Japan
Gelovit	2.5% gel	Berenguer Infall ES

Androstanolone is almost identical to the body's own dihydrotestosterone which, as we know, is formed by the peripheral conversion of testosterone. Some therefore call Androstanolone a synthetic dihydrotestosterone. This steroid has a predominantly androgenic effect and, due to its structure, cannot be converted into estrogen. For a fast buildup of power and muscle mass Androstanolone is of little value. It used to be the athlete's favorite competition steroid since it helped to obtain a harder muscle through a lower fat content by increasing the androgen level without aromatizing. Numerous athletes used Androstanolone during workouts for doping-tested championships since the substance remains in the body for only a short time and the testosterone/epitestosterone value is not influenced. Another positive characteristic is that the injectable version is not liver-toxic. Today, however, Androstanolone is rarely used by athletes. One reason for this is that almost all European and American compounds are no longer commercially available. The other reason is that most athletes use the still readily available Masteron which has similar effects. Neither the original nor a fake of Androstanolone is available on the black market.

CATAPRES

Substance: clonidine hydrochloride

Trade names

Catanidin	0.150 mg, 0.30 mg tab.;	Bender A
Catapres	0.100 mg, 0.20 mg, 0.3 mg tab.;	Boehringer U.S.
		Mylan Pharm. U.S.
		Wyatt Pharm.U.S.
Catapres (o.c.)	0.100 mg, 0.20 mg, 0.3 mg tab.;	Warner Chilcott U.S.
		Par Pharm. U.S.
		Elkin-Sinn U.S.
		Lederle Labs U.S.
Catapresan	0.075 mg, 0.15 mg, 0.3 mg tab.;	Boehringer G, FI,DK, A, ES GR, CZ, NO
Catapresan	0.075 mg, 0.15 mg tab.;	Bender A
Clonidin	0.150 mg, 0.30 mg, tab.;	3M Medica G
Clonidine	0.100 mg, 0.20 mg, 0.3 mg tab.;	Schein U.S.
Clonidine (o.c.)	0.100 mg, 0.20 mg, 0.3 mg tab.;	Barr Labs U.S.
Clonidine HCL	0.100 mg, 0.20 mg, 0.3 mg tab.;	Pure Pack U.S.
Clonisin	0.150 mg tab.;	Leiras FIC.-ratio- pharm (o.c)
0.075 mg, 0.15 mg, 0.3 mg tab.;		Ratiopharm G
Clonistada (o.c)	0.150 mg, 0.30 mg, tab.;	Stadapharm G
Combipres	0.100 mg, 0.20 mg, 0.3 mg tab.;	Par Pharm. U.S.
Dixarit	0.025 mg drag.;	Boehringer Ingelh. G
Haemiton	0.075 mg, 0.15 mg, 0.3 mg tab.; Dresden G	Arzneimittelwerk
Mirfat	0.150 mg, 0.30 mg, tab.;	Merckle G
Paracefan	0.1 mg tab.;	Boehringer G, B

Note: The above list contains only a small selection of available compounds. Only the tablet form has been listed. The substance clonidine hydrochloride may be administered in various other forms including capsules, injectable solutions, ampules, and eyedrops. Forty additional compounds are available abroad which, due to the limited space, have not been listed here.

Catapres is an antihypertensive drug. In school medicine it is used to reduce high blood pressure. High blood pressure caused by steroids can be lowered by taking Catapres. Athletes became interested in this drug when medical research reported that Catapres stimulates the endogenous production of the growth hormones. It should also be taken before going to sleep at night and in the morning immediately after getting up. Some athletes take a 0.3 mg tablet at night and a 0.15 mg tablet on an empty stomach immediately after waking up in the morning. The nightly dose increases the concentration of growth hormones for several hours, which then again can be increased by taking the morning dose. The achieved serum concentration is significantly above the normal value so that Catapres does have a considerable anabolic effect. Athletes, however, rarely use it since it has several undesirable side effects such as lethargy, fatigue, dry mouth, potency disturbances, and vertigo. Those who have a low blood pressure and a low heart rate should be extremely careful when using it. One hundred tablets are available for approx. $60. on the black market.

Catapresan from Germany

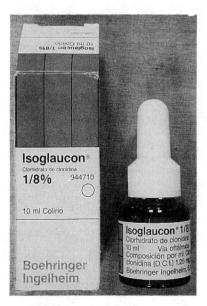

Isoglaucon, eye drops with Clonidine from Spain!

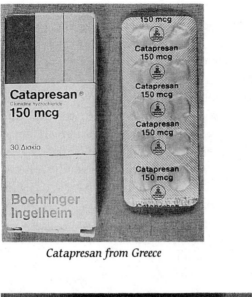

Catapresan from Greece

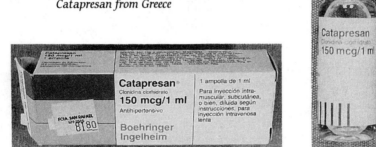

Catapresan from South America

CLENBUTEROL

Substance: clenbuterol hydrocloride

Trade names

Broncodil	0.01 mg tab.;	Von Boch I
Broncoterol	0.02 mg tab.;	Quimedical PT
Cesbron	0.02 mg tab.;	Fidelis PT
Clenasma	0.02 mg tab.;	Biomedica Foscama
Clenbuter.Pharmachim	0.02 mg tab.;	Sopharma Sofia BG
Contrasmina	0.02 mg tab.;	Falqui I

Contraspasmina	0.02 mg tab.;	Arzneimittel Werk Dresden G
Monores	0.01 mg tab.;	Valeas I
Monores	0.02 mg tab.;	Valeas I
Novegam	0.02 mg tab.;	Chinoin Mexico
Prontovent	0.02 mg tab.;	Salus I
Spiropent	0.02 mg tab.;	Thomae G, Bender A, De Angeli I, Europharma ES, Promeco Mexico, Boehringer BG, HU, CZ
Spiropent mite	0.01 mg tab.;	Thomae G
Spasmo-Mucosolvan	0.02 mg tab.;	Thomae G
Ventolase	0.02 mg tab.;	Juste ES
Veterinary:		
Ventipulmin	0.016 mg/gr.;	Richter A, BL-Vetmedica G

Note:

The substance Clenbuterol hydrochloride is also available in various other forms of administration, including syrups, drops, liquids, dosing aerosols, injectable solutions, and granules. Since athletes usually prefer tablets, manufacturers and trade names offering this oral version are listed.

Clenbuterol is a very interesting and remarkable compound. It is not a steroid hormone but a beta-2-symphatomimetic. Its effects, however, can by all means be compared to those of steroids. Similar to a combination of Winstrol Depot and Oxandrolone, Clenbuterol can cause a solid, highly qualitative muscle growth which goes hand in hand with a significant strength gain. Clenbuterol, above all, has a strong anticatabolic effect, which means it decreases the rate at which protein is reduced in the muscle cell, consequently causing an enlargement of muscle cells. For this reason, numerous athletes use Clenbuterol after steroid treatment to balance the resulting catabolic phase and thus obtain maximum strength and muscle mass. A further aspect of Clenbuterol is its distinct fat-burning effect. Clenbuterol burns fat without dieting because it increases the body temperature slightly, forcing the body to burn fat for this process. Clenbuterol, in the meantime, is not only a favorite competition compound among professional bodybuilders. An especially intense fat-burning occurs when Clenbuterol is combined with the LT3-thyroid hormone compound Cytomel. Due to the higher body temperature Clenbuterol magnifies the effect of anabolic/androgenic steroids taken simultaneously, since the protein processing is increased.

The dosage depends on body weight and can be optimized by measuring the body temperature. Athletes usually take 5-7 tablets, 100-140 mcg per day. For women 80-100 mcg/day are usually sufficient. It is important that the athlete begin by taking only one tablet on the first day and then increasing the dosage by one tablet each of the following days until the desired maximum dosage is reached. Following, there are several schedules for taking Clenbuterol. On the one hand, emphasis is placed on the burning of fat; on the other hand, importance is placed on a balanced relationship between strength and muscle growth as well as fat reduction. For more details we refer the reader to the German book: *Clenbuterol - Das Mittel der Zukunft* by Manfred Bachmann (currently being translated into English). The compound is usually taken over a period of 8-10 weeks. Since Clenbuterol is not a hormone compound it has no side effects typical of anabolic steroids. For this reason it is also liked by women. Possible side effects of Clenbuterol include restlessness, palpitations, tremor (involuntary trembling of fingers), headache, increased perspiration, insomnia, possible muscle spasms, increased blood pressure, and nausea. Note that these side effects are of a temporary nature and usually subside after 8-10 days, despite continuation of the product. In the meantime, Clenbuterol is well distributed on the black market and costs between $0.70 and $1.20 per 0.02 mg tablet. Throughout Europe the substance clenbuterol hydrocloride must be prescribed by a physician. Clenbuterol is not officially available in the U.S.

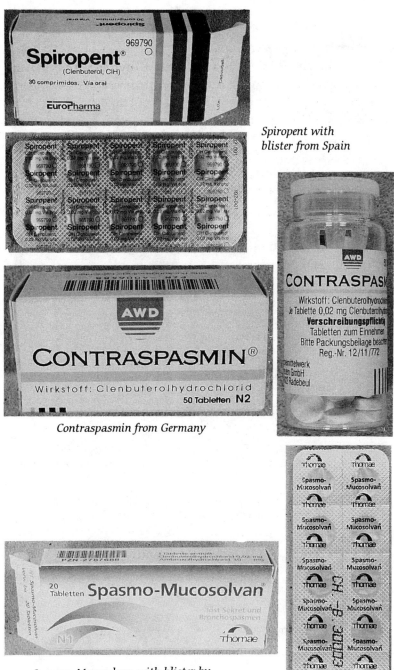

*Spiropent with
blister from Spain*

Contraspasmin from Germany

*Spasmo-Mucosolvan with blister by
Thomae / Germany (20 tabs - box)*

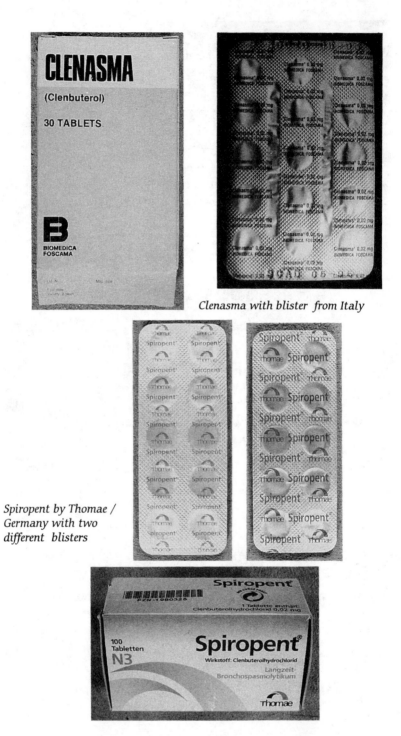

CLENASMA

(Clenbuterol)

30 TABLETS

B

BIOMEDICA
FOSCAMA

Clenasma with blister from Italy

*Spiropent by Thomae /
Germany with two
different blisters*

Spiropent

100
Tabletten
N3

Spiropent®

Wirkstoff: Clenbuterolhydrochlorid

Langzeit-
Bronchospasmolytikum

Thomae

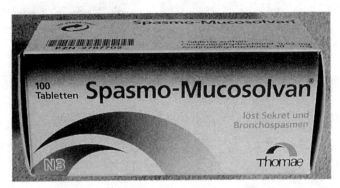

Spasmo-Mucosolvan from Germany (100 tabs - box)

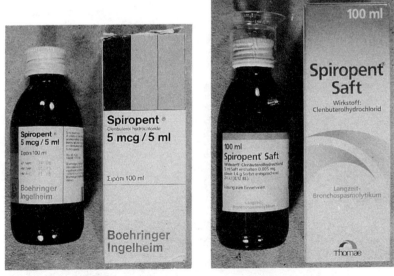

Liquid Spiropent from Greece

Liquid Spiropent from Germany (100ml)

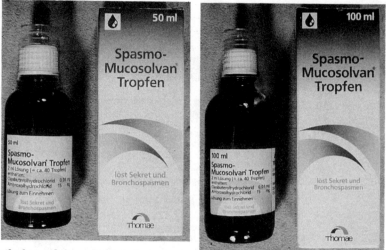

Clenbuterol drops with Ambroxol
hydrochlorid, from Germany (50ml)

. . . . . 100 ml

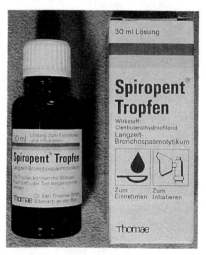

Spiropent drops by
Thomae / Germany

Another box of Clenasma
from Italy

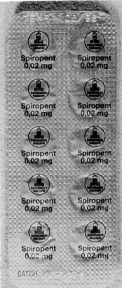

*Spiropent
blister from
Greece*

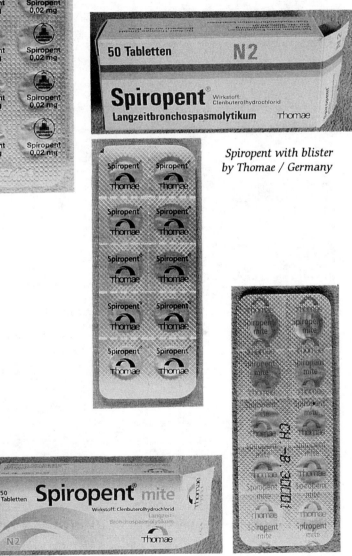

*Spiropent with blister
by Thomae / Germany*

Spiropent mite from Germany

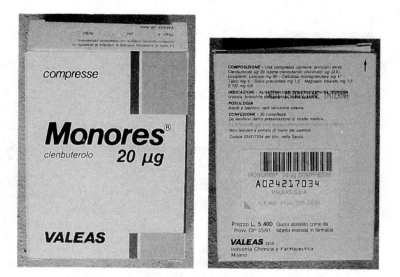

Monores, front, back and blister, Clenbuterol by Valeas / Italy

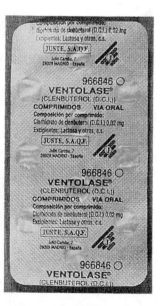

Ventolase, another Clenbuterol from Spain

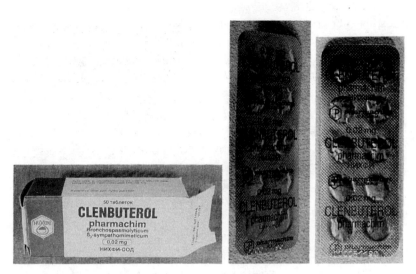

Clenbuterol pharmachim, this is the real version from Bulgaria

CLOMID

Substance: clomiphene citrate

Trade names

Ardomon	50 mg tab.;	Med-Hel GR
Clom 50 (o.c)	50 mg tab.;	Salutas G
Clomid	50 mg tab.;	Merell Dow B, CH, U.S.; Merell FR, GB; Lepetit I; Hauser-Chepharin A
Clomifen	25 mg cap.;	Lab Casen ES
Clomifen	50 mg tab.;	Leiras FI
C.-ratioph. (o.c)	50 mg tab.;	Ratiopharm G
Clomiphen Citrate	50 mg tab.;	Anfarm GR
Clomiphen-Merck	50 mg tab.;	Merck A
Clomipheni citras	50 mg tab.;	Centrafarm NL
Clomivid	50 mg tab.;	Draco DK, S
Clostilbegyt	50 mg tab.;	Egis HU, Bulgaria
Clostilbegyt	50 mg tab.;	Medphano G

Clostilbegyt (o.c)	50 mg tab.;	Med Pharm G, Thiemann G
Dufine	50 mg tab.;	Inibsa PT
Dyneric	50 mg tab.;	Marion Merrell Dow G
Gravosan	50 mg tab.;	Leciva CZ
Indovar	50 mg tab.;	Jaba PT
Klomifen	50 mg tab.;	Belupo YU; Mulda TK; Yurtoglu TK
Kyliformon	50 mg tab.;	Kylifor GR
Omifin	50 mg tab.;	Merrell ES, Mexico
Pergotime	50 mg tab.;	Icapharm S; Serono G, DK, FR; Serono/Zyma-Golen Belgium, Nordisc ab NO
Pioner	50 mg tab.;	Remedina GR
Prolifen	50 mg tab.;	Chiesi I
Serofene	50 mg tab.;	Serono Argentina, Mexico
Serophene	50 mg tab.;	Interlabo CH; Pharma-Im port NL; Serono GB, U.S., Teva A, CZ
Serpafar	50 mg tab.;	Faran GR, BG
Tokormon	50 mg tab.;	Genepharm GR

Clomid is not an anabolic/androgenic steroid. Since it is a synthetic estrogen it belongs, however, to the group of sex hormones. In school medicine Clomid is normally used to trigger ovulation. Those who cannot make much of this should read the package insert of Merrell Dow Pharma GmbH Company enclosed with the compound. Under "application" one reads the following: "To trigger the release of an ovum (ovulation) in women who want children and have certain ovary malfunctions..." Some might ask now what such a compound is doing in the drug arsenal of athletes. Those who know the effect of Clomid will immediately understand why it is used by numerous athletes. Clomid, by setting in motion the process of releasing hormones, stimulates the release of gonadotropin and triggers ovulation in women with anovulatory cycles and who are sterile because of this. Although this is actually a drug destined for women its effect on men is undisputed. The manufacturer of Dyneric, the Merrell Dow Pharma GmbH, writes in its package insert for the German version of Clomid: "Dyneric causes an improved activity between mid-brain, pituitary gland, and ovaries." What, however, is not mentioned is that Dyneric also improves the activity between mid-brain (hypothalamus), pituitary gland (hypophysis), and testes in men. Clomid has a strong influence on the hypothalamohypophysial testicular axis. It stimulates the hypophysis to release more gonadotropin so that a faster and higher release of FSH (follicle stimulating hormone) and LH (luteinizing hormone) occurs. This results in an elevated endogenous (body's own) testosterone level. Clomid is especially effective when the body's own testosterone production, due to the intake of anabolic/androgenic steroids, is suppressed. In most cases Clomid can normalize the testosterone level and the spermatogenesis (sperm development) within 10-14 days. For this reason Clomid is primarily taken after steroids are discontinued. At this time it is extremely important to bring the testosterone production to a normal level as quickly as possible so that the loss of strength and muscle mass is minimized. Even better results can be achieved if Clomid is combined with HCG or when Clomid is used after the intake of HCG. The difference between Clomid and HCG lies in the fact that Clomid has a direct influence on the hypothalamus and the hypophysis, thus regenerating the entire regulating cycle while HCG imitates the effect of the luteinizing hormone (LH) which stimulates the Ledig's cells to produce more testosterone. Since HCG, unlike Clomid, leads to a distinctly elevated plasmatestosterone level within a few hours, many athletes first take HCG and then Clomid (see also HCG).

Paradoxically, although Clomid is a synthetic estrogen it also works as an antiestrogen. The reason is that Clomid has only a very low estrogenic effect and thus the stronger estrogens which, for example, form during the aromatization of steroids, are blocked at the receptors. These would include those that develop during the aromatizing of steroids. This does not prevent the steroids from aromatizing but the increased estrogen is mostly deactivated since it cannot attach to the receptors. The increased water retention and the possible signs of feminization can thus be reduced or even completely avoided. Since the antiestrogenic effect of Clomid is lower than those found in Proviron, Nolvadex, and Teslac it is mainly taken as a testosterone stimulant. From the german book Doping by Brigitte Berendonk, the reader can learn that Clomid is not only used in bodybuilding: "During the 1980's Clomiphene (table 2) has been used, a medication that promotes the production of the body's own stimulating hormone, gonadotropin, which in turn increases the testosterone level. It is, for example, administered to women as a so-called antiestrogen to trigger ovulation ("ovulation stimulator"). Clomiphene (usually the Hungarian compound Clostilbegyt) was used by rowers (resp. Prof. Dr. Herbert Gürtler) and weightlifers (Dr. Lathan; p. 187) since the late 1970's. Increasingly, it was used in other sports disciplines as well, including track and field athletics. Riedel, at the time, happily made the handwritten entry in his notebook: "Substance that is not an anabolic: generally traceable but is not a doping substance." The dosages were horrendous. I found entries of up to 15 times 100 mg daily and the report that the positive effect lasts up to 20 days after the last tablet is taken. And it was already assured since 1982 that the increased testosterone production after doping with Clomiphene did not reveal traits of the T/E quotient (testosterone/epitestosterone quotient, the author) during doping tests."

Side effects of Clomid are very rare if reasonable dosages are taken. Possible side effects are climacteric hot flashes and occasional visual disturbances which can manifest themselves in blurred vision, giving flickering or flashing. Should visual disturbances occur, the manufacturer recommends discontinuing Clomid treatment. Inadequate liver functions cannot be excluded; however, they are very unlikely. In women enlargement of the ovaries and abdominal pain can occur since Clomid stimulates the ovaries. When taking Clomid multiple pregnancies are possible as well. As for the dosage, 50-100 mg/day (1-2 tablets) seems to be sufficient. The tablets are usually taken with fluids after meals. If several tablets are taken it is recommended that they be administered in equal doses distributed throughout the day. The duration of intake should not exceed 10 to 14 days. Most athletes begin with 100 mg/day, taking one 50 mg tablet every morning and evening after meals. After the fifth day the dosage is often reduced to only one 50 mg tablet per day. It is normally not necessary to take the compound for more than ten days in order to increase the endogenous testosterone production. Since Clomid should not be taken for a prolonged time its application as an antiestrogen must be excluded because, for that purpose, it would have to be taken for several weeks. Clomid is relatively expensive. A package with 10 tablets costs approx. $35 - 45 on the black market. Fortunately, since the intake is only for a brief time, the financial burden usually becomes acceptable. The foreign compounds such as the Spanish Omifin are considerably cheaper and cost less than $2 per tablet. The tablets of the Merrell Dow Company (Dyneric, Omifin, Clomid) are beige, indented, and have an "M" engraved on the back, imprinted with two circles. Fakes of Dyneric, Clomid, Omifin, and other compounds are not available at this time.

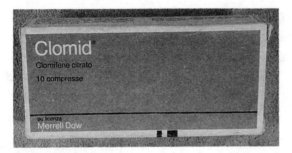

Clomid, front, back and blister, Clomiphene by Merrel Dow / Italy

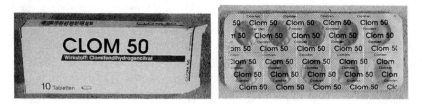

Clom 50 with blister from Germany

Omifin with blister from Spain

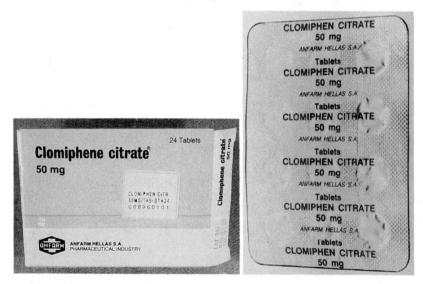

Clomiphene citrate from Greece

Clomifen from Spain, box and blister

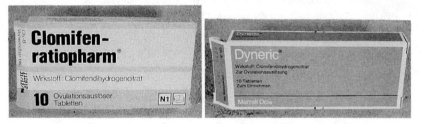

Clomifen by ratiopharm from
Germany

Dyneric from Germany

CYCLOFENIL

Substance: cyclofenil

Trade names

Fertodur (o.c.)	200 mg tab.;	Schering G, CH, I
Fertodur	200 mg tab.;	Schering PT, GR, TK, Mexico
Neoclym	200 mg tab.;	Poli I
Ondogyne (o.c.)	400 mg tab.;	Roussel F
Rehibin	100 mg tab.;	Serono GB
Sexovid	100 mg tab.;	Teikiku Zoki Japan
Sexovid (o.c.)	100 mg tab.;	Leo ES

Cyclofenil is not an anabolic/androgenic steroid. However, since it is an estrogen it belongs to the group of sex hormones. Some of you might shake your heads now and ask what this medicine has to do with bodybuilding, since everyone knows that the female hormone estrogen is one of the main enemies of every athlete. Dear Reader, let us surprise you. Cyclofenil works as an antiestrogen and, at the same time, increases the body's own testosterone production. Since Cyclofenil itself is only a very weak and mild estrogen it occupies the estrogen receptors, and prevents the stronger estrogens from bonding with the receptors thereby becoming active. As a matter of fact, this works so well that some athletes take Cyclofenil during the steroid treatment in order to maintain a low estrogen level. The result is a lower water retention produced by the steroids and less gynecomastia. The athlete has a harder appearance, making this is a compound that can potentially be taken during the preparation for a competition. Bodybuilders, however, use it less frequently since they prefer the more readily available Nolvadex and Proviron compounds.

The main reason for taking Cyclofenil is the previously-mentioned increase in the production of endogenous testosterone. In this respect it has an effect similar to Clomid (see Clomid). The Canadian physician, Dr. Mauro G. Pasquale, who is highly respected among experts, confirms this in his book *Drug Use and Detection in Amateur Sports, Update Five* goes even one step further and compares its effect to HCG's. "It would appear that Cyclofenil has effects on athletes similar to both Clomid and to HCG." This works since Cyclofenil has a direct effect on the hypothalamo–hypophysial testicular axis obviating a negative feedback. Since the body is always eager to maintain its balance, when the testosterone level is high, the testes signal the hypothalamus to release less gonadotropin. The hypophysis, in turn, releases less gonadotropin and the testes are only slightly stimulated. This self-regulating of the body is called a negative feedback. And this process is eliminated by the intake of Cyclofenil so that the body continues to produce testosterone even at an elevated testosterone level. There is no question that the body is capable of producing considerably more testosterone than it does. The problem is only that it does not see a reason to do so and thus it initiates a negative feedback. Bill Phillips in his *Anabolic Reference Update*, March 1990, no. 17 described this process very aptly. He said that it is like removing the regulator of a vehicle's carburetor, making the engine run at full speed. It was shown, however, that the body discovers this "swindle" after four to six weeks and deactivates the effect of Cyclofenil. For this reason athletes take the compound for no more than six weeks, then they discontinue its use for two to three months. Based on our experience, the dosage lies between 400 and 600 mg/day. Lower dosages usually do not show satisfying results. Cyclofenil, for this purpose, is either used during steroid treatment, after the treatment, before competitions with doping tests, or by "natural bodybuilders". Like HCG and Clomid, Cyclofenil is ineffective in women since it has a positive influence on the male hormone system. Even in men, the increased testosterone level attributed to the effect of Cyclofenil, is not high enough to speak of drastic improvements; however, strength gains, a slight gain in body weight, a noticeable increase in energy, and a higher regeneration are possible. These results are noticeable particularly in advanced athletes who have little or no experience with steroids. Cyclofenil needs a response time of approximately one week before it becomes effective.

The side effects are so minimal that we are somewhat surprised that Schering Company has taken Cyclofenil (Fertodur) off the market in Germany, Switzerland, and Italy. The only plausible reason for this action could be that the sales figures did not justify a further production. In a few cases athletes experience a light acne, increased sexual desire, and hot flashes. The first two secondary symptoms are especially indicative that the compound is actually effective. After discontinuance some athletes report a depressed mood and a slight decrease in physical strength. Those who take Cyclofenil as an antiestrogen during steroid treatment could experience a rebound effect when the compound is discontinued.

In the meantime, it is very difficult to find Cyclofenil and it is rarely found on the black market. The Mexican Fertodur by Schering contains 16 tablets of 200 mg each which are welded into aluminum foil with the name "Fertodur Tabletas" printed on top. Such a package costs $25 - 30 on the black market. Since Cyclofenil is a prescription drug it cannot be found in food preparations. In the U.S., a few years ago some supplement companies actually offered Cyclofenil-containing products and the products actually contained Cyclofenil. Since in the U.S. Cyclofenil is not approved by the FDA (Food and Drug Administration), the manufacturer was pressured to discontinue further manufacturing. Should somebody, however, offer you a "supplement" which apparently contains Cyclofenil, you certainly will not get what you want. There are no available fakes for the pharmaceutical versions.

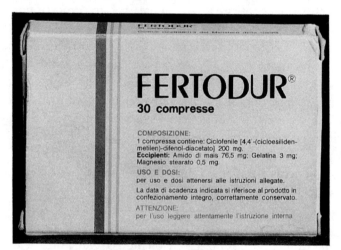

Fertodur, front and back, Schering / Italy

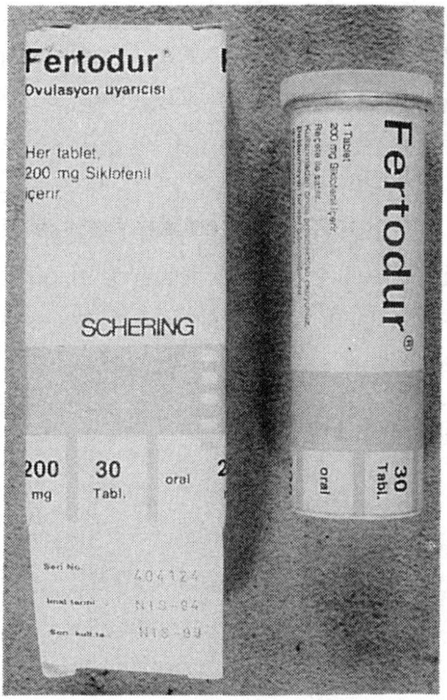
Fertodur
Ovulasyon uyarıcısı
Her tablet
200 mg Siklofenil
içerir
SCHERING
200 mg
30 Tabl.
oral
Fertodur®
30 Tabl.
oral

Fertodur by Schering / Turkey

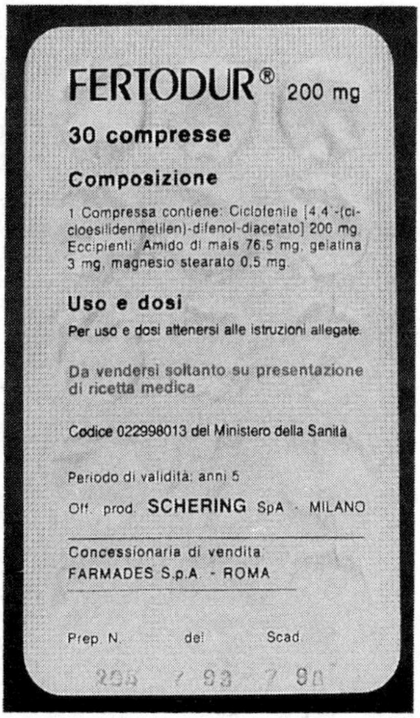
FERTODUR® 200 mg
30 compresse
Composizione
1 Compressa contiene: Ciclofenile [4,4'-(cicloesilidenmetilen)-difenol-diacetato] 200 mg. Eccipienti: Amido di mais 76,5 mg, gelatina 3 mg, magnesio stearato 0,5 mg.
Uso e dosi
Per uso e dosi attenersi alle istruzioni allegate.
Da vendersi soltanto su presentazione di ricetta medica
Codice 022998013 del Ministero della Sanità
Periodo di validità: anni 5
Off. prod. SCHERING SpA - MILANO
Concessionaria di vendita:
FARMADES S.p.A. - ROMA
Prep. N. del Scad.

Fertodur blister by Schering / Italy

CYTADREN

Substance: aminoglutethimide

Trade names

Aminoglutethimid	250 mg tab.;	The chem. pharm. & Res. inst. BG
Aminoglutethimide	250 mg tab.;	Farmitalia-Carlo Erba GB
Cytadren	250 mg tab.;	Ciba U.S.
Mamomit	100 mg tab.;	Pliva YU
Orimeten	250 mg tab.;	Ciba G, ES, GB, A, B, CH, I, NO, NL, S, FI, TK, PT, BG, HU, CZ, GR
Orimetene	250 mg tab.;	Ciba FR, GR
Rodazol	250 mg tab.;	Rodleben G

Cytadren is not an anabolic/androgenic steroid. Since it is a steroidbiosynthesial inhibitor it belongs to the group of sex hormones. Cytadren inhibits the buildup of androgens, estrogens, and the suprarenal cortical hormones (glucocorticoids and mineralocorticoids). Let us first take a look at the latter two points since they explain why athletes are interested in this compound. Cytadren has a highly antiestrogenic effect since, on the one hand, it inhibits the body's own estrogen production and, on the other hand, it obviates the conversion of androgens into estrogens. This is especially encouraging since it helps to keep the estrogen level of bodybuilders low. The second highly interesting point is that Cytadren prohibits the buildup of adrenocortical hormones. It obviates the production of endogenous cortisone like no other compound by inhibiting the conversion of cholesterol into cortisone. For this reason, Cytadren, in school medicine, is used for the treatment of Cushing's syndrome, a hyperfunction of the adrenal glands which causes the body to overproduce cortisone. Consequently, it reduces the cortisone level, which has several advantages for the athlete. Cortisone is a catabolic hormone and catabolic is the exact opposite of anabolic. Cortisone prevents the protein synthesis in the muscle cell, resulting in a muscular atrophy by breaking down amino acids in the muscle cell. The human body constantly releases cortisone and reacts to stress situations such as intense training by increasing its cortisone release. Natural bodybuilders, therefore, after a short time, experience a stagnation in their development since the release of the body's cortisone is higher than the anabolic effect of working out. The more advanced the athlete and the harder his workout, the more his cortisone level will increase.

If the release of cortisone can be successfully obviated or at least considerably reduced the ratio of anabolic hormones to catabolic hormones in the body shifts in favor of the former. This results in an increase in muscle mass and body strength. And Cytadren achieves exactly these results; however, there is one problem. Cytadren reduces the cortisone level so effectively that the body tries to balance this by hypophysially producing more ACTH (adenocorticotropic hormone), thus stimulating the secretion of cortisone by the adrenal glands. Thus in school medicine, when treating Cushing's syndrome, a low dose of oral hydrocortisone is used to prevent the hypophysis from producing ACTH. The dose is so low that the cortisone level in the blood does not rise substantially. And this is exactly the problem. Cytadren reduces the cortisone level which the body balances by producing ACTH, thus neutralizing the effect of Cytadren. If exogenous hydrocortisone is taken no ACTH is produced; however, this also reduces the effect of Cytadren. It is therefore necessary to find an administration schedule that prevents or delays the body's own production of ACTH. Since the body does not show abrupt reactions when the cortisone level is lowered by the intake of Cytadren, the compound must be taken over several days before the body begins reacting. If Cytadren is only taken for a period of two days and then discontinued for two entire days, it seems logical that the body will not have enough time to react accordingly, thus interrupting the production of ACTH in the hypophysis. Similar to Clenbuterol, an alternating administration schedule with two days of administration and two days of abstinence is created. Another problem needs to be solved since Cytadren, as mentioned earlier, inhibits the body's own production of androgen. Cytadren, therefore, should not be used by natural bodybuilders. The solution to this problem is to take a long-term effective testosterone such as Testosterone enanthate simultaneously. Testoviron Depot 250, for example, can be considered as one such possible compound.

As for the question of dosage, we have arrived at a very interesting point. In school medicine the dosage for the treatment of Cushing's syndrome is between 2 and 7 tablets per day. Since not enough athletes have used this compound so far, we do not have enough experimental data. Due to the fact that the cortisone level of athletes is not as high as in persons who suffer from a hyperfunction of the adrenal glands, it is probable that lower dosages are sufficient. From what we have heard so far, 2-4 tablets of 250 mg each per day seems to be an appropriate dose. The tablets are always taken individually, in regular intervals throughout the day, and taken best during meals. It is important to begin the intake by "sneaking in," which means that you begin by taking only one tablet and then slowly and evenly increasing the dosage until the respective maximum dosage is reached. How long should it be taken? This question is difficult to answer but, considering that the body can sometimes increase the production of ACTH, it is advised that the compound is not used longer than 4-6 weeks. (We must also consider potential side effects, which we will discuss in a minute.) Another interesting aspect: Cytadren is (as of yet) not on any doping list. We have heard from reliable informants that a combination of Cytadren, growth hormones, and a low quantity of injectable testosterone is the new hit among athletes of any field, since it allows the athlete to pass any doping test.

Thus the side effects of Cytadren need to be looked at and they are, unfortunately, numerous and sometimes very severe. The most common side effects are fatigue and dizziness. Lack of concentration, restlessness, depression, apathy, and sleeping disorder are less common but possible. Even rarer and mostly depending on the doses are nausea, vomiting, gastrointestinal pain, diarrhea, and headaches. A possible rash and the already-mentioned fatigue and dizziness are usually initial symptoms and these can be minimized by taking slowly increasing dosages, or they may simply disappear. The package insert of Ciba-Geigy GmbH Germany also states that in some cases there is an inadequate thyroid function which requires treatment. It is therefore recommended that the thyroid gland be supervised by a physician during intake of Cytadren. Another problem that can occur is liver disease. Cases of reduced counts of the white blood cells, the blood platelets, and even of all blood cells have been reported. Those who plan to try Cytadren should carefully read the package insert. It has been our experience that athletes, due to the reduced cortisone level, complain about joint pain and are also exposed to a higher risk of getting injured. There is no question that Cytadren is effective when taken according to the two-day alternating administration schedule; however, the athlete should carefully consider the cost/benefit factor prior to taking the compound. Cytadren is in U.S. pharmacies only available by prescription. A package with 100 tablets of 250 mg each costs $190.-, so that Cytadren is not a budget-priced compound. Each package contains 10 push-through strips of 10 tablets each. The tablets are indented on one side with an imprinted "G" on both the right and left of the breakage line. On the other side of the tablet the letters "CG" are punched in. Cytadren is rarely found on the black market.

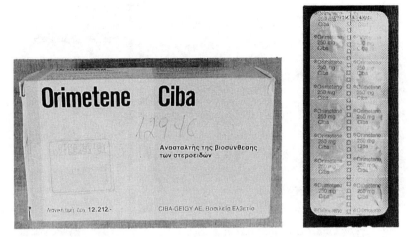

Orimetene, box and blister, by Ciba - Geigy / Greece

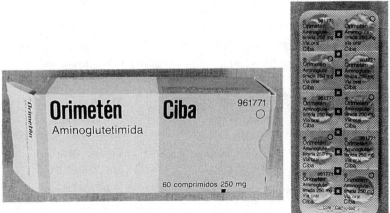

Orimetene by Ciba/ Spain

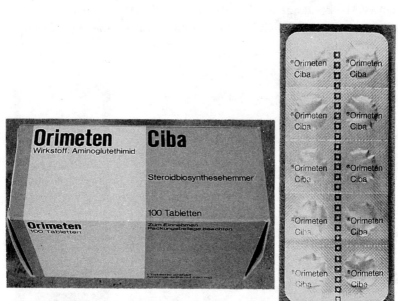

Orimeten by Ciba / Germany, box and blister

CYTOMEL

Substance: liothyronine sodium

Trade names

Cynomel	5 mcg, 24 mcg tab.;	Uhlmann-Eyrard CH
Cynomel	25 mcg tab.;	Merrell Dow FR, Dincel TK
Cyronine (o.c.)	25 mcg, 50 mcg tab.;	Major U.S.
Cytomel	5 mcg tab.;	Smith Kline U.S.; Smith Kline & French Canada, NL
Cytomel	25 mcg tab.;	Smith Kline Rit ̇B, Smith Kline U.S.; Smith Kline & French Canada, NL

Cytomel		50 mcg tab.; Smith Kline U.S.
Cytomel Tabs	5, 25, 50 mcg tab.;	Schein U.S.
Euthroid (o.c.)	50 mcg tabl.;	Parke Davis U.S.
Linomel	25 mcg tab.;	Smith Kline Argentina
Liothyronin	20 mcg tab.;	Nycomed NO, S
Neo-Tiroimade	5 mcg, 25 mcg tab.;	Made PTI
Ro-Thyronine	25 mcg, 50 mcg tab.;	Robinson U.S.
T3 (o.c.)	25 mcg, 50 mcg tab.;	Uni-Pharme U.S.
T3	25 mcg, 50 mcg tab.;	Uni-Pharme Israel
T3	25 mcg, 50 mcg tab.;	Unipharma GR
Tertroxin	20 mcg injection solution;	Glaxo DK
Tertroxin	20 mcg tab.;	Glaxo DK, South Africa, CZ, GB
Thybon,-forte	20 mcg, 100 mcg tab.;	Hoechst G
Thyrotardin	100 mcg dry substance;	Henning Berlin G Inject
Ti-Tre	5 mcg, 20 mcg tab.;	Glaxo I
Tiromel	25 mcg tab.;	Ibrahim TK
Tironina (o.c.)	25 mcg tab.;	Abello ES
Trijodthyronin	20 mcg tab.;	Nycomed S
Trijod. Sanabo	25 mcg tab.;	Sanabo A
Trijodthyr. 50	50 mcg tab.;	Berlin-Chemie G
Trijodthyr. Leo	25 mcg tab.;	Leo ES

Cytomel is not an anabolic/androgenic steroid but a thyroid hormone. As a substance it contains synthetically manufactured liothyronine sodium which resembles the natural thyroid hormone tricodide-thyronine (L-T3). The thyroid of a healthy person usually produces two hormones, the better known L-thyroxine (L-T4) and the aforementioned L-triiodine-thyronine (L-T3). Since Cytomel is the synthetic equivalent of the latter hormone, it causes the same processes in the body as if the thyroid were to produce more of the hormone. It is interesting to note that L-T3 is clearly the stronger and more effective of these two hormones. This makes Cytomel more effective than the commercially available L-T4 compounds such as L-thyroxine or Synthroid. The manufacturer of the German L-T3 compound, Hoechst AG, ascribes the following characteristics to its Thybon drug, making it clear that L-T3 is superior to L-T4: "The synthetically manufactured thyroid hormone, L-triiodine-thyronine (L-T3), included in Thybon, in experimental and clinical testing has proven to be 4-5 times more biologically active and to take effect more quickly than L-thyroxine (L-T4)." In school medicine Cytomel is used to treat thyroid insufficiency (hypothyroidism). Among other secondary symptoms are obesity, metabolic disorders, and fatigue. Bodybuilders take advantage of these charcteristics and stimulate their metabolism by taking Cytomel, which causes a faster conversion of carbohydrates, proteins, and fats. Bodybuilders, of course, are especially interested in an increased lipolysis, which means increased fatburning. Competing bodybuilders, in particular, use Cytomel during the weeks before a championship since it helps to maintain an extremely low fat content, without necessitating a hunger diet. Athletes who use low dosages of Cytomel report that by the simultaneous intake of steroids, the steroids become more effective, most likely as the result of the faster conversion of protein.

Until recently, Cytomel was used by bodybuilders—and female bodybuilders, in particular—on a daily basis over several months to remain "hard" and in good shape all year round. Believe us when we tell you that to a great extent several bodybuilders who are pictured in "muscle magazines" and display a hard and defined look in photos, eat fast food and iron this out by taking Cytomel. The overstimulated thyroid burns calories like a blast furnace. Nowadays, instead of Cytomel, athletes use Clenbuterol which is becoming more and more popular. Those who combine these two compounds will burn an enormous amount of fat. The next time you read that a certain pro bodybuilder approaching a championship competition is still eating 4000 calories a day, you will know why. Cytomel is also popular among female bodybuilders. Since women generally have slower metabolisms than men, it is extremely difficult for them to obtain the right form for a competition given today's standards. A drastic reduction of food and calories below the 1000 calorie/day mark can often be avoided by taking Cytomel. Women, no doubt, are more prone to side effects than men but usually get along well with 50 mcg/day. A short-term intake of Cytomel in a reasonable dosage is certainly "healthier" than an extreme hunger diet.

As for the dosage, one should be very careful since Cytomel is a very strong and highly effective thyroid hormone. It is extremely important that one begins with a low dosage, increasing it slowly and evenly over the course of several days. Most athletes begin by taking one 25 mcg tablet per day and increasing this dosage every three to four days by one additional tablet. A dose higher than 100 mcg/day is not necessary and not advisable. It is not recommended that the daily dose be taken all at once but broken down into three smaller individual doses so that they become more effective. It is also important that Cytomel not be taken for more than six weeks. At least two months of abstinence from the drug needs to follow. Those who take high dosages of Cytomel over a long period of time are at risk of developing a chronic thyroid insufficiency. As a consequence, the athlete might be forced to take thyroid medication for the rest of his life. It is also important that the dosage is reduced slowly and evenly by taking fewer tablets and not be ended abruptly. Those who plan to take Cytomel should first consult a physician in order to be sure that no thyroid hyperfunction exists.

Possible side effects such as medication are described in the package insert by the German pharmaceutical group Hoechst AG for their compound Thybon: "Exceeding the individual limits of compatibility for liothyronine or taking an overdose, especially, if the dose is increased too quickly at the beginning of the treatment, can cause the following clinical symptoms for a thyroid hyperfunction): heart palpitation, trembling, irregular heartbeat, heart oppression, agitation, shortness of breath, excretion of sugar through the urine, excessive perspiration, diarrhea, weight loss, psychic disorders, etc., as well as symptoms of hypersensitivity." Our experience is that most symptoms consist of trembling of hands, nausea, headaches, high perspiration, and increased heartbeat. These negative side effects can often be eliminated by temporarily reducing the daily dosage. Caution, however, is advised when taking Cytomel since, especially in the beginning, the effect can be quick and sometimes drastic. Athletes do not use the injectable version of L-T3, this is normally used as "emergency therapy for thyrotoxic coma." Those who use Cytomel over several weeks will experience a decrease in muscle mass. This can be avoided or delayed by simultaneously taking steroids. For the most part, since Cytomel also metabolizes protein, the athlete must eat a diet rich in protein.

L-T3 can usually be found quite easily. 100 tablets of 0.05 mg each cost approx. $40. The product by Schein Company, according to the dealer catalog, with the same substance concentration and quantity of tablets, costs $24.29. It is unlikely that there will be fakes.

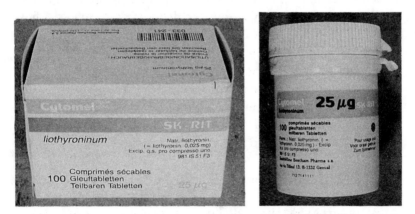

Cytomel from Belgium, box and container

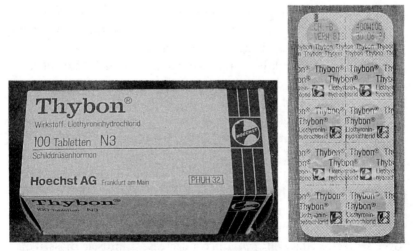

Thybon by Hoechst / Germany, box with blister

DANOCRINE

Substance: danazol

Trade names

Anargil	100 mg, 200 mg cap.;	Medochemie Ltd.CZ
Danatrol	50 mg cap.;	Winthrop I, ES, GR
Danatrol	100 mg cap.;	Winthrop I, ES, GR, B, CH, NL
Danatrol	200 mg cap.;	Winthrop I, ES, GR,B, CH, GR,NL, PT, Läakefarmos FI
Danatrol (o.c.)	50 mg, 100 mg, 200 mg tab.;	Sanofi Winthrop U.S.
Danazol (o.c.)	200 mg tab.;	Geneva U.S., Martec Pharm. U.S. Warner Chilcott U.S.
Danocrine	50 mg cap.;	Sanofi Winthrop U.S.
Danocrine	100 mg, 200 mg cap.;	Sanofi Winthrop DK, S, U.S.
Danogar (o.c.)	50 mg, 100 mg, 200 mg tab.;	Sanofi Winthrop U.S.
Danokrin	200 mg cap.;	Kwizda A, Winthrop GB
Danol (o.c.)	50 mg, 100 mg 200 mg tab.;	Sanofi Winthrop U.S.
Danol-1/2	100 mg, 200 mg cap.;	Winthrop GB
Danoval	100 mg, 200 mg cap.;	Krka YU
Ladogal	200 mg cap.;	Winthrop Argentina
Ladogal (o.c.)	50 mg, 100 mg, 200 mg tab.;	Sanofi Winthrop U.S.
Ladogar (o.c.)	50 mg, 100 mg, 200 mg tab.;	Sanofi Winthrop U.S.
Mastodanatrol(o.c.)	100 mg tab.;	Sterling-Winthrop FR
Winobanin	100 mg, 200 mg cap.;	Sanofi Winthrop G

Danocrine is an antigonadotropin. In school medicine it is used to treat hormone-related disorders. One such disorder, for example, is the hormone-related breast enlargement in men, better known as gynecomastia. Bodybuilders can use Danocrine to minimize possible feminization caused by the aromatizing of steroids. It is our experience that the daily dose should be around 400 mg. Danocrine has a mild androgenic effect but no anabolic effect. The possible side effects such as virilization symptoms, hot flashes, perspiration, increased libido, increased liver values, and high blood pressure through retention of fluids are highly dependent on the dose and they usually decrease again later. It is difficult to find Danocrine on the black market since it is rarely used by athletes. The official price for 100 capsules of 200 mg each is $330. Fakes are not known at this time.

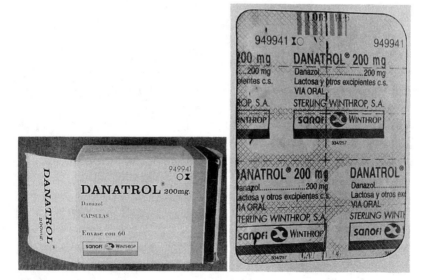

Danatrol with blister by Sanofi-Winthrop from Spain (200mg)

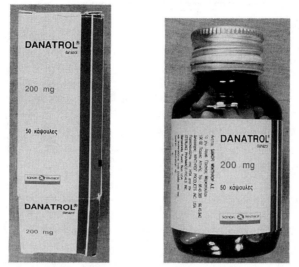

Danatrol box and glass bottle by Sanofi-Winthrop / Greece (200ml)

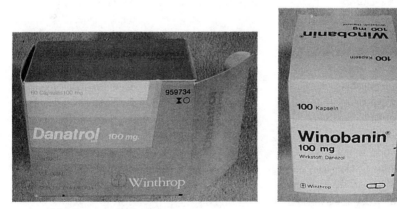

Danatrol from Spain (100mg)

Winobanin from Germany (100mg)

DECA-DURABOLIN

Substance: nandrolone decanoate

Trade names

Anaboline	50 mg/ml;	Adelco GR
Androlone-D 200 (o.c.)	200 mg/ml;	Keene U.S.
Deca-Durabolin	25 mg/ml;	Bender A; Donmed South Africa; Organon G, B, CH, DK, ES, GB, GR, I, NL, PL, FI, Hermes/ Organon YU
Deca-Durabolin	50 mg/ml;	Organon G, B, CH, DK, ES, FR, GB,U.S, GR, I, NL, PL,FI; Mexico, Thailand Hermes/Organon YU, Steris U.S., Bender A, Donmed South Africa
Deca-Durabolin '100'	100 mg/ml;	Organon NL
Deca-Durabolin	100 mg/ml;	Organon GB, GR, FI, Canada, U.S., Steris U.S.
Deca-Durabolin	200 mg/ml;	Steris U.S.
Deca-Durabol	25, 50, 100 mg/ml;	Organon S
Elpihormo	50 mg/ml;	Chemica GR
Extraboline	50, ml;	Genepharm GR
Hybolin Decanoate	50, 100 mg/ml;	Hyrex U.S.
Jebolan	50 mg/ml;	Etem TK
Nandrolone Dec.	50, 100, 200 mg/ml;	Steris U.S.
Nandrol. Dec. (o.c.)	100 mg/ml;	Lyphomed U.S., Quad U.S.
Nandrobolic L.A. (o.c.)	100 mg/ml;	Forest U.S.
Neo-Durabolic (o.c.)	100, 200 mg/ml;	Hauck U.S.
Nurezan	50 mg/ml;	RafarmGR
Retabolil	25 mg/ml;	Gedeon Richter U,BG
Retabolil	50 mg/ml;	Gedeon Richter HU,BG

Retabolin	50 mg/ml;	Medexport Russia
Sterobolin (o.c.)	50 mg/ml;	Orion FL
Turinabol Depot (o.c.)	50 mg/ ml;	Jenapharm G
Turinabol Depot	50 mg/ml;	Jenapharm BG, CZ
Ziremilon	50 mg/ml;	Demo GR

Veterinary:

Anabolicum	25 mg/ml; 10 ml/50 ml	Bela-Pharm G
Norandren 50	50 mg/ml; 10 ml/50 ml	Brovel Mexico

Deca-Durabolin is a brand name of Organon Company, the manufacturer of the drug containing the substance nandrolone decanoate. Although nandrolone decanoate is still contained in many generic compounds, almost every athlete connects this substance with Deca-Durabolin. Organon introduced Deca during the early 1960's as an injectable steroid available in various strengths. Most common are the administrations of 50 mg/ml and 100 mg/ml. Deca-Durabolin is the most widespread and most commonly used injectable steroid. Deca's large popularity can be attributed to its numerous possible applications and, for its mostly positive results. Deca's main characteristic is clearly defined on the package insert by Organon GmbH Company: "The distinct anabolic effect of nandrolone decanoate is mirrorred in the positive nitrogen balance." As described in a previous chapter, nitrogen, in bonded form, is part of protein. Deca-Durabolin causes the muscle cell to store more nitrogen than it releases so that a positive nitrogen balance is achieved. A positive nitrogen balance is synonymous with muscle growth since the muscle cell, in this phase, assimilates (accumulates) a larger amount of protein than usual. The same manufacturer, however, points out on the package insert that a positive nitrogen balance and the protein-building effect that accompany it will occur only if enough calories and proteins are supplied. One should know this since, otherwise, satisfying results with Deca cannot be obtained. The highly anabolic effect of Deca-Durabolin is linked to a moderately androgenic component, so that a good gain in muscle mass and strength is obtained. At the same time, most athletes notice considerable water retention which, no doubt, is not as distinct as that with injectable testosterones but which in high doses can also cause a smooth and watery appearance. Since Deca also stores more water in the connective tissues, it can temporarily ease or even cure existing pain in joints. This is especially good for those athletes who complain about pain in the shoulder, elbow, and knee; they can often enjoy pain-free workouts during treatment with Deca-Durabolin. Another reason for this is that Deca blocks the cortisone receptors, thus allowing less cortisone to reach the muscle cells and the connective tissue cells. Athletes use Deca, depending on their needs, for muscle buildup and in preparation for a competition.

Deca is suitable, even above average, to develop muscle mass since it promotes the protein synthesis and simultaneously leads to water retention. The optimal dose for this purpose lies between 200 and 600 mg/week. Scientific research has shown that best results can be obtained by the intake of 2 mg/pound body weight. Those who take a dose of less than 200 mg/week will usually feel only a very light anabolic effect which, however, increases with a higher dosage. The anabolic and consequent buildup effect of Deca-Durabolin, up to a certain degree, depends on the dosage. In the range of approx. 200 to 600 mg/week, the anabolic effect increases almost proportionately to the dosage increase. If more than 600 mg/week are administered, the relationship of the positive to the negative effects shifts in favor of the latter. In addition, at a dosage level above 600 mg/week, the anabolic effect no longer increases proportionately to the dosage increase, so that 1000 mg/week do not guarantee significantly better results than 600 mg/week. Most male athletes experience good results by taking 400 mg/week. Steroid novices usually need only 200 mg/week. Deca works very well for muscle buildup when combined with Dianabol and Testosterone. The famous Dianabol/Deca stack results in a a fast and strong gain in muscle mass. Most athletes usually take 15-40 mg Dianabol/day and 200-400 mg Deca/week. Even faster results can be achieved with 400 mg Deca/week and 500 mg Sustanon 250/week. Athletes report an enormous gain in strength and muscle mass when taking 400 mg Deca/week, 500 mg Sustanon 250/week, and 30 mg Dianabol/day. Deca is a good basic steroid which, for muscle buildup, can be combined with many other steroids.

Although Deca-Durabolin is not an optimal steroid when preparing for a competition, many athletes also achieve good results during this phase. Since Deca is a long-term anabolic, there is risk that with a higher dosage, the competing athlete will retain too much water. This problem can usually be avoided when the athlete is injected with the faster-acting Durabolin, which contains the substance nandrolone-phenylpropionate. A conversion into estrogen, that means an aromatizing process, is possible with Deca-Durabolin but usually occurs only at a dose of 400 mg+/week. During competitions with doping tests Deca must not be taken since the metabolites in the body can be proven in a urine analysis up to 18 months later. Those who do not fear testing can use Deca as a high-anabolic basic compound in a dosage of 400 mg/week. The androgens contained in 400 mg/week also help to accelerate the body's regeneration. The risk of potential water retention and aromatizing to estrogen can be successfully prevented by combining the use of Proviron with Nolvadex. A preparatory stack often observed in competing athletes includes 400 mg/week Deca-Durabolin, 50 mg/day Winstrol, 228 mg/week Parabolan, and 25 mg/day Oxandrolone.

Although the side effects with Deca are relatively low with dosages of 400 mg/week, androgenic-caused side effects can occur. Most problems manifest themselves in high blood pressure and a prolonged time for blood clotting, which can cause frequent nasal bleeding and prolonged bleeding of cuts, as well as increased production of the sebaceous gland and occasional acne. Some athletes also report headaches and sexual overstimulation. When very high dosages are taken over a prolonged period, spermatogenesis can be inhibited in men, i.e the testes produce less testosterone. The reason is that Deca-Durabolin, like almost all steroids, inhibits the release of gonadotropin from the hypophysis.

Women with a dosage of up to 100 mg/week usually experience no major problems with Deca. At higher dosages androgenic-caused virilization symptoms can occur, including deep voice (irreversible), increased growth of body hair, acne, increased libido, and possibly clitorishypertrophy. Women who experience disturbance even at a weekly dose of only 50 mg/week of Deca-Durabolin, are often better off taking the earlier-mentioned and faster-acting Durabolin. Unlike the long-acting Deca, when Durabolin is administered once or twice weekly in a dosage of 50 mg, no concentration of undesired amounts of androgens occur. Since most female athletes get on well with Deca-Durabolin a dose of Deca 50 mg+/week is usually combined with Oxandrolone 10 mg+/day. Both compounds, when taken in a low dosage, are only slightly androgenic so that masculinizing side effects only rarely occur. Deca, through its increased protein synthesis, also leads to a net muscle gain and Oxandrolone, based on the increased phosphocreatine synthesis, leads to a measurable strength gain with very low water retention. Other variations of administration used by female athletes are Deca and Winstrol tablets, as well as Deca and Primobolan S-tablets.

Since Deca-Durabolin has no negative effects on the liver it can even be used by persons with liver diseases. Exams have shown that a combined application of Dianabol/Deca-Durabolin increases the liver values which, however, return to normal upon discontinuance of the 17-alpha alkylated Dianabol and continued administration of Deca. Even a treatment period with Deca-Durabolin over several years could not reveal a damage to the liver. For this reason Deca combines well with Andriol (240-280 mg/day) since Andriol is not broken down through the liver and thus the liver function is not influenced either. Older and more cautious steroid users, in particular, like this combination.

A great disadvantage of Deca-Durabolin is its high price. In the U.S. a 50 mg ampule costs approx. $10 - 12. In a catalog of a large American pharamaceutical company the 50 mg ampules are offered at $11.79. A 200 mg/ml ampule costs $19.49. Since the weekly dose is around 200-400 mg/week, treatment can become very expensive. On the black market, one can especially find the Dutch and Greek Deca-Durabolin in strengths of 200 mg/2 ml ampules; they usually cost around $30 per ampule. Those who have access to the generic Greek 50 mg products such as Anaboline, Ziremilon, or Extraboline, receive a product of equally good quality at a slightly lower price. We doubt whether the Russian Retabolin and the Hungarian Retabolil are of good quality. At least from the standpoint of their price these products are very interesting.

Because of its great popularity and the high demand that goes along with it, there are many fakes of Deca-Durabolin. Some of the most popular include the brown 10 m/injection vial "Nandrolone-Decanoate" by International Pharmaceuticals and the 30 ml and 50 ml brown glass vials supposedly by the manufacturer "National Products CA-U.S." Also, Deca fakes are mostly sold in brown and white 2ml glass ampules with supposedly 100 mg/ml. In Europe, original Deca is never sold in a glass ampule or vial with more than 2ml injection solution. The ampules and vials by Organon Company all come with an adhesive label or sticker and no simple stamp imprint which, as on most fakes, is directly placed on the glass. If somebody offers you individual ampules without its appertaining packaging you should be very skeptical about the compound (and salesperson). The drug "Nandrolone Decanoate" by International Pharmaceuticals comes with an adhesive label on the 10 ml vial is individually packaged, but it is still a fake. There are also several fakes of the Dutch Deca-Durabolin "100" by Organon Company. It is relatively easy to recognize the original since it comes in a prick-through ampule with a red cap. The Greek Deca is bought by dealers on Crete in large quantities with little difficulty, since Crete receives a certain yearly allotment from the Greek mainland. Its subsidy by the government allows for a low price. The Mexican Deca unfortunately is manufactured only in a 50 mg version which means quite voluminous injections for its user. Since it is not as simple to imitate the Redi-ject versions one can assume that he or she is dealing with an original Deca compound if it originated in Mexico. There are always two Redi-ject injections in one original package. The ampules by Organon are of brown glass, with an aluminum cap and a white label with blue and black print. The probability of receiving an original Mexican Deca is very low.

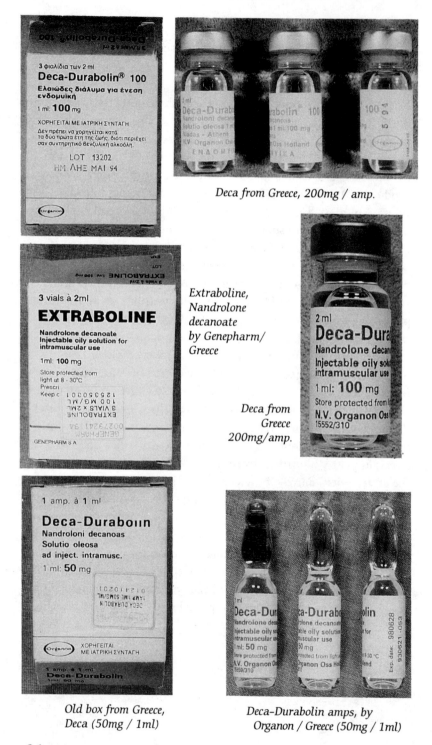

3 φιαλίδια των 2 ml
Deca-Durabolin® 100
Ελαιώδες διάλυμα για ένεση
ενδομυική

1 ml: **100** mg

ΧΟΡΗΓΕΙΤΑΙ ΜΕ ΙΑΤΡΙΚΗ ΣΥΝΤΑΓΗ

Δεν πρέπει να χορηγείται κατά
τα δύο πρώτα έτη της ζωής, διότι περιέχει
σαν συντηρητικό βενζυλική αλκοόλη.

LOT 13202
HM ΛΗΞ ΜΑΙ 94

Deca from Greece, 200mg / amp.

3 vials à 2ml
EXTRABOLINE
Nandrolone decanoate
Injectable oily solution for
intramuscular use

1ml: **100** mg

Store protected from
light at 8 - 30°C

GENEPHARM S A

*Extraboline,
Nandrolone
decanoate
by Genepharm/
Greece*

2 ml
Deca-Dura
Nandrolone decan
Injectable oily sol
intramuscular use
1 ml: **100** mg
Store protected from
N.V. Organon Oss
15552/310

*Deca from
Greece
200mg/amp.*

1 amp. à 1 ml
Deca-Duraboiin
Nandroloni decanoas
Solutio oleosa
ad inject. intramusc.

1 ml: **50** mg

ΧΟΡΗΓΕΙΤΑΙ
ΜΕ ΙΑΤΡΙΚΗ ΣΥΝΤΑΓΗ

*Old box from Greece,
Deca (50mg / 1ml)*

*Deca-Durabolin amps, by
Organon / Greece (50mg / 1ml)*

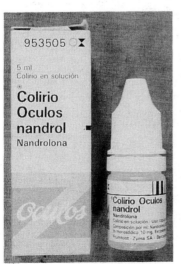

1 φύσ 1 ml
Deca-Durabolin
Nandrolone decanoate
Ενέσιμο ελαιώδες διάλυμα
για ενδομυική χρήση

1 ml: 50 mg

Διατηρείται σε θερμοκρασία 8–30 °C
Προστατεύεται από το φως
Χορηγείται με ιατρική συνταγή
Να φυλάσσεται μακρυά από παιδιά.

ΛΙΑΝΙΚΗ ΤΙΜΗ ΔΡΧ.

ΗΜ. ΛΗΞΗΣ:
Exp. date;   980428

ΠΑΡΤΙΔΑ:
Lot: 930401-004

(Organon)

1 ampolla de 1 ml   740480
Deca-Durabolín 50
Decanoato de nandrolona

Composición por ampolla:
Decanoato de nandrolona   50 mg
Excipiente c. s.

Inyección intramuscular

(Organon)

1 ampolla de 1 ml
Deca-Durabolín 50

New box Deca (50mg / 1ml) Greece

*Deca-Durabolin 50 by
Organon / Spain*

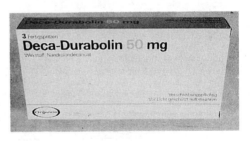

3 Fertigspritzen
Deca-Durabolin 50 mg
Wirkstoff: Nandrolondecanoat

Verschreibungspflichtig
Vor Licht geschützt aufbewahren

(Organon)

*Rediject syrings from Germany
(50mg) 3 in a box*

953505

5 ml
Colirio en solución

Colirio
Oculos
nandrol
Nandrolona

Colirio Oculos
nandrol
Nandrolona

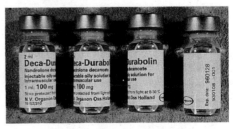

2 ml
Deca-Dur
Nandrolone dec
Injectable oily so
Intramuscular
1 ml: 100 mg
N. V. Organon

ca-Durabo
rolone decanoat
ble oily solution
ular use
100 mg

urabolin
canoate
solution for
use

Exp. date: 960128
930108 -001

*Eyedrops with Nandrolona
from Spain*

*Deca-Durabolin from the
Netherlands (200mg /amp)*

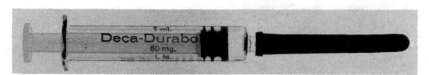

Rediject syring with blister by Organon / Mexico (50mg / 1ml)

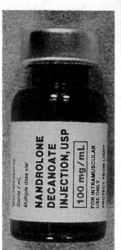

*Nandrolone Decanoate
by Steris / U.S.*

DIANABOL

Substance: methandrostenlone/methandienone

Trade names

Anabol Tablets	5 mg tab.;	L.P. Standard Labs. Co. Thailand
Anabolin (o.c.)	5 mg tab.;	Leiras FI
Anabolin (o.c.)	0.5% cream;	Leiras FI
Andoredan	5 mg tab.;	Takeshima-Kodama Japan
Bionabol	2 mg tab.;	Pharmacia Co. Dupnitza BG
Bionabol	5 mg tab;	Pharmacia Co. Dupnitza BG
Dialone (o.c.)	5 mg tab.;	Major U.S.

Dianabol (o.c.)	5 mg tab.;	Ciba GB, G, U.S.
Encephan	5 mg tab.;	Sato Japan
Metanabol	5 mg tab.;	Polfa PL
Metanabol	1 mg tab.;	Polfa PL
Metanabol	0.5% cream;	Polfa PL
Methandrostenolonum	5 mg tab.;	Russia
Nerobol	5 mg tab.;	Galenika YU, Gedeon Richter HU
Nerobol	5 mg tab.;	Gedeon Richter BG
Pronabol-5	5 mg tab.;	P&B Labs. Private Ltd.I ndia
Stenolon	5 mg tab.;	Leciva CZ
Stenolon	1 mg tab.;	Leciva CZ
Trinergic	5 mg cap.;	India
Naposim	5 mg tab.;	Rumania

Veterinary:

Anabolikum 2.5%	25 mg/ml; 50 ml	Meca G
Metandiabol	25 mg/ml; 50 ml	Quimper Mexico

"Dianabol (17-alpha-methyl-17beta-hydroxil-androsta-1.4dien-3-on) is a new, orally applicable steroid with a great effect on the protein metabolism. The effect of Dianabol promotes the protein synthesis, thus it supports the buildup of protein. This effect manifests itself in a positive nitrogen balance and an improved well-being. The calcium balance is positively influenced as well: Dianabol promotes the calcium deposits in the bones. Dianabol is indicated in the treatment of all diseases and conditions in which an anabolic (protein-buildup promoting) effect and a generally roborizing (entire organism strengthening) effect can be obtained." (Excerpt from the package insert of the former German anabolic Dianabol of Ciba Aktiengesellschaft, Wehr/Baden).

Dianabol is an oral anabolic which was developed in 1956 by the American Dr. John Ziegler in collaboration with Ciba-Geigy Company. In the U.S. it was introduced on the market in 1960 and within a short time it was available in many countries. In the course of a few years Dianabol became the most favored and most used anabolic by athletes in all disciplines. On 05/01/1982 Ciba-Geigy took all human-use Dianabol versions off the market because of its high potential for misuse. Ciba-Geigy gave as its reason for this step the increasing improper use of Dianabol in some developing countries where the compound was used as an appetite stimulant and for the improvement of the conversion of proteins in children and women. Three years later, on 05/01/1985, Ciba-Geigy's injectable Dianabol for veterinary medicine was taken off the market. Since Ciba-Geigy's patent rights for the substance methandrostenolone (or methandienone) had already expired a few years earlier, a continuous supply for athletes was guaranteed. In the meantime, several manufacturers in various countries have marketed this substance under their own generic name. (See list with various trade names.)

Dianabol is similar to the chemical structure of 17-alpha methytestosterone. Dianabol, therefore, has a very strong anabolic and androgenic effect which manifests itself in an enormous buildup of strength and muscle mass in its users. Dianabol is simply a "mass steroid" which works quickly and reliably. A weight gain of 2 - 4 pounds per week in the first six weeks is normal with Dianabol. The additional body weight consists of a true increase in tissue (hypertrophy of muscle fibers) and, in particular, in a noticeable retention of fluids. Dianabol aromatizes easily so that it is not a very good drug when one works out for a competition. Excessive water retention and aromatizing can be avoided in most cases by simultaneously taking Nolvadex and Proviron so that some athletes are able to use Dianabol until three to four days before a competition.

The dosage spectrum, in particular for bodybuilders, weightlifters, and powerlifters, is very wide. It ranges from two tablets per day up to twenty or more tablets per day. Those athletes who believe that they absolutely must take a two-figure amount of tablets should think about the interesting statement that the Ciba-Geigy Company made about its compound Dianabol: "The most distinct measure of the effect of Dianabol is the increase in body weight. There seems to be no direct correlation between the increase of body weight and the amount of the dosage." The German authors R. Häcker and H. de Mar++es confirm this in their book *Hormonelle Regulation und psychophysische Belastung im Leistungssport*. On page 55 it reads: "A simple correlation between the administered dosage and the amount of concentration in the blood could not be found either." This obviously does not mean that every athlete should take only one 5 mg tablet; however, this statement, together with the year-long empirical values from numerous athletes, helps determine a reasonable dosage range. Accordingly, an effective daily dose for athletes is around 15-40 mg/day. The dosage of Dianabol taken by the athlete should always be coordinated with his individual goals. Steroid novices do not need more than 15-20 mg of Dianabol per day since this dose is sufficient to achieve exceptional results over a period of 8-10 weeks. When the effect begins to slow down in this group after about eight weeks and the athlete wants to continue his treatment, the dosage of Dianabol should not be increased but an injectable steroid such as Deca-Durabolin in a dosage of 200 mg/week or Primobolan in a dosage of 200 mg/week should be used in addition to the Dianabol dose; or he may switch to one of the two abovementioned compounds. The use of testosterone is not recommended at this stage as the athlete should leave some free play for later. For those either impatient or more advanced, a stack of Dianabol 20-30 mg/day and Deca-Durabolin 200-400 mg/day achieves miracles. Daniel Duchaine makes it plain in his book Underground Steroid Handbook 2, page 33, by quoting an old pro, "If you can't grow on Deca and D-bol, you're not gonna grow anything, no matter how fancy it is."

In fact, athletes who are not ambitious to compete will make highly satisfying progress with Dianabol. Competing athletes, more advanced athletes, and athletes weighing more than 220 pounds do not need more than 40 mg/day, and in very rare cases 50 mg/day. It does not make sense to increase the number of Dianabol tablets immeasurably since fifteen tablets do not double the effect of seven or eight. Daily dosages of 60 mg+ usually are the result of the athlete's ignorance or his plain despair, since in some athletes, due to the continued improper intake of steroids, nothing seems to be effective any longer. The simultaneous intake of Dianabol and Anadrol 50 is not a good idea since these two compounds have similar effects. The situation can be compared to the intake of ten or more tablets of one of these drugs per day. Those who are more interested in strength and less in body mass can combine Dianabol with either Oxandrolone or Winstrol tablets. The additional intake of an injectable steroid does, however, clearly show the best results. To build up mass and strength, Sustanon or Testosterone enanthate at 250 mg+/week and/ or Deca-Durabolin 200 at mg+/week are suitable. To prepare for a competition, Dianabol has only limited use since it causes distinct water retention in many athletes and due to its high conversion rate into estrogen it complicates the athlete's fat breakdown. Those of you without this problem or who are able to control it by taking Nolvadex or Proviron, in this phase should use Dianabol together with the proven Parabolan, Winstrol Depot, Masteron, Oxandrolone, etc.

Since Dianabol's half-life time is only 3.2-4.5 hours (1) application at least twice a day is necessary to achieve a somewhat even concentration of the substance in the blood. Scientific tests continue to show that on days of intense workout compared to rest days, the half-life time of Dianabol is reduced even further so that an application three times daily appears sensible. Since Dianabol is also 17-alpha alkylated and thus largely protected against a loss in effect, it is recommended that the tablets be taken during meals so that possible gastrointestinal pains can be avoided. On the third day after discontinuing the intake of Dianabol, proof of the substance methandrostenolone (methandienone) in the blood is negative. This means that the tablets are no longer effective. The athlete, however, should not proceed under the assumption that a urine test will be negative since the elimination of the metabolites of the substance methandrostenolone through the urine continues much longer. The maximum substance concentration of Dianabol reaches the blood after 1-3 hours. A simple application of only 10 mg results in a 5-fold increase in the average testosterone concentration in the male (2). An important reason why Dianabol works well in all athletes is that the endogenous cortisone production is reduced by 50-70%. Thus, Dianabol considerably slows down the rate at which protein is broken down in the muscle cell.

Women should not use Dianabol because, due to its distinct androgenic component, considerable virilization symptoms can occur. There are, however, several female bodybuilders and, in particular, female powerlifters who use Dianabol and obtain enormous progress with 10-20 mg/day. Women who do not show a sensitive reaction to the additional intake of androgens or who are not afraid of possible masculinization symptoms get on well with 2-4 tablets over a period not to exceed 4-6 weeks. Higher dosages and a longer time of intake bring better results; however, the androgens begin to be noticeable in the female organism. No woman who continues to care about her femininity should take more than 10 mg/day and 50-100 mg of Deca-Durabolin/week over 4-6 weeks.

Although Dianabol has many potential side effects, they are rare with a dosage of up to 20 mg/day. Since Dianabol is 17-alpha alkylated it causes a considerable strain on the liver. In high dosages and over a longer period of time, Dianabol is liver-toxic. Even a dosage of only 10 mg/day can increase the liver values; after discontinuance of the drug, however, the values return to normal. Since Dianabol quickly increases the body weight due to high water retention, a high blood pressure and a faster heartbeat can occur, sometimes requiring the intake of an antihypertensive drug such as Catapresan. Additive intake of Nolvadex and Proviron might be necessary as well, since Dianabol strongly converts into estrogens and in some athletes causes gynecomastia ("bitch tits") or worsens an already existing condition. Because of the strongly androgenic component and the conversion into dihydrotestosterone, Dianabol, in some athletes, can trigger a serious acne vulgaris on the face, neck, chest, back, and shoulders since the sebaceous gland function is stimulated. If a hereditary predisposition exists Dianabol can also accelerate a possible hair loss which again can be explained by the high conversion of the substance into dihydrotestosterone. Dianabol has significant influence on the endogenous testosterone level. Studies have shown that the intake of 20 mg Dianabol/day over 10 days reduces the testosterone level by 30-40% (3). This can be explained by Dianabol's distinct antigonadotropic effect, meaning that it inhibits the release of the gonadotropic FSH (follicle stimulating hormone) and LH (luteinizing hormone) by the hypophysis. Another disadvantage is that, after discontinuance of the compound, a considerable loss of strength and mass often occurs since the water stored during the intake is again excreted by the body. In high dosages of 50 mg +/day aggressive behavior in the user can occasionally be observed which, if it only refers to his workout, can be an advantage. In order to avoid uncontrolled actions, those who have a tendency to easily lose their temper should be aware of this characteristic when taking a high D-bol dosage. Despite all of these possible symptoms Dianabol instills in most athletes a "sense of well-being anabolic" which improves the mood and appetite and in many users, together with the obtained results, leads to an improved level of consciousness and a higher self-confidence.

For years, the steroid black market has been the only supply source for athletes to get Dianabol where, proverbially, D-bol is available in all colors, forms, sizes, and under any imaginable name. Those, however, who are only interested in original compounds, should make sure that the selected compound is part of the list with common trade marks for methan-drostenolone (methandienone) or that the compound looks like the one in the photos following this description. According to our experience the Thailandian Anabol tablets and the Indian Pronabol-5 are the best compounds. The "Thai-landians," as they are often called by their users, can be easily identified. They are pentagonally shaped, of pink color, and indented. One thousand tablets are packaged in a plastic bag which is contained in a labelled plastic box the size of a drinking glass (see photo). Note that the manufacturing date and not the expiration date is printed on the label. The plastic box is usually also shrink-wrapped. The price for a 1000-package lies around $500-$1000 on the black market. The Indian Pronabol-5, simply called "Pronas," is enclosed in an oblong box with ten strips of 10 tablets each. These tablets are round, white, and indented on one side. The original Pronas can be easily recognized since they come in a silver aluminum strip with a double bottom, and have a purple imprint so that the tablets are invisible. Since the fake Pronabols are indented as well one must make certain not to purchase tablets in bulk or tablets contained in a normal push-through strip. Original "Pronas", cost approximately $100 per package on the black market. Other easily available original compounds are the Polish Metanabol and the Czech Stenolon.

For a long time the Polish Metanabol was packaged in a small brown glass vial of 20 tablets each. Unfortunately, the tablets are not indented or marked so the contents of the vials can be easily substituted. Since 1994, Metanabol has only been available in blister strips of 10 tablets each, of orange color, and with their own packaging. The Czech Stenolon tablets have two indents on one side and come in push-through strips of 20 tablets. Each push-through strip is included in a yellow-grey package. Note that there is no package insert since the entire user information is printed on the back of the small carton. On the black market usually only individual strips without packaging can be found since the packaging takes up too much room when smuggled. Because of the interesting price of these two compounds it is not unusual to find athletes who take twenty or more tablets daily. The Rumanian Naposim contains 20 tablets in a small plastic box with each tablet having an engraved triangle on one side.

The Russian Dianabol is packaged in push-through strips of ten tablets each. Ten push-through strips are contained in a green box or are held together by a black rubber band and a rag similar to toilet paper. The imprint on the push-through strips is either blue or black. The tablets are not indented and it is of note that the substance amount is given in grams (0.005g/tabl.) Since the price is low the Russian Dianabol is often taken in two-digit quantities. Although the tablets cost only 2-4 cents in Russia, a price of $0.50 is quite acceptable on the black market. The situation with the Russian compound is a little different since, in the meantime, numerous athletes have experienced unusual side effects with these tablets. They range from nausea, vomiting, and elevated liver values to real cases of illness which have forced one or more athletes to stay in bed for several days. These tablets, however, have one thing in common: there is no doubt that they work powerfully. Due to the unusual number of side effects and simultaneously the positive effect, there is speculation that the Russian Dianabol is a simple 17-alpha methyltestosterone. Since Dianabol as already mentioned, is a derivative of it, the two substances have similar effects. The fine difference, however, is that oral 17-alpha methyltestosterone is clearly more androgenic and therefore causes more strain on the the liver.

Our opinion is that processing of the 17-alpha methyltestosterone in methandrostenolone was probably not carried out completely in the Russian Dianabol; consequently, several tablets contain a mix. It is also possible that during manufacturing of the Russian Dianabol old, expired, tablets were mixed with the produced substance and made into new tablets. We want to explicitly emphasize, however, that these are only speculations. Unfortunately, there are already fakes of the Russian tablets available. They are only recognized as such after 1-2 weeks of their intake when "nothing happens." As said before, in our experience the best results can be obtained with the Thailandian Anabol tablets and the Indian Pronabol-5.

(1) Hormonelle Regulation und psychophysische Belastung im Leistungssport, p. 55; R. Häcker and H. De Marees;
(2) Hormonelle Regulation und psychophysische Belastung im Leistungssport, p. 57; R. Häcker and H. De Marees;
(3) Hormonelle Regulation und psychophysische Belastung im Leistungssport, p. 55; R. Häcker and H. De Marees;

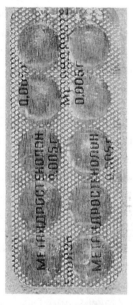

Methandrostenoloni, D-bol from Russia, box, 10 blisters are held together by a black rubber band

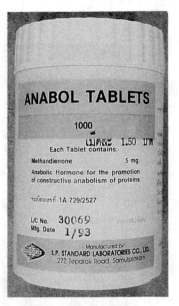

Anabol tablets, D-bol from Thailand,
1000 in a plastic can

Naposim, D-bol from
Rumania

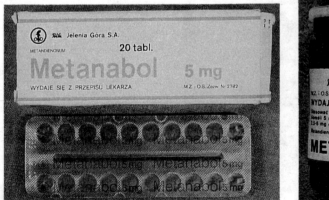

New box and blister of Metanabol
from Poland

Old version
of Metanabol

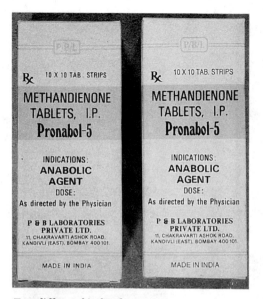

℞ 10 X 10 TAB. STRIPS

METHANDIENONE
TABLETS, I.P.
Pronabol-5

INDICATIONS:
**ANABOLIC
AGENT**
DOSE:
As directed by the Physician

P & B LABORATORIES
PRIVATE LTD.
11, CHAKRAVARTI ASHOK ROAD,
KANDIVLI (EAST), BOMBAY 400 101.

MADE IN INDIA

℞ 10 X 10 TAB. STRIPS

METHANDIENONE
TABLETS, I.P.
Pronabol-5

INDICATIONS:
**ANABOLIC
AGENT**
DOSE:
As directed by the Physician

P & B LABORATORIES
PRIVATE LTD.
11, CHAKRAVARTI ASHOK ROAD,
KANDIVLI (EAST), BOMBAY 400 101.

MADE IN INDIA

*Two different kinds of
Pronabol-5, D-bol from India*

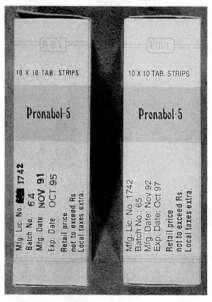

10 X 10 TAB. STRIPS

Pronabol-5

10 X 10 TAB. STRIPS

Pronabol-5

Mfg. Lic. No. 1742
Batch No.: 64
Mfg. Date: NOV 91
Exp. Date: OCT 95

Retail price
not to exceed Rs
Local taxes extra.

Mfg. Lic. No. 1742
Batch No.: 65
Mfg. Date: Nov 92
Exp. Date: Oct 97

Retail price
not to exceed Rs.
Local taxes extra.

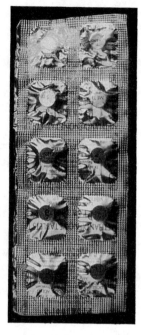

Pronabol-5 blister

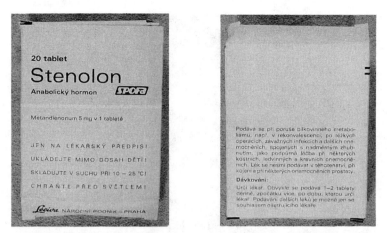

Stenolon by Leciva, D-bol from the former CZ, front, back and foil strip

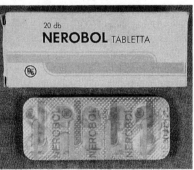

Nerobol with blister, D-bol from Hungary

*Liquid D-bol for
veterinary use by
Quimper / Mexico,
Metandiabol box
and vial*

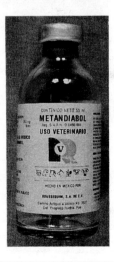

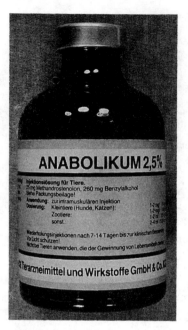

ANABOLIKUM 2,5%

Injektionslösung für Tiere.
25 mg Methandrostenolon, 260 mg Benzylalkohol
Siehe Packungsbeilage!
Anwendung: zur intramuskulären Injektion
Dosierung: Kleintiere (Hunde, Katzen): 1-2 mg
Zootiere: 1-2 mg
sonst: 2-4 ml

Wiederholungsinjektionen nach 7-14 Tagen bis zur klinischen Besserung
Vor Licht schützen!
Nicht bei Tieren anwenden, die der Gewinnung von Lebensmitteln dienen

Tierarzneimittel und Wirkstoffe GmbH & Co.

Veterinary D-bol from Germany, Anabolikum 2.5% by Meca

DURABOLIN

Substance: nandrolone phenylpropionate

Trade names

Activin (o.c.)	10 mg/ml;	Aristegvi ES
Anabolin (o.c.)	50 mg/ml;	Alto U.S.
Anabolin-IM (o.c.)	50 mg/ml;	Alto U.S.
Anabolin-LA-100 (o.c.)	100 mg/ml;	Alto U.S.
Androlone (o.c.)	50 mg/ml;	Keene U.S.
Durabolin	25 mg/ml;	Organon B, ES, FR, GB, NL, FI,Canada, U.S.,Opopharma CH, Pliva YU Medika/Santa TKi, Donmed South Africa
Durabolin	50 mg/ml;	Organon GB, PT, U.S., Canada, Pliva YU
Durabolin	100 mg/2 ml;	Organon U.S.
Equibolin-50 (o.c.)	100 mg/2 ml;	Vortech U.S.

Fenobolin	20 mg/ml;	Medexport Russia
Fherbolico (o.c.)	50 mg/ml;	Fher ES
Hybolin Improved	25, 50 mg/ml;	Hyrex U.S.
Nandrobolic (o.c.)	25 mg/ml;	Forest U.S.
Nandrol.Phenprop. (o.c.)	50 mg/ml;	Quad U.S.
Nerobolil (o.c.)	25 mg/ml;	Gedeon Richter HU
Nerobolil	25 mg/ml;	Gedeon Richter BG
Nu-Bolic (o.c.)	25 mg/ml;	Seatrace U.S.
Superanabolon	25 mg/ml;	Leciva CZ
Turinabol (o.c.)	25 mg/ml;	Jenapharm G
Turinabol	25 mg/ml;	Jenapharm BG, Germed CZ

Durabolin, as its name already suggests, is very similar to the popular Deca-Durabolin. It is almost a precursor of Deca since it was put on the market by Organon in 1959, three years before Deca. The main difference lies in the compounds' different durations in the body. Durabolin, since phenylpropionate is added to nandrolone, leaves the body much faster than Deca, which contains the substance nandrolone decanoate. While Deca needs to be injected once a week, Durabolin must be injected more frequently and in regular intervals. The substance nandrolone-phenylpropionate quickly gets into the blood, where it remains active for two to three days. Athletes who hope for optimal results inject Durabolin every third day, or even every two days. The dosage is around 50-100 mg per injection, or a total of 150-300 mg/week. Those who have access to the 50 mg version should take advantage of it since it is less expensive than the 25 mg version, which is normally more easily available. In addition, the 1-2 ml injections are more pleasant than the 2-4 ml. Durabolin has a distinct anabolic effect which assists the protein synthesis and allows the protein to be stored in the muscle cell in large amounts. This is combined with a moderate androgenic component which stimulates the athlete's regeneration and helps maintain the muscle mass during a diet. It shows that Durabolin stores much less water in the body than Deca-Durabolin. For this reason, Durabolin is more suitable for a preparation for a competition while Deca should be given preference for the buildup of strength and muscle mass. Durabolin, however, can be used for this purpose as well. The gains are fewer and slower than with Deca but of a higher quality and remain, for the most part, after discontinuing the compound. A stack suitable for this purpose would be, e.g. 50 mg Durabolin every 2 days, 50 mg Testosterone propionate every 2 days, and 20 mg Winstrol tablets every day.

Compared to Deca-Durabolin the side effects of Durabolin are few and less frequent. Although Deca is usually well tolerated in men when taken in a dosage of 200-400 mg/week, male athletes who react sensitively to the androgenic residual effect can experience problems as can women. Water retention, high blood pressure, an elevated estrogen level, and virilization symptoms occur less often with Durabolin. Female athletes therefore take Durabolin in weekly intervals since, due to its short duration of effect, no undesirable concentration of androgen takes place. They achieve good results with 50 mg Durabolin/week, 50 mg Testosterone propionate every 8-10 days, and 8-10 mg Winstrol/day, or 10 mg Oxandrolone/day. Three to four day intervals between the relative injections are to be observed. Durabolin is one of the safest non-toxic steroids offering satisfactory results. Durabolin has no negative effect on the liver function so it can even be taken in cases of liver disease. Side effects occur only in rare cases and in persons who are extremely sensitive. Virilization symptoms in women such as huskiness, deep voice, hirsutism, acne, and increased libido are possible but occur only rarely if reasonable dosages are taken at reasonable intervals. Men usually experience no symptoms with Durabolin. Since the release of gonadotropin in the hypophysis is inhibited, there is a chance that the body's own testosterone production in a male athlete will be lower when the compound is taken over a prolonged time and in excessive doses.

The main disadvantages of Durabolin, for most athletes, consist of its poor availability on the black market, the fact that frequent injections are needed, and the high cost. Durabolin, i.e. the substance "nandrolone phenylpropionate," unlike Deca-Durabolin is rarely found on the black market. When an athlete accidentally finds Durabolin it is usually the unfit 25 mg version. The original Spanish package of Organon with three ampules of 25 mg each, costs approx. $24-36.- on the black market. All of Organon's original ampules have a white paper label with black print and no imprint which is branded into or painted onto the glass. American Durabolin is available in 25 mg/ml, 5 ml vials, and 50 mg/ml in 2 vials. The official retail price for one 5 ml vial is $16.29 while the 2 ml version costs $14.29. There are (so far) no fakes available.

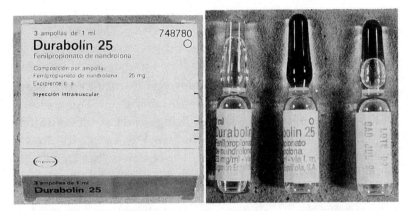

Durabolin 25 by Organon / Spain (25mg / amp.) 3 in a box

Superanabolon by Leciva / CZ, 5 amp / box (25mg / 1ml)

DYNABOLON

Substance: nandrolone undecanoate

Trade names

Dynabolon	80.5 mg/ml;	Farmasister I
Dynabolon	80.5 mg/ml	Crinos I
Dynabolon	80.5 mg/ml;	Theramex FR
Psychobolan (o.c.)	80.5 mg/ml;	Theramex GR

Along with Anadur, Deca-Durabolin, and Durabolin, this is another steroid containing the substance nandrolone. Dynabolon is a favorite among athletes since it brings good results with few side effects. Although it is often compared to "Deca", its effect is milligram per milligram stronger. The reason is that Dynabolon is slightly androgenic with an anabolic effect, thus it strongly promotes the protein synthesis. The increased androgenic component helps the athlete achieve a good strength increase and an accelerated regeneration. Those who have had good results with Deca will usually respond even better to Dynabolon. Athletes report a distinct, quickly effective, solid gain in muscles, which goes hand in hand with a significant gain in strength. The increase in body weight and the improved strength are the result of the water retention in tissues and joints. Dynabolon does not strongly aromatize in dosages below 4 ml/week. Dynabolon is effective for 1-2 weeks, thus requiring more frequent injections than Deca. Bodybuilders who work with this compound usually inject it twice a week. The minimum dosage is 2ml/week. A weekly dosage of 4 ml (equal to 322 mg) is usually sufficient for most athletes to achieve satisfactory results. This requires the injection of 2 ml (equal to 161 mg or 2 ampules) twice weekly. Higher dosages would certainly bring even better gains but often go hand in hand with distinct water retention. Such dosages also aromatize so strongly that antiestrogens must be taken to maintain the quality of the muscles. Women do well with 1 ml/week and rarely show virilization symptoms if the compound is not taken for more than six weeks. Female athletes rarely use

Dynabolon since they normally prefer Durabolin, which has a shorter duration of effectiveness.

The side effects in men are quite rare and usually occur only in sensitive persons or when high dosages are taken. Possible side effects such as high blood pressure and elevated cholesterol levels, as well as acne or gynecomastia usually disappear without treatment after use of the product is discontinued. Dynabolon is tolerated quite well by the liver so that increased liver values occur only in rare instances. Unlike Deca it should not be taken if a hepatic disease or dysfunction exists.

Dynabolon is hardly found on the American black market while in Italy and France the versions of Theramex are quite popular. In Germany the French Dynabolon of Theramex Company, Monaco, is often available. In small numbers, through various channels, these products then reach the U.S. This is a small yellow box which always contains only one ampule. As with all French steroids, the expiration date is printed on an extra-label which is attached to the back of the package. In addition, the ampule is shrink-wrapped and can be opened by removing a small piece of aluminum. The ampule itself contains 1 ml neutralized olive oil with 80.5 mg nandrolone undecanoate and usually costs between $15 and $20 on the black market. The red label on the ampule is branded into the glass and can be felt. It cannot be removed by fingernail or be scratched off. So far, no fakes of Dynabolon are available.

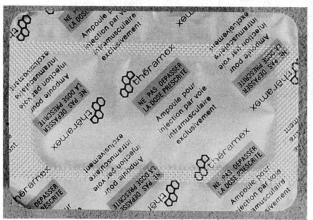

Dynabolon, Theramex / France, box,
blister and ampule

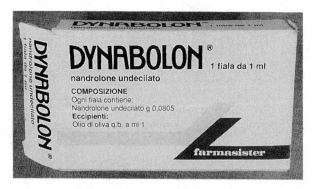

Dynabolon by Farmasister / Italy

EPHEDRINE

Substance: ephedrine hydrochloride

Trade names

Ceepa (o.c.)	24 mg tab.;	Geneva U.S.
Central (o.c.)	elex.	Central U.S.
Dymetadrine	25 mg tab.;	AST Research U.S.
Efedrin (o.c.)	20 mg tab.;	ACO S
Efedrin	25 mg tab.;	Leiras FI
Efedrin DAK	20 mg tab.;	DAK Labs DK
Efedrina Level	50 mg tab.;	Laboratorio Level S.A. ES
Ephedrine HCL	25 mg tab.;	Strength Systems U.S.
Ephedrine HCL	25 mg tab.;	NVE Pharmaceuticals U.S.
Ephedrine HCL	25 mg tab.;	T&M U.S.
Eph. HCl-Antos (o.c.)	50 mg tab.;	Merania A
Ephedrin Spofa	25 mg tab.;	Slovakofarma CZ
Ephedrini HCL (o.c.)	50 mg tab.;	Brocacef NL; Interpharm NL; Magnafarm NL; OPG NL; Pharbita NL; Pharmachemie NL
Ephedrinum HCL	25 mg tab.;	Polfa PL
Ephedroides 3	30 mg tab.;	Richelet FR
Lardet Expectorant (o.c.)	24 mg tab.;	Standex U.S.
Mudrane GG (o.c.)	16 mg tab.;	Poythress U.S.
Perspiran N	25 mg tab.;	Gödecke G
Perspiran N prot.	48 mg tab.;	Gödecke G
Pyrralan Expectorant (o.c)	30 mg tab.;	Lannet U.S.
Quadrinal	24 mg tab.;	Knoll U.S.
Quibron Plus	25 mg tab.;	Bristol U.S.
Rhinoguttae	10 mg tab.;	Ex-Fna NL
Stopastheme	10 mg cap.;	Granions FR
Tedral-SA (o.c.)	48 mg tab.;	Parke Davis U.S.
T-E-P (o.c.)	24 mg tab.;	Stanlabs U.S.
Theodrine	24 mg tab.;	Rugby U.S.
Theopheyllin (o.c.)	24 mg tab.;	H.L.Moore U.S.
Vencipon N	12.21 mg drg	Artesan G, A

Note: The substance ephedrine hydrochloride is also part of numerous injectable solutions, drops, nasal sprays, syrups, ointments, powders, and fluids which, however, are not listed here since athletes usually prefer tablets.

Ephedrine belongs to the group of sympathomimetics. Although it is not a hormone compound, we would still like to describe it briefly since it offers the athlete three interesting effects. First, ephedrine has clear fatburning characteristics. On the one hand, this occurs since ephedrine produces heat in the body (thermogenesis). Simplified, ephedrine slightly increases the body temperature so that the body burns more calories than usual. On the other hand, ephedrine stimulates the thyroid gland to transform the weaker LT-4 (L-thyroxine) into the stronger LT-3 (liothyronine), thus accelerating the metabolism. The fatburning effect, with the additional intake of both methylzanthine caffeine and aspirin, can almost be doubled. Scientific research has shown that the combination of 25 mg ephedrine, 200 mg caffeine, and 300 mg aspirin is ideal to produce a synergetic effect. Those who apply this combination three times daily, approximately 30 minutes prior to a meal, will significantly burn fat. Competing bodybuilders have appreciated this for quite some time. Second, ephedrine has anticatabolic characteristics. Thus it is especially useful for maintaining the muscle system while dieting. Finally, athletes often use ephedrine as a "training booster." Since it has a mild amphetamine-like effect on the central nervous system (CNS) it improves the concentration, vigilance, and the interplay of nerves and muscles. For this purpose, 25-50 mg ephedrine are taken approximately one hour before a workout. The athlete feels an immediate boost in energy which during workout can manifest itself in a 5-10% increase in strength. Again, also in this case, the effect can be improved by taking caffeine and aspirin (s.a.). It is important to note that ephedrine, administered for this purpose, is not to be taken more than three times a week; otherwise, the body gets accustomed to it and the "boost effect" decreases, and much higher dosages are needed.

Side effects can manifest themselves in the form of more rapid heart beat, insomnia, tremors (light trembling of the fingers), headaches, dizziness, high blood pressure, and lack of appetite. The last characteristic, however, is much appreciated by athletes on a diet. Ephedrine must not be taken when high blood pressure, a severe hyperfunction of the thyroid gland, irregular heart rhythm, or a recent myocardial infarction are present. In Europe ephedrine is a prescription drug which is mostly available in combination with other substances. Such a combination compound, for example, is the German drug Perspiran N, which contains an additional 25 mg ephedrine hydrochloride and 125 mg theophylline per tablet. Theophylline increases the effect of ephedrine. The Spanish Efedrina Level of Laboratorio Level S.A. Company can be found on the black market. A 50 mg tablet usually costs $10. The tablets are indented, with "EFEDRINA" stamped on the back. Twenty-four tablets are packaged in a small white plastic box with a pull-off label. It is interesting to note that in the U.S. the substance ephedrine hydrochloride is not a prescription drug and is freely available while other stimulants and medicines used in sports are either unavailable or available only at high risk on the black market. In special magazines for bodybuilders one can always find ads freely offering Ephedrine. Until the time that this condition changes, Ephedrine is of no importance on the black market.

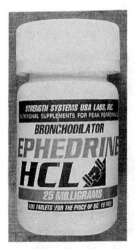

Ephedrine by Strength Systems

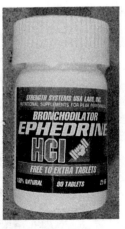

Another one by Strength Systems

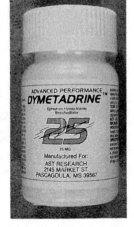

Dymetadrine by AST

Ephedrine from France

Efedrina Level box

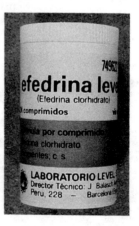

Efedrina Level from Spain

Zusammensetzung:
1 Dragee enthält:
Ephedrinhydrochlorid 12,21 mg
(entsprechend 10 mg Ephedrin)
Phenolphthalein 30 mg
Apothekenpflichtig! Reg.-Nr. V 12

ARTESAN Pharma · 3130 Lüchow
Depot für Österreich:
Overta Importges. mbH, Graz Spez.-Reg.-Nr. 8546

60 Dragees
zum Einnehmen

VENCIPON »N«

Zur kurzfristigen, höchstens vier Wochen dauernden,
unterstützenden Behandlung ernährungsbedingten
Übergewichts.

Vencipon with blister, ephedrine from Germany

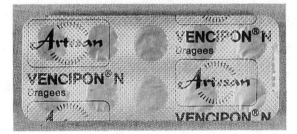

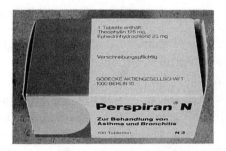

1 Tablette enthält:
Theophyllin 125 mg,
Ephedrinhydrochlorid 25 mg

Verschreibungspflichtig

GÖDECKE AKTIENGESELLSCHAFT
1000 BERLIN 10

Perspiran® N

Zur Behandlung von
Asthma und Bronchitis

100 Tabletten N 3

Perspiran with blister, ephedrine from Germany

EQUIPOISE

Substance: boldenone undecylenate

Trade names

Boldebal-H	50 mg/ml;	Ilium Troy Lab. Australia
Equipoise (o.c.)	25 mg, 50 mg/ml;	Squibb Canada, Mexico, U.S.
Equipoise	25 mg, 50 mg/ml;	Solvay Vet. Canada, Mexico, U.S.
Ganabol	25 mg, 50 mg/ml;	Laboratorios V.M. Columbia, Panama, Guatemala, El Salvador, Honduras, Ecuador, Dom. Rep.,Bolivia, Peru, Chile, Paraguay, Venezuela
Pace	25 mg/ml;	Jurox Labs Australia
Sybolin	25 mg/ml;	Manufacturer unknown, Australia
Vebonol	25 mg/ml;	Ciba-Geigy G, CH, Australia

Today, the substance boldenone undecylenate can only be found in steroids for veterinary medicine. The American Equipoise is for horses; the Columbian Ganabol is used for cattle; and the German Vebonol for dogs. Athletes do not care, which shows the enormous popularity and far-reaching application of these steroid compounds. Boldenone undecylenate is also very effective in humans and offers the athlete interesting characteristics which other steroids simply do not have. It does not make a difference to the athlete whether he uses Equipoise, Pace, Ganabol, or Vebonol since the effect is always the same. Most American bodybuilders use Equipoise since, unlike the other veterinary compounds, it is available on the black market.

Equipoise has a relatively high anabolic effect which is usually connected with a moderately distinct androgenic component. For this reason, Equipoise is not the steroid that will cause enormous gains in strength and muscle mass in the shortest time. Equipoise has a very favorable effect on the organism's nitrogen balance so that the main effect consists of a distinctly increased protein synthesis in the muscle cell. The resulting gain in body weight consists of a solid quality increase of the muscles which occurs slowly and evenly. The high quality is caused by low water retention of the substance. An additional advantage is that Equipoise aromatizes only slightly, thus making it an effective drug to use when preparing for competitions. Athletes who are dieting combine Equipoise with Winstrol Depot and report a dramatic increase in muscle hardness. Together with a sufficiently high supply of calories and protein this combination offers its users a large increase in strength and a rapid gain in quality muscles. Many will notice that Equipoise stimulates the appetite. The advantages achieved can usually be well-maintained over several weeks after use of the compound is discontinued. Equipoise also stimulates the erythropoiesis which is manifested by improved development and the formation of red blood cells. Bodybuilders thus experience an improved pump effect during workout and an improved vascularity.

For most male athletes the weekly dosage is usually 150-300 mg. Often since only the 25 mg version can be found, frequent or very voluminous injections are necessary. For most athletes 50 mg (corresponding to a 2 ml injection) taken every second day is sufficient. Advanced and ambitious bodybuilders usually take higher doses (50 mg daily) and achieve dramatic results. Women also usually respond well to Equipoise and with 50-100 mg/week they gain good muscles with a low water retention. A dosage in this range is usually well tolerated. Higher dosages can cause virilization symptoms such as deep voice, increased production of the sebaceous gland and acne, increased libido and in some cases increased hair growth on the face and legs. Men have few problems with Equipoise. Since water and salt retentions are low, the blood pressure usually does not increase. Acne, gynecomastia, and increased aggressiveness occur only in rare instances. The feared "steroid fever," which can occur when using veterinary steroids, is rare with Equipoise since the product by Squibb is highly sterile and pure. Those who experience flu-like symptoms when they begin taking the compound should reduce the dosage for a short time. Feeling feverish together with not feeling well, disappears after a few days. On a positive note, Equipoise is not liver-toxic. Ciba-Geigy confirms this in their German packet insert when in reference to the compound Vebonol: "Thanks to its special structure Vebanol has no negative influence on the liver."

The main disadvantages of Equipose are its high price and the fact that it is not always available on the black market. The German Vebonol, for example, is available in a glass vial with a 10 ml injection solution. The vial is made of normal window glass with a gold-orange screw cap. The adhesive paper label has rounded corners and cannot be removed from the vial. The expiration date and batch denomination are well visible and have been imprinted later in black ink unlike the rest of the label. The expiration date and batch denomination can be easily smeared. The injection solution has a light-yellow color. The 10 ml vial is also packaged in a small matching box. The long gold strip running diagonally through all four sides of the box is eye-catching, whereas the strip on the label of the glass vial is green. The price on the black market for a 10 ml vial is usually around $90. The most famous and widespread fake Boldenone undecylenate is a 50 ml glass vial made by Squibb Inc., Toronto, Canada, with a green label. It is imprinted with "Boldone" and contained in a label which has square edges and can be easily removed. The fact is that Squibb Company does not manufacture a veterinary steroid with the name "Boldone" and that the expiration date and batch number are in the same blue color and print as the rest of the label. This helps identify this compound as a fake. Original Equipoise is not easy to find; the same is true for the Columbian Ganabol and the Australian Pace and Sybolin.

Ganabol from Columbia is available in four different sizes: 10, 50 and 100 ml vials and —this is no typing error— in 250 ml glass bottles. (It is impossible to call them vials.) All bottles are made of brown glass and packaging as well as the label are in a bright green. As a contrast, several animals are pictured in red color. If there is no special marking on the box, it includes 25 mg of the substance per ml. There is also a 50 mg/ml substance version; this can be recognized by the number "50" (which refers to milligram) printed in red on yellow background and located in the left corner of the box. Ganabol costs approx. $8 per ml on the black market; the 100 ml vial costs approx. $800. Currently there are no available fakes.

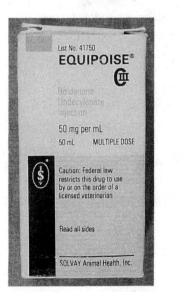 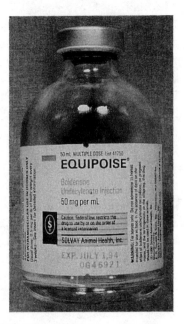

Equipoise, box and vial by Solvey / U.S.

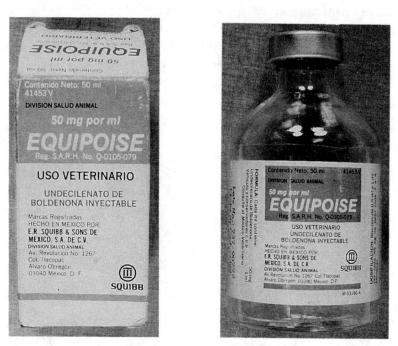

Equipoise, box and vial by Squibb / Mexico

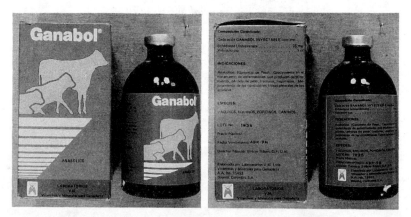

Ganabol, box and vial by Laboratorios' V.M., Middle and South America

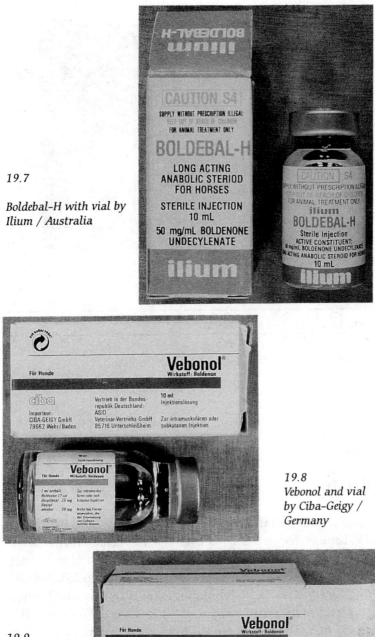

19.7

Boldebal–H with vial by Ilium / Australia

19.8
Vebonol and vial by Ciba–Geigy / Germany

19.9
Another package of Vebonol from Germany

 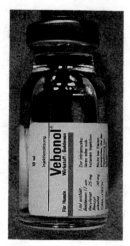

Vebonol vial from Germany

ESICLENE

Substance: formebolone

Trade names

Esiclene	1 mg drops;	LPB I; Biofarma PT
Esiclene	4 mg/2ml	LPB I;
Esiclene	5 mg tab.;	LPB I; Biofarma PT
Hubernol (o.c.)	1 mg drops;	ICN Hubber ES
Hubernol (o.c.)	5 mg drag.;	ICN Hubber ES

Esiclene is a steroid that is somewhat different from the others. The substance formebolone is available in various forms of administration. For athletes only the injectable version is of interest. Because of its anabolic effect, Esiclene is not well suited as a steroid for athletes. In bodybuilding, however, it is a highly valued and commonly used compound since it has the unusual characteristic of allowing any muscle to increase in diameter and size within the shortest period. How is this possible? Esiclene stimulates the muscle tissue located at the point of injection. The tissue defends itself or shall we say, reacts with a local inflammation.

This is manifested by an accumulation of tissue fluid from the lymph system which is the cause for the swelling or enlargement of the injected muscle. In order to avoid any misunderstandings we want to explicitly emphasize once more that the liquid is not accumulating in the skin but actually in the muscle tissue. Now it should also be clear why all other forms of administration of the compound will bring no results for bodybuilders. Since an inflammation is normally painful, each Esiclene ampule also includes 20 mg lidocaine, a mild painkiller. The injection itself is not painful but an unpleasant feeling at the point of injection is noted for about a day. Since the substance dissolves in water, Esiclene's duration of effect is limited so that the swelling begins to decrease after about one day, and after at most 4-5 days the muscle is back to its normal size. For this reason, bodybuilders use Esiclene only during the last 7-14 days before a competition to shape up less-developed muscle groups. In order to compensate for the decrease in swelling, the compound is usually injected daily. Smaller muscle groups such as biceps, triceps, deltoid muscles and calves are especially suitable and thus preferred over others.

Over a period of 1-2 weeks a temporary growth gain of 1-1,5 inches on arms and calves can be obtained. At most, two or three different muscles are usually injected at the same time. Often the athlete starts with a 1 ml injection; during the following days it is increased to 2 ml = 1 ampule per muscle. Esiclene, for this purpose, is injected with insulin needles. Esiclene is also popular among women since it is highly effective. It has also been proven that Esiclene, as is common for water-dissolved steroids, helps the athlete to achieve a better muscle hardness over the entire body during the course of his preparation for a competition. Some bodybuilders use Esiclene over a longer period in regular intervals, usually 2 ml every 5-7 days, in order to stimulate the growth of an extremely obstinate arm or calf muscle. Apart from the pain at the point of injection and, in some cases, a somewhat awkward-looking muscle, Esiclene has no significant negative side effects. It is difficult to find Esiclene on the black market. Six ampules are included in a box with a pull-out plastic bed. One ampule contains 2 ml of injection liquid with 4 mg of dissolved substance. This compound is very inexpensive. In Italy the box of 6 costs approx. $5. On the black market an ampule normally sells for $6 - 10. There are currently no fakes available.

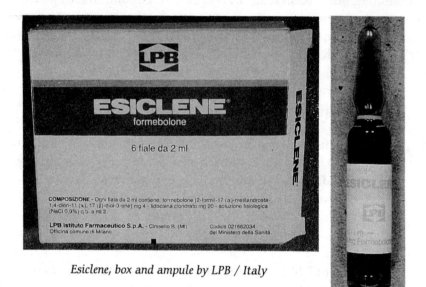

Esiclene, box and ampule by LPB / Italy

ESTANDRÓN

Substance:		
Testosterone propionate		20 mg
Testosterone phenylpropionate		40 mg
Testosteronisocaproate		40 mg
Estradiol phenylpropionate		4 mg
Estradiol benzoate		1 mg

Trade names

Ambosex	105 mg/ml;	Gedeon Richter BG
Estandrón	105 mg/ml;	Organon ES
Estandron	105 mg/ml;	Organon PT, A

This injectable steroid is a mix of three different testosterone esters and a smaller portion of estradiol, a female sex hormone. The testosterone composition of Estandrón is similar to that found in Sustanon but contains one less testosterone substance (Testosterone decanoate). Like all other injectable testosterone compounds Estandrón is also extremely suitable for a rapid build up of strength and muscle mass. It is highly androgenic and has a distinct protein-improving and anticatabolic effect. Estandrón also improves the body's ability to regenerate; it lubricates joints by storing fluid in the connective tissue, and it increases the glycogen level n the muscle cells.

At first it appears a little unusual that estradiol is included in Estandrón. Why in the world are estrogens included in a steroid compound whose main component is the male sex hormone testosterone? The answer is simple: Estandrón's target group is not men but women. The steroid developed by Organon Company is a combination of androgens/estrogens which in school medicine is used in the treatment of climacteric disorders (various physical conditions occuring in women in menopause) and of osteoporosis. The antagonistic (contrasting) sexual effects are distinct. To get the facts straight: the estradiol included in Estandrón neutralizes the androgenic effect of the three testosterone esters, thereby reducing or avoiding androgenic-caused masculinization symptoms in women.

This is a combination which offers bodybuilders advantages and disadvantages. The advantage consists of the fact that women who do not want to give up the performance-enhancing characteristics of testosterone but, at the same time, who show a sensitive reaction to the androgenic component, can achieve good gains without too much worry about virilization symptoms. The same is true for men who may experience acne, hair loss or a prostate condition when taking additional testosterone. In these cases the estradiol in the compound is able to counteract these conditions. Since small amounts of estrogens are also anabolic and in particular stimulate blood circulation, this could also be one of the reasons why Estandrón gives its users an enormous pump and a considerable increase in mass. Another positive aspect is also the fact that estrogens reinforce the storage of calcium in bones. Unfortunately, the estradiol mixture can lead to the formation of edemas and weight gain in both sexes. This results in excessive water retention and the risk of formation of subcutaneous fat deposits with increases in the dosage. A considerable risk of gynecomastia in male bodybuilders is also present. Competing bodybuilders and athletes who, because of testosterone injections, grow very rapidly should stay away from Estandrón. Further, the endogenous testosterone production is reduced considerably and the blood pressure often rises as well.

The dosage for male bodybuilders usually lies between 3 and 5 ml/ week. In order to minimize androgenic-caused side effects some "delicate" men combine Estandrón with the milder and predominantly anabolic steroids and achieve quite satisfying results. An example might be an intake of 3 ml Estandrón/week and 200 mg Primobolan Depot/week or 200 mg Deca-Durabolin/week. Those who would like to gain body mass as quickly as possible and who do not care about its consistency or quality, will be satisfied by taking 5 ml Estandrón/week, 200 mg Deca-Durabolin/week, and 30 mg Dianabol/day. Women are usually content with 1-2 ml Estandrón/ week. Most female bodybuilders achieve good gains and losing their femininity while taking 20 mg Winstrol tablets/day and 1-2 Estandrón/week.

The Spanish Estandrón can sometimes be found on the steroid black market, one ampule selling for $10 - 12. Like all ampules of the Organon Company, neither the Spanish, Portuguese, nor the Austrian alternative shows a simple print but comes with a white paper label with black print. An advantage is that there are no fakes of these lesser known steroids.

In the U.S., there are several drugs with a composition similar to Estandrón. We would like to mention, for example, the Depo-Testadiol compound by the Schein Company which contains 50 mg Testosterone cypionate and 2 mg estradiol per ml. According to the dealer catalog the 10 ml vial costs $13.79. The generic version of the same strength costs $7.

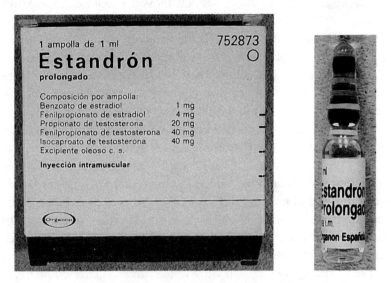

1 ampolla de 1 ml	752873

Estandrón
prolongado

Composición por ampolla:
Benzoato de estradiol	1 mg
Fenilpropionato de estradiol	4 mg
Propionato de testosterona	20 mg
Fenilpropionato de testosterona	40 mg
Isocaproato de testosterona	40 mg
Excipiente oleoso c. s.	

Inyección intramuscular

Organon

Estandrón, box and ampule by Organon / Spain

FINAJECT

Substance: trenbolone acetate

Trade names

Finaject (o.c.)	30 mg/ml;	Roussel France
Finajet (o.c.)	30 mg/ml;	Hoechst Great Britain
Finaplix	20 mg pellets	Hoechst-Roussel Agri-Vet Company U.S.

Finaject was an injectable steroid of veterinary medicine which was extremely popular in bodybuilding and powerlifting during the 1980's. "Was"?, some of you will wonder. Well, we can easily explain this. All those of you who still do not know, do not believe, do not want to realize the facts, or still let unscrupulous black market dealers convince you to purchase Finaject, should pay attention to the following statement: ORIGINAL FINAJECT HAS NOT BEEN

MANUFACTURED IN NINE YEARS! (Finaplix will be discussed at the end of this chapter.) Since 1987 neither Finaject nor Finajet has been manufactured in either France or Great Britain, nor in any other country worldwide. Residual supplies are available at this time; however, in all likelihood they are used up or superposed (past their expiration dates). For this reason, trade with faked Finaject is booming on the black market where the athlete can find a 30 ml or 50 ml vial of dark-brown glass that usually comes with a red cap. The label or sticker is in French and shows the compound as "Finaject 30." The manufacturer is apparently Distrivet s.a., 35 bd des Invalides, 75007 Paris by "Groupe Roussel UCLAF." The expiration date and manufacturing date are either missing or printed in the same type as the rest of the label. In some cases the vial comes in an additional package (see photo in chapter on Fakes.) The multicolored imprint on the carton can be wiped off with your finger if you wet the label and apply some pressure when rubbing. This would never be the case on an original package. All fakes are lacking traces of the substance "trenbolone acetate." So what does this compound contain? An analysis made in September '93 showed a very small amount of "testosterone enanthate." This finding, however, does not mean much, since the next vial that is analyzed might contain something completely different. The 50 ml oil solution costs $350 - 400. on the black market, which is a lot of money for a little "Testo." No matter what, the best you can do is stay clear of compounds with the imprint "Finaject." The same is obviously true for the English Finajet.

Although it does not make much sense to describe in detail a compound and its characteristics when it is no longer available (yes, we will talk about Finaplix) we would like to make an exception here. Some day perhaps "Fina" will be produced again, although this seems unlikely. Too many times in Europe it was illicitly abused in the treatment of animals destined for food processing. This shows what a high potential for abuse there is. Finaject is a very strong and androgenic compound which also has a high anabolic effect. It gives its users a fast and powerful strength gain without causing excessive gain in body weight. The reason is that "Fina" does not cause a water retention in the body. This was the reason why it was so popular among powerlifters who had to stay within a certain weight class. The strength gain is comparable to the famous "mass steroids" Dianabol, Anapolon 50, and Testosterone. What is special about Finaject is the substance trenobolone acetate which plays an active role during fatburning. It was a favorite among competing bodybuilders during preparation for championships since it helped athletes whose fat content was already relatively low to obtain a good muscle hardness and density. When the nutrition was right, it was possible that one could obtain with Finaject simultaneously both a high strength gain and a qualitatively high muscle gain; and the entire muscle system continued to get harder.

Since Finaject is the acetate form of trenbolone, its effect lasts only a short time and frequent administration is necessary. Most athletes inject 1 ml (30 mg) every second day. Higher dosages such as, for example, 30 mg/day or 60 mg every two days, however, were not unusual since an enormous strength gain and also a strong but still high-quality muscle gain was obtained. Finaject does not aromatize since its substance is not changed into estrogens. In combination with Winstrol it has a dramatic effect on the body's appearance. To achieve a gigantic strength gain bodybuilders used to combine 30 mg Finaject every 1-2 days and 50 mg Winstrol Depot every 1-2 days (also known as Strombaject) during preparation for a competition and the buildup phase. No other combination gives the athlete such an incredible hardness and such a defined muscle gain. The possible physical change obtainable in only a few weeks is enormous enough to shock some non-involved observers. Believe us, competing bodybuilders love this combination especially. Finaject was also part of probably the most effective stack for mass buildup. Together with Dianabol or Anadrol 50, and testosterone, "Fina" builds up strength and mass in record time. So much about the positive aspects of Finaject which, unfortunately, are often spoiled by its considerable negative side effects.

"Fina" is quite kidney-toxic and after a certain time of intake, it may cause pain in the kidneys. The first sign of possible kidney damage manifests itself in a very dark-colored urine. Some athlete will probably still remember the day when he excreted blood in his urine for the first time. It is important that Fina not be taken in high dosages over a prolonged period of time. It must also be observed that the amount of fluids is increased to at least one gallon/day so that the kidneys are well flushed. Finaject has considerable androgenic-caused side effects both in women and men. Athletes often report headaches, nasal bleeding, high blood pressure, oily skin with acne, and in part an enormous increase in aggressiveness. The high blood pressure is surprising since "Fina" does not cause water and salt retention which are normally the main cause of this condition. The skin can also considerably worsen which again manifests itself in a higher production of the sebaceous gland resulting in severe acne and larger pores. Especially negative is the characteristically high aggressiveness of athletes. "Fina" gets into your brain and can cause considerable mood swings in its users. One is extremely irritable and can "act out" quite abruptly. Daniel Duchaine in his *Underground Steroid Handbook 2* hits the nail on the head: "Someone on Finajet is no fun to be with." Women, in short time, can experience most undesirable cosmetic changes which often are irreversible. Despite this, many top female bodybuilders and powerlifters have included "Fina" in their training program for competitions. Finject is no steroid for male/female leisure bodybuilders and, if at all, should only be used by advanced and ambitious competitive athletes. Sensible women refuse to take it. Although "Fina" does not aromatize, its users often report gynecomastia. We believe that the reason for this is that during the late 1980's many athletes—and today all users—do not inject original but faked "Fina." Since the fake usually turns out to be a common testo this seems to explain the feminization symptoms. Original "Fina" was often recognized by the pain it caused at the point of injection even hours after the injection. Some athletes complained about hot flashes, nausea, and, in the event of veterinary compounds, "steroid fever." The original "Fina"—as mentioned before—has not been manufactured in years and many have been replaced by Parabolon which is made in France and comes from the field of human medicine. Parabolan, as a substance, also contains trenbolone but without the acetate form (see Parabolan).

As promised we conclude by discussing Finaplix which has become increasingly popular in recent years. When we previously talked about Finaject or Finajet, we referred exclusively to the injectable solution dissolved in oil. Finaplix, however, is a little more difficult because there is no place to insert a needle and draw a solution. Finaplix is a veterinary drug which is not for injection but is to be "shot" into your system. You have read correctly: animals are shot with Finaplix using an implant pistol. Finaplix is only available in this one form of administration, in the form of pellets which are small, cylindrical implants similar to tablets. We hope but do not guarantee that no one will hold such a pistol at his behind and pull the trigger. Athletes who are afraid of injections apparently have even drunk the content of ampules! We can only explicitly warn you not to do so. Back to its form of administration: Two different sizes are available. Finaplix-s stands for 70, Finaplix-h for 100 pellets which are enclosed in a cartridge. These pellets are obviously not intended to be swallowed. Their basic chemical structure is developed in such a way as to break down very slowly; that is, the substance release is delayed. Once implanted, its substance is expected to work for a certain time in a way similar to progesterone or estradiol patches for women. One way of administering the substance found in the pellets consists of first grinding the pellets into powder by use of a mortar and pestle. Then the powder is put into a container, adding 2 ml of distilled water or sesame oil. (Two pellets should be enough, since one pellet contains 20 mg trenbolone acetate.) Then combine powder and liquid and draw up the solution using a syringe. At this point we want to emphasize once more that this procedure has a great number of risks. The injectable solution was not created under sterile lab conditions and an injection could cause infections and many other complications.

Another way of administration which is far less dangerous, can be prepared as follows: the ground pellets are mixed with a mixture of 50% water and 50% DMSO (dimethyl sulfoxide). Then the mixture is put on the skin and allowed to soak in. Dimethyl sulfoxide is used to transport the substance trenbolone through the skin. Using this method approximately 40 mg of the substance can get into the blood without much harm. On the black market a box of 100 pellets costs up to $300. So far we have not seen any fakes.

HALOTESTIN

Substance: fluoxymesterone

Trade names

Android-F (o.c.)	10 mg tab.;	Brown U.S.
Halotestin	2 mg tab.;	Upjohn U.S.
Halotestin	5 mg tab.;	Upjohn U.S., DK, FR, GR, I, S, NL, FI, NO, Phillippines; Galenika YU
Halotestin	10 mg tab.;	Upjohn U.S.
Halotestin	10 mg tab.;	Warner-Chilcott U.S.
Hysterone Tabs (o.c.)	20 mg tab.;	Major U.S.
Ora-Testryl (o.c.)	5 mg tab.;	Squibb Mark U.S.
Stenox	2.5 mg tab.;	Atlantis Laboratories Mexico
Ultandren (o.c.)	1 mg tab.;	Ciba GB
Ultandren (o.c.)	5 mg tab.;	Ciba GB

Halotestin is an oral steroid which was introduced on the market by Upjohn Company in 1957. Its fluoxymesterone substance is a precursor of methyltestosterone which, through changes in the chemical structure, was made much more androgenic than testosterone. The anabolic component of Halotestin is only slightly pronounced. Based on its characteristics Halotestin is used mainly when the athlete is more interested in a strength buildup rather than in a muscle gain. Powerlifters and weightlifters who must stay within a certain weight class often use Halotestin because they are primarily interested in a strength gain without adding body weight. In bodybuilding this drug is almost exclusively taken during preparation for a competition. Since the substance is strongly androgenic while at the same time aromatizing very poorly, Halotestin helps the athlete obtain an elevated androgen level while keeping the estrogen concentration low. With a lower body fat content Halotestin gives the bodybuilder a distinctive muscle hardness and sharpness. Although the muscle diameter does not increase, it appears more massive since the muscle density is improved. The fact that a daily dose of up to 20 mg does not cause water and salt retention makes it even more desirable. During a diet, Halotestin helps the athlete get through difficult, intense training while increasing the aggressiveness of many users. This is another reason why it is so popular among powerlifters, weightlifters, football players, and, in particular, boxers. The generally observed dose is normally 20-40 mg/day. Bodybuilders are usually satisfied with 20-30 mg/day while powerlifters often take 40 mg/day or more. The daily dosage is usually split into two equal amounts and taken mornings and evenings with plenty of fluids. Since the tablets are 17-alpha alkylated, they can be taken during meals without any loss in effect.

Those who are tired of taking Dianabol tablets will find Halotestin an interesting alternative. In the meantime we know several bodybuilders who have combined Halotestin with injectable, mostly anabolic, steroid preparations such as Anadur, Deca-Durabolin, Primobolan Depot, or Equipoise. The quick strength gain induced by Halotestin can usually be turned into solid, high-quality muscle tissue by taking the above steroids. This is an especially welcome change for athletes who easily retain water and have to fight against swollen breast glands. Many will be surprised at what progress can be achieved by a simple combination of 30 mg Halotestin/day and 100 mg Equipoise every two days over a four-week period.

"So far, so good," you will say, but unfortunately, this is not so since Halotestin is a very toxic steroid. Besides Anadrol 50 and Methyltestosterone it is the oral steroid with the most side effects. Those who would like to try Halotestin should limit the intake to 4-6 weeks and take no more than 20-30 mg daily. Fluoxymesterone puts extremely high stress on the liver and is thus potentially liver-damaging. Other frequently-observed side effects are increased production of the sebaceous gland (which goes hand in hand with acne), nasal bleeding, headaches, gastrointestinal pain, and reduced production of the body's own hormones. Men become easily irritable and aggressive. Gynecomastia and high blood pressure caused by edemas do not occur with Halotestin. Do not be surprised, however, when on Halotestin's package insert you read the words "gynecomastia" and "edemas." This standard warning, due to legal provisions, is included in all strong androgenic steroids. Women should avoid Halotestin since it can cause substantial and in part irreversible virilization symptoms.

Halotestin is rarely found on the American black market. Sometimes the Italian, Greek, or French version of Upjohn shows up. The 5 and 10 mg tablets are very expensive. One hundred 10 mg tablets cost approx. $100 on the black market. A strip with ten tablets of 5 mg each in a French pharmacy costs 39 francs, equal to approx. $8. The Italian Halotestin costs about the same but contains 20 tablets filled in a glass vial. The Greek Halotestin is packaged in a small glass vial containing twenty tablets of 5mg each with a plastic tear-off top. In Greece the box costs $5. The Italian, Greek, and French Halotestin tablets are all indented with the UPJOHN imprint on the back.

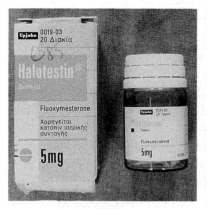

Halotestin from Greece, box and glass
container by Upjohn

Halotestin from the Phillipines, box
and glass container by Upjohn

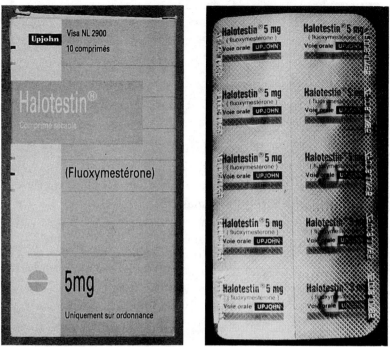

Halotestin from France, box and blister by Upjohn

HCG (HUMAN CHORIONIC GONADOTROPIN)

Substance: chorionic gonadotropin

Trade names

A.P.L.	5000 I.U., 10000 I.U., 20000 I.U. amp.;	Wyeth-Ayerst U.S.
Biogonadyl	500 I.U., 2000 I.U. amp.;	Biomed PL
C.G. (o.c.)	10000 I.U. amp.;	Sig U.S.
Choragon	1500 I.U., 5000 I.U. amp.;	Ferring G
Chorex	5000 I.U., 10000 I.U. amp.;	Hyrex U.S.
Chorigon (o.c.)	10000 I.U. amp.;	Dunhall U.S.
Chorion-Plus (o.co.)	10000 I.U. amp.;	Pharmex U.S.
Choron 10	1000 I.U., 10,000 I.U. amp.	Forest U.S.

Corgonject (o.c.)	5000 I.U. amp.;	Mayrand U.S.
Follutein (o.c.)	10000 I.U. amp.;	Squibb Mark U.S.
Gestyl	1000 I.U. amp.;	Organon BG
Glukor (o.c.)	10000 I.U. amp.;	Hyrex U.S.
Gonadotraphon	500 I.U., 1000 I.U. 5000 I.U. amp.;	Paines+Byrne GB
Gonadotrafon LH	125 I.U., 250 I.U., 1000 I.U. amp.;	Amsa I
Gonadotrafon LH	2000 I.U., 5000 I.U., amp.;	Amsa I
G. chor. "Endo"	500 I.U., 1500 I.U., 5000 I.U. amp.;	Organon FR
Gonadotropyl	5000 I.U. amp.;	Roussel Mexico
Gonic (o.c.)	1000 I.U. amp.;	Hauck U.S.
Gonic	1000 I.U. amp.;	Roberts U.S.
Harvatropin	10000 I.U. amp.;	Harvey U.S.
H.C.G. (o.c.)	1000 I.U., 10000 I.U. amp.;	Huffman U.S.
H.C.G.	5000 I.U., 10000 I.U. amp.;	Pharmed Group U.S.
HCG	5000 I.U., 10000 I.U. amp.;	Steris U.S.
HCG Lepori	500 I.U., 1000 I.U., 2500 I.U. amp.;	Lepori ES
Neogonadil Bruco	1000 I.U. amp.;	Opocrin I(o.c.)
Physex	1500 I.U., 3000 I.U., amp.;	Leo DK, NO
Physex Leo	500 I.U., 1500 I.U., 5000 I.U. amp.;	Leo ES
Praedyn	1500 I.U., 3000 I.U. amp.;	Leciva CZ
Predalon	500 I.U., 5000 I.U. amp.;	Organon G
Pregnesin	250 I.U., 500 I.U., 1000 I.U. amp.;	Serono G, CZ
Pregnesin	2500 I.U., 5000 I.U. amp.;	Serono G, CZ
Pregnyl	10000 I.U. amp.;	Organon U.S.
Pregnyl	100 I.U. amp.;	Organon I, BG
Pregnyl	500 I.U., 1500 I.U., 5000 I.U. amp.;	Organon A, B, CH, GB, BG, GR, I, NL, PL, S, FI; YU; CZ, NO, HU, Medika/ Santa TK
Pregnyl	1500 I.U., 5000 I.U. amp.;	Organon Mexico
Primogonyl (o.c.)	250 I.U., 500 I.U. amp.;	Schering A
Primogonyl	250 I.U., 500 I.U. amp.;	Schering CH, G,CZ
Primogonyl	1000 I.U., 5000 I.U. amp.;	Schering G, CH,

		YU, CZ
Profasi	10000 I.U. amp.;	Serono CH, B, Mexico, S, FI, GB,NO, NL
Profasi	500 I.U. amp.;	Serono CH, GB, Mexico, HU, FR
Profasi	1000 I.U. amp.;	Serono HU, NL
Profasi	1500 I.U. amp.;	Serono FR
Profasi	2000 I.U., 5000 I.U. amp.;	Serono A, B, CH, DK, HU, GB, GR, S,FR, NL, NO, Mexico
Profasi HP	5000 I.U., 10000 I.U. amp.;	Serono U.S.
Profasi HP	250 I.U., 2000 I.U., 5000 I.U. amp;	Serono I
Profasi HP	500 I.U., 1000 I.U., amp;	Serono I
Profasi HP	500 I.U., 1000 I.U., 2500 I.U. amp;	Serono ES
Rochoric (o.c.)	10000 I.U. amp.;	Rocky-Mount. U.S.

Veterinary:		
Brumegon	1000 I.U. amp.;	Hydro G
Choriolutin	1500 I.U., 5000 I.U;	Albrecht G
Chor.Gonadotropin	10000 I.U.	Steris U.S.
Chorulon vet.	Injection solution	Intervet DK
Chorvlon (o.c.)	1500 I.U. amp.;	Werfft-Chemie A
Ekluton	1500 I.U., 5000 I.U.;	Vemie G
Gonadoplex vet.	Injection solution;	Leo DK
HCG	10000 I.U.	Steris U.S.
Ovogest	1500 I.U., 5000 I.U.;	Hydro G
Ovo-Gonadon	500 I.U.;	Alvetra G
Prolan vet.	Injection solution;	Bayer S

Human chorionic gonadotropin, or HCG, is not an anabolic/androgenic steroid but a natural protein hormone which develops in the placenta of a pregnant woman. HCG is formed in the placenta immediately after nidation (1). It has luteinizing characteristics since it is quite similar to the luteinizing hormone (LH) in the anterior pituitary gland. During the first 6-8 weeks of a pregnancy the formed HCG allows for continued production of estrogens and gestagens in the yellow bodies (corpi luteum). Later on, the placenta itself produces these two hormones. HCG is manufactured from the urine of pregnant women since it is excreted in unchanged form from the blood via the woman's urine, passing through the kidneys. The commercially available HCG is sold as a dry substance and can be used both in men and women. In women injectable HCG allows for ovulation since it influences the last stages of the development of the ovum, thus stimulating ovulation. It also helps produce estrogens and yellow bodies.

The fact that exogenous (2) HCG has characteristics almost identical to those of the luteinizing hormone (LH) which, as mentioned, is produced in the hypophysis, makes   HCG so very interesting for athletes. In a man the luteinizing hormone stimulates the Leydig's cells in the testes; this in turn stimulates production of androgenic hormones (testosterone). For this reason athletes use injectable HCG to increase the testosterone production. HCG is often used in combination with anabolic/androgenic steroids during or after treatment. As mentioned, oral and injectable steroids cause a negative feedback after a certain level and duration of usage. A signal is sent to the hypothalamohypophysial testicular axis since the steroids give the hypothalamus an incorrect signal. The hypothalamus, in turn, signals the hypophysis (3) to reduce or stop the production of FSH (follicle stimulating hormone) and of LH. Thus, the testosterone production decreases since the testosterone-producing Leydig's cells in the testes, due to decreased LH, are no longer sufficiently stimulated. Since the body usually needs a certain amount of time to get its testosterone production going again, the athlete, after discontinuing steroid compounds, experiences a difficult transition phase which often goes hand in hand with a considerable loss in both strength and muscle mass. Administering HCG directly after steroid treatment helps to reduce this condition because HCG increases the testosterone production in the testes very quickly and reliably. In the event of testicular atrophy caused by megadoses and very long periods of usage, HCG also helps to quickly bring the testes back to their original condition (size). Since occasional injections of HCG during steroid intake can avoid a testicular atrophy, many athletes use HCG for two to three weeks in the middle of their steroid treatment. It is often observed that during this time the athlete makes his best progress with respect to gains in both strength and muscle mass. The reasons for this is clear. On the one hand, by taking HCG the athlete's own testosterone level immediately jumps up and, on the other hand, a large concentration of anabolic substances in the blood is induced by the steroids. Many bodybuilders, powerlifters, and weightlifters report a lower sex drive at the end of a difficult workout cycle, immediately before or after a competition, and especially toward the end of a steroid treatment. Athletes who have often taken steroids in the past usually accept this fact since they know that it is a temporary condition. Those, however, who are on the juice all year round, who might suffer psychological consequences or who would perhaps risk the breakup of a relationship because of this should consider this drawback when taking HCG in regular intervals. A reduced libido and spermatogenesis due to steroids, in most cases, can be successfully cured by treatment with HCG.

Most athletes, however, use HCG at the end of a treatment in order to avoid a "crash," that is, to achieve the best possible transition into "natural training." A precondition, however, is that the steroid intake or dosage be reduced slowly and evenly before taking HCG. Although HCG causes a quick and significant increase of the endogenic plasmatestosterone level, unfortunately it is not a perfect remedy to prevent the loss of strength and mass at the end of a steroid treatment. The athlete will only experience a delayed re-adjustment, as has often been observed. This is also confirmed by the physician Dr. Mauro Di Pasquale in his book Drug Use and Detection in Amateur Sports: "HCG is used by athletes to try to decrease the negative effects which occur when coming off prolonged dosages of anabolic steroids. These athletes believe that by using HCG, they can stimulate their own testes to produce testosterone, thereby getting back to a normal state faster. This, however, is faulty reasoning. Although HCG does stimulate endogenous testosterone production, it does not help in re-establishing the normal hypothalamic/pituitary testicular axis. The hypothalamus and pituitary are still in a refractory state after prolonged steroid usage, and remain this way while HCG is being used, because the endogenous testosterone produced as a result of the exogenous HCG represses the endogenous LH production. Once the HCG is discontinued, the athlete must still go through a re-adjustment period. This is merely delayed by the HCG use." For this reason experienced athletes often take Clomid and Clenbuterol following HCG intake or they immediately begin another steroid treatment. Some take HCG merely to get off the "steroids" for at least two to three weeks.

Many bodybuilders, unfortunately, are still of the opinion that HCG helps them become harder while preparing for a competion by breaking down subcutaneous fat so that indentations and vascularity are better exposed. A look at the book *The Practical Use of Anabolic Steroids with Athletes* by Dr. Robert Kerr should eliminate all doubts: The HCG package insert states clearly that HCG "has no known effect of fat mobilization, appetite or sense of hunger, or body fat distribution." It further states, "HCG has not been demonstrated to be effective adjunctive therapy in the treatment of obesity, it does not increase fat losses beyond that resulting from caloric restriction." A remarkable characteristic of HCG is its biphasic response. The American physician Dr. William N. Taylor writes in his book *Anabolic Steroids and the Athlete:* "Apparently, regardless of the dose used, a biphasic response of plasma testosterone to a single injection to HCG, has been reported. The initial peaked rise in plasma testosterone levels occurs approximately two hours after the single injection of HCG, and the second peaked level occurs some 48 to 96 hours after the inital single HCG injection. Throughout this period the mean plasma testosterone level is elevated, and both the magnitude of the peak values and the magnitude of the mean plasma levels seem to be dose dependent in at least some studies."

Thus the question arises: what dosage is needed in order to obtain a sufficiently high testosterone level? Since neither scientific nor medical literature indicates the usage of HCG in athletes, one can only start with empirical data. To avoid complete reliance on speculations we would, once more in this context, like to refer to the book *Anabolic Steroids and the Athlete* by Dr. William N. Taylor. In the chapter *HCG and its Function in Men* one reads: "In 1980, Padron et al. reported that in normal men the administration of 6000 I.U. of HCG in a single injection resulted in elevated testosterone levels for six days after the injection." Also, in the same chapter Taylor writes that at a dosage of 1500 I.U. the pharmatestosterone level increases by 250-300% (2.5-3fold) compared to the initial value. Taking these observations and combining them with general empirical values, one comes to the conclusion that the athlete should inject one HCG ampule every 5 days. Since the testosterone level, as explained, remains considerably elevated for several days, it is unnecessary to inject HCG more than once every 5 days. The relative dose is at the discretion of the athlete and should be determined based on the duration of his previous steroid intake and on the strength of the various steroid compounds. As we know, the elevation of the HCG-caused plasmatestosterone level depends on the dosage. Thus athletes who take steroids for more than three months and athletes who use primarily the highly androgenic steroids such as Anadrol 50, Sustanon 250, Testosterone enanthate/cypionate, Dianabol, etc. should take a relatively high dosage. The effective dosage for athletes is usually 2000-5000 i.U. per injection and should—as already mentioned—be injected every 5 days. HCG should only be taken for a few weeks. We are of the opinion that intake for more than 4 weeks is neither necessary nor sensible. If HCG is taken by male athletes over many weeks and in high dosages, it is possible that the testes will respond poorly to a later HCG intake and a release of the body's own LH. This could result in a permanent inadequate gonadal function. B. Phillips, *Anabolic Reference Guide,* *5th issue*: "Cycles on the HCG should be kept down to around 3 weeks at a time with an off cycle of at least a month in between. For example, one might use the HCG for 2 or 3 weeks in the middle of a cycle, and for 2 or 3 weeks at the end of a cycle. It has been speculated that the prolonged use of HCG could permanently repress the body's own production of gonadotropins. This is why short cycles are the best way to go."

Dr. William N. Taylor, *Anabolic Steroids and the Athlete states* "...that large doses of HCG produce what is speculated to be a transient loss of testicular receptors for HCG, which gives rise to a desensitization of the testes to HCG."

HCG can in part cause side effects similar to those of injectable testosterone. A higher testosterone production also goes hand in hand with an elevated estrogen level which could result in gynecomastia. This could manifest itself in a temporary growth of breasts or reinforce already existing breast growth in men. Farsighted athletes thus combine HCG with an antiestrogen. Male athletes also report more frequent erections and an increased sexual desire. In high doses it can cause acne vulgaris and the storing of minerals and water. The last point must especially be observed since the water retention which is possible through the use of HCG could give the muscle system a puffy and watery appearance. Athletes who have already increased their endogenous testosterone level by taking Clomid and intend subsequently to take HCG could experience considerable water retention and distinct feminization symptoms (gynecomastia, tendency toward fat deposits on the hips). This is due to the fact that high testosterone leads to a high conversion rate to estrogens. In very young athletes HCG, like anabolic steroids, can cause an early stunting of growth since it prematurely closes the epiphysial growth plates. Mood swings and high blood pressure can also be attributed to the intake of HCG. Dr. Bob Goldman in his book *Death in the Locker Room* notes: "One interesting aspect is that with abuse of this drug men might finally realize what it feels like to be pregnant, for with enough use, they may experience nausea, vomiting, and "morning sickness" syndrome women enjoy..." A few years ago it was speculated whether or not the biologically active HCG could possibly transmit the AIDS virus. It was shown, however, that this is not in any way possible.

HCG is also suitable as "over bridge" doping before a competition with doping controls. This was especially common in the former East Germany which had centrally guided doping practices, as the author Brigitte Berendonk lays open several times in her book

Doping: "These over bridging recommendations in the habilita-
tion paper by Riedel, 1986, for the jumping disciplines of track
and field athletics—already given in his dosage suggestions (on
p.205)—were mildly beautified compared to reality... This HCG
regulating hormone which was taken to increase the body's own
testosterone synthesis, in practice was often used in amounts
above the 3000 I.U. recommended by Riedel. Riedel, on another
occasion, suggests injections of up to 4000 I.U. every 5th day
(see p. 33) and all the fraud protocols had in common that a last
amount of 3000 I.U. HCG was injected on the day before the
competition (track and field) or even on the day of the competition (Dr. Lathan's practice with the weightlifters of East Germany). The reason was that the East Germans had discovered
(Clausnitzer et al. 1982; Riedel 1986) that when the testosterone
level was increased by the intake of HCG the critical T/E quotient
was hardly changed and discovery through testing became impossible." HCG and the already discussed Clomid are options for
increasing the endogenous testosterone concentration without a
pronounced change of the T/E ratio.

HCG's form of administration is also unusual. The substance
choriongonadotropin is a white powdery freeze-dried substance
which is usually used as a compress. Based on the low structural
stability of this compress it can easily fall apart, thus giving the
impression of a reduced volume. This is, however, insignificant
since there is neither a loss in effect nor a loss of substance. Each
package, for each HCG ampule, includes another ampule with an
injection solution containing isotonic sodium chloride. This liquid, after both ampules have been opened in a sterile manner, is
injected into the HCG ampule and mixed with the dried substance.
The solution is then ready for use and should be injected intramuscularly. If only part of the substance is injected the residual
solution should be stored in the refrigerator. It is not necessary to
store the unmixed HCG in the refrigerator; however, it should be
kept out of light and below a temperature of 25° C.

HCG is a relatively expensive compound. Pregnyl costs approx.
$36 -45 for 3 ampules of 5000 I.U. each and the relative solu-

tion ampules. The other compounds have a similar price and are $12 -15 for 5000 I.U. The 5000 I.U. ampules are the most economic and, in our opinion, also the most sensible for bodybuilders, powerlifters, and weightlifters. There are currently only a few fakes of HCG. Since the dry substance of HCG is somewhat similar to the dry substance of Somatropin (4) often "cheap" HCG is sold as "expensive" HGH on the black market. This circumstance was probably Ben Johnson's downfall during his second positive doping test with his increased testosterone/epitestosterone value in early 1993 (see also growth hormones).

(1) Embedding of the fertilized ovum cell in the mucous membrane of the cervix uterus;
(2) Exogenous in this context means injectable;
(3) Anterior pituitary gland;
(4) Substance of STH (somatotropic hormone) better known as growth hormone.

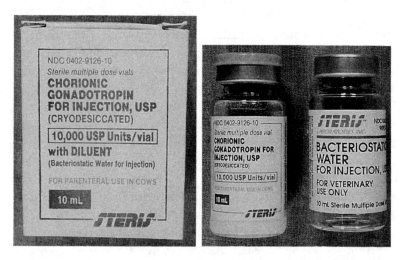

HCG by Steris / U.S.

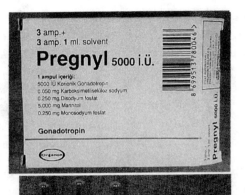

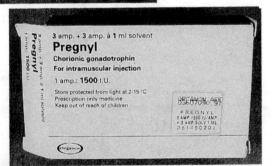

HCG from Turkey, box and amps by Organon

3 amp.+
3 amp. 1 ml. solvent

Pregnyl 5000 i.Ü.

1 ampul içeriği:
5000 IÜ Korionik Gonadotropin
0.050 mg Karboksimetilselüloz sodyum
0.250 mg Disodyum fosfat
5.000 mg Mannitol
0.250 mg Monosodyum fosfat

Gonadotropin

3 amp. + 3 amp. à 1 ml solvent
Pregnyl
Chorionic gonadotrophin
For intramuscular injection
1 amp.: **1500** I.U.

Store protected from light at 2-15 °C
Prescription only medicine
Keep out of reach of children

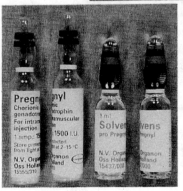

Pregnyl from Greece, box and amps

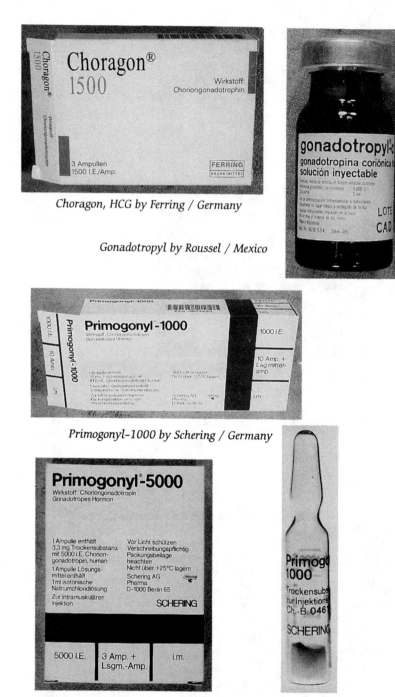

Choragon, HCG by Ferring / Germany

Gonadotropyl by Roussel / Mexico

Primogonyl-1000 by Schering / Germany

Primogonyl-5000 by Schering / Germany

Primogonyl amp

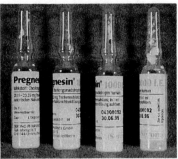

Pregnesin from Germany, box and ampules

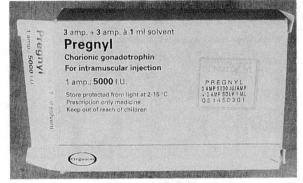

Pregnyl 5000 I.U. by Organon / Greece

Pregnyl 5000 I.U., HCG pens solution from Greece, introduced in Holland

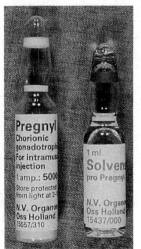

HCG Lepori amp. from Spain

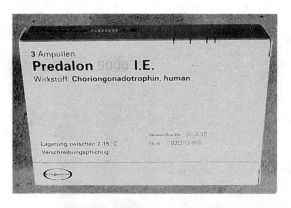

Predalon 5000 I.U. from Germany

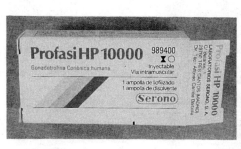

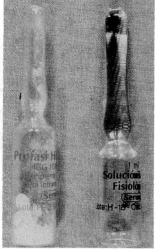

Profasi HP 10000 by Serono

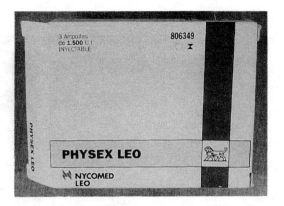

HCG by Leo / Spain, 1500 I.U. per amp.

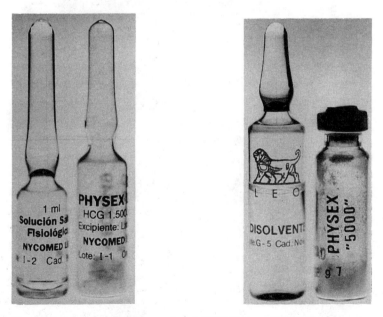

New and old ampules of Physex Leo, 1500 I.U. new, 5000 I.U. old version

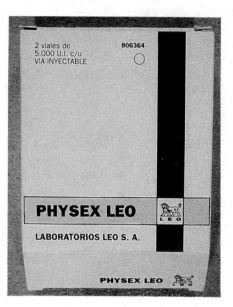

Physex Leo, HCG 5000 I.U.
from Spain, old package

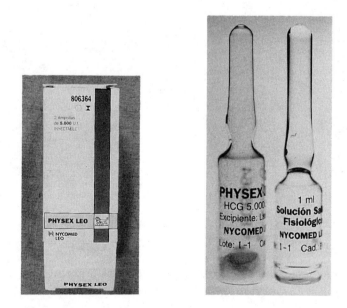

Physex Leo, HCG 5000 I.U., box and amp. by Nycomed Leo /
Spain, new version

HUMAN GROWTH HORMONE

Substance: Somatropin

Trade names

Corpormon	4 I.U.;	Nikken Japan
Crescormon (o.c.)	4 I.U.;	Globopharm CH; Kabi GR, YU; Kabi Vitrum U.S.
Crescormonn (o.c.)	4 I.U.	Kabi-Fides ES
Genotr	2, 3, 4 I.U.	Kabi pharmacia NO 16, 32 I.U.
Genotonorm	4 I.U.	Kabi B; Kabipfrimmer ES
Genotropin	2 I.U.	Kabi pharmacia S, BG, A, GR, NL
Genotropin	3 I.U.	Kabi pharmacia S, BG, A, GR, NL
Genotropin	3 I.U.;	Kabi pharmacia G, DG, S; BG, A, HU, PL, CZ GR, NL, CH, FI, Pierrel I
Genotropin	12 I.U.;	Kabi pharmacia S, DK, PT, CZ, NO, CH
Genotropin	16 I.U.;	Kabi pharmacia G, DK, FI, S, A, PT, HU, GR,NL, CH
Geno, Kabi Quick	2, 3 I.U.	Kabi Pharmacia G
Grorm (o.c.)	4 I.U.	Serono G, CH, ES, I
Grorm	2, 4 I.U.	Institutio farmacologio serono CZ
Humatrope	4 I.U.	Lilly G, DK, ES, S, GB, FI, B, HU, GR, CZ, NO, NL, I Serum und Impfinstitut CH
Humatrope	5mg sol.;	Lilly U.S.
Humatrope	16 I.U.;	Lilly G, DK, FI, GB, ES, GR, NO, NL, CH
Norditropin	4 I.U.;	Nordisk PL; Nordisk Gentofte DK;Novo-Nordisk A, ES, I, NO, Novo HU,Novo Industri BG
Norditropin	12 I.U.;	Novo-Nordisk G, FI; CH, NO, NL, ES Novo GB; FI, HU, Nordisk Gentofte DK; Nordisk B, PL Novo Industri BG, CZ, Santa GR
Norditropin	24 I.U.;	Novo Industri CZ, Novo HU, FI, Santa GR Novo Nordisk NO, A, ES, DK, NL
Norditrop. Pen Set	24 I.U.	Novo-Nordisk G
Nutropin	10 mg sol.;	Genentech U.S.

Protropin	10 mg sol.;	Genentech U.S.
Saizen	2 I.U.	Serono G, CH, ES
Saizen	4 I.U.	Serono G, A, CH, ES, I, GB, GR, FI, HU, FR, S, CZ
Saizen	10 I.U.	Serono S, FI, GB, CH, CZ, HU, FR, ES
Somatohorm	4 I.U.	Biomed PL
Somatonorm	4 I.U.	Kabi-vitrum CZ, Kabi pharmacia ES, FR
Somat. Sero (o.c.)	4 I.U.	Serotherapeutisches Institut A
Zomacton	4, 12 I.U.	Ferring G

"Wow, is this great stuff. It is the best drug for permanent muscle gains. This is the only drug that can remedy bad genetics as it will make anybody grow. GH use is the biggest gamble that an athlete can take, as the side effects are irreversible. Even with all that, we LOVE the stuff." (Daniel Duchaine, *Underground Steroid Handbook*, 1982.)

As with no other doping drug, growth hormones are still surrounded by an aura of mystery. Some call it a wonder drug which causes gigantic strength and muscle gains in the shortest time. Others consider it completely useless in improving sports performance and argue that it only promotes the growth process in children with an early stunting of growth. Some are of the opinion that growth hormones in adults cause severe bone deformities in the form of overgrowth of the lower jaw and extremities. And, generally speaking, which growth hormones should one take —the human form, the synthetically manufactured version, recombined or genetically produced form— and in which dosage? All this controversy about growth hormones is so complex that the reader must have some basic information in order to understand them. The growth hormone is a polypeptide hormone consisting of 191 amino acids. In humans it is produced in the hypophysis and released if there are the right stimuli (e.g. training, sleep, stress, low blood sugar level). It is now important to understand that the freed HGH (human growth hormone) itself has no direct effect but only stimulates the liver to produce and release insulin-like growth factors and somatomedins. These growth factors are then the ones that cause various effects on the body. The problem, however, is that the liver is only capable of producing a limited amount of these substances so that the effect is limited. If growth hormones are injected they only stimulate the liver to produce and release these substances and thus, as already mentioned, have no direct effect.

During the mid 1980's only the human, biologically-active form was available as exogenous source of intake. It was obtained from the hypophysis of dead corpses, an expensive and costly procedure. In 1985 the intake of human growth hormones was linked with the very rare Creutzfeld-Jakob disease, an invariably fatal brain disease characterized by progressive dementia. In response, manufacturers removed this version from the market. Today, human growth hormones are no longer available for injection. Fortunately, science has not been asleep and has developed the synthetic growth hormone which is genetically produced either from Escherichia coli (E coli) or from the transformed mouse cell line. It has been available in numerous countries for years (see list with trade names).

The use of these STH somatotropic hormone compounds offers the athlete three performance-enhancing effects. STH (somatotropic hormone) has a strong anabolic effect and causes an increased protein synthesis which manifests itself in a muscular hypertrophy (enlargement of muscle cells) and in a muscular hyperplasia (increase of muscle cells.) The latter is very interesting since this increase cannot be obtained by the intake of steroids. This is probably also the reason why STH is called the strongest anabolic hormone. The second effect of STH is its pronounced influence on the burning of fat. It turns more body fat into energy, leading to a drastic reduction in fat or allowing the athlete to increase his caloric intake. Third, and often overlooked, is the fact that STH strengthens the connective tissue, tendons, and cartilages, which could be one of the main reasons for the significant increase in strength experienced by many athletes. Several bodybuilders and powerlifters report that through the simultaneous intake with steroids STH protects the athlete from injuries while increasing his strength. You will say that this sounds just wonderful. What is the problem, however, since there are still some who argue that STH offers nothing to athletes? There are, by all means, several athletes who have tried STH and who were sadly disappointed by its results. However, as with many things in life, there is a logical explanation or perhaps even more than one:

1. The athlete simply has not taken a sufficient amount of STH regularly and over a long enough period of time. STH is a very expensive compound and an effective dosage is unaffordable by most people.

2. When using STH the body also needs more thyroid hormones, insulin, corticosteroids, gonadotropins, estrogens and —what a surprise!—androgens and anabolics. This is also the reason why STH, when taken alone, is considerably less effective and can only reach its optimum effect by the additive intake of steroids, thyorid hormones, and insulin, in particular. But we must point out in this case that STH has a predominantly anabolic effect. There are three hormones which are needed at the same time in order to allow for maximum anabolic effect. These are STH, insulin, and an LT-3 thyroid hormone, such as, for example, Cytomel. Only then can the liver produce and release an optimal amount of somatomedin and insulin-like growth factors. This anabolic effect can be further enhanced by taking a substance with an anticatabolic effect. These substances are—everybody should probably know by now—anabolic/androgenic steroids or Clenbuterol. Then a synergetic effect takes place. Are you still wondering why pro bodybuilders are so incredibly massive but, at the same time, totally ripped while you are not? It is "Polypharmacy at its finest," as W. Nathaniel Phillips described to the point in his book *Anabolic Reference Guide* (5th Issue, 1990). But coming back once more to the "anabolic formula": STH, insulin, and L-T3. Most athletes have tried STH during preparation for a competition in that phase when the diet is calorie-reduced. The body usually reacts by reducing the release of insulin and of the L-T3 thyroid hormone. And, as was described under point 2, this is not an advantageous condition when STH is expected to work well. Well, we almost forgot. Those who combine Clenbuterol with STH should know that Clenbuterol (like Ephedrine) reduces the body's own release of insulin and L-T3. True, this seems a little complicated and when reading it for the first time it might be a little confusing;

however it really is true: STH has a significant influence on several hormones in the human body; this does not allow for a simple administration schedule. As said, STH is not cheap and those who intend to use it should know a little more about it. If you only want to burn fat with STH you will only have to remember user information for the part with the L-T3 thyroid hormone as is printed by Kabi Pharmacia GmbH for their compound Genotropin: "The need of the thyroid hormone often increases during treatment with growth hormones."

3. Since most athletes who want to use STH can only obtain it if prescribed by a physician, the only supply source remains the black market. And this is certainly another reason why some athletes might not have been very happy with the effect of the purchased compound. How could he, if cheap HCG was passed off as expensive STH? Since both compounds are available as dry substances, all that would be needed is a new label of Serono's Saizen or Lilly's Humatrope on the HCG ampule. It is no longer fun when somebody is paying $200 for 5000 I.U. of HCG, only worth $12, and thinking that he just purchased 4 I.U. of STH. And if you think this happens only to novices and to the ignorant, ask Ben Johnson. "Big Ben," who during three tests within five days showed an above-limit testosterone level, was not a victim of his own stupidity but more likely the victim of fraud. "According to statistics by the German Drug Administration, 42% of the HGH vials confiscated on the North American black market are fakes." (*Der Spiegel*, no. 11, 1993.) One can only say, "Poor Ben." Even *Deutsche Apothekerzeitung* is aware of this problem. The magazine wrote in its issue no. 26 of 07/01/93 in the article "Wachstumshormon-Präparate: Arzneimittelfälschungen in Bodybuilder-Szene": "The currently-known cases are traded with Dutch or Russian labels... In addition to a display of labels in the Dutch or Russian language the fakes are distinguished from the original product, insofar as the dry substance is not present as lyophilic but present as loose powder. The fakes confiscated so far use the name "Humatrope 16" under the name of Lilly Company (with Dutch denomination) or "Somatogen" (in Russian)." Nowhere can this much money be made except by faking STH. Who has ever held

original growth hormones in his hand and known how they should look?

4. In a few very rare cases the body reacts by developing antibodies to the exogenous STH, thus making it ineffective.

Before discussing the extremely difficult matter of dosage and intake the following question suggests itself: Generally speaking who is taking growth hormones? A whole lot of athletes as the following quotation suggests: "Charlie Francis, the Canadian athletic trainer of Ben Johnson tells how he improved the performance of Ben and numerous other Olympic athletes by the use of growth hormones in 1983. Francis also had conclusive evidence that the U.S.-American field and track athletes were using growth hormones. In a 1989 interview with a pro bodybuilder, an interview not meant for publication, this massive athlete made clear that he was convinced that almost all professional top athletes were using Protropin. He also said that it did not bother him if the IFBB were to introduce doping tests for men in 1990 as long as there would be no testing for growth hormonesô (*Anabolic Reference* Update, June 1989, no. 11). "It is highly suspected that the top Ms. O competitors use this product to help them attain their incredibly rippled muscles while still looking like women." (*Anabolic Reference Guide*, 5th Issue, 1990, W. N. Phillips.) Most top bodybuilders using Growth Hormone (GH) feel that insulin activates it. One top pro was rumored to have been using 12 I.U. of GH per day in preparation for his last WBF contest. He swears that GH only works with insulin." (*Muscle Media 2000*, October/November 1993, no. 34.)" And shortly before the 1984 Olympic Games in Los Angeles, U.S. researchers succeeded in synthetically manufacturing the hormone. This hormone which cannot be detected with current testing methods immediately prepared American athletes throughout the country for the games in California. After reports of success the drug became the secret runner on the doping market. The football pro Lyle Alzado, who died of brain tumor, shortly before his death confessed that he had taken HGH for 16 weeks — and he claimed that 80% of all American football pros do so, too. Ben Johnson, who in 1988 in Seoul was caught with anabolics, admitted to the investigating committee of the Canadian government that he had tried the Growth Hormone. He had paid $10,000 for ten bottles of HGH. According to Johnson, his physician, George Astaphan, had also designed programs for his colleagues Mark McKoy, Angella Issajenko, and Desai Williams. Hurdle sprinter Juli Rochelean who today runs records for Switzerland under the name Baumann procured HGH on the black market of the bodybuilder scene in Montreal... Among women Gail Devers won the 100 meters (1992 Olympic Games in Barcelona, the auth.) after having just overcome a severe thyroid condition, a well-known side effect of taking HGH. Such suspicions are reinforced by current market data. The two U.S. companies Genentech and Eli Lilly produced about 800 million dollars of HGH in 1992. Genentech alone reported an eleven percent production increase compared to last year. Chemists incessantly emphasize that the drug should only be manufactured for use by persons with stunted growth. The U.S.Food and Drug Administration, however, sees it differently: the U.S. government currently includes HGH on the list of forbidden drugs and threatens up to five years of prison for illegal possession of the drug." (*Der Spiegel*, no. 11 of 03/15/93). "Many of the top strength athletes use HGH and the cost of its use ran as high as $30,000/year for one particular pro bodybuilder. Short term users (8 week duration) will spend up to $150 per daily dosage. And because the top athletes are rumored to use it, HGH lust in the lower ranks has become more rampant." (Daniel Duchaine, *Underground Steroid Handbook 2*.)

The question of the right dosage, as well as the type and duration of application, is very difficult to answer. Since there is no scientific research showing how STH should be taken for performance improvement, we can only rely on empirical data, that is experimental values. The respective manufacturers indicate that in cases of hypophysially stunted growth due to lacking or insufficient release of growth hormones by the hypophysis, a weekly average dose of 0.3 I.U/week per pound of body weight should be taken. An athlete weighing 200 pounds, therefore, would have to inject 60 I.U. weekly. The dosage would be divided into three intramuscular injections of 20 I.U. each. Subcutaneous injections (under the skin) are another form of intake which, however, would have to be injected daily, usually 8 I.U. per day. Top athletes usually inject 4–16 I.U./day. Ordinarily, daily subcutaneous injections are preferred. Since STH has a half-life time of less than one hour, it is not surprising that some athletes divide their daily dose into three or four subcutaneous injections of 2–4 I.U. each. Application of regular, small dosages seems to bring the most effective results. This also has its reasons: When STH is injected, serum concentration in the blood rises quickly, meaning that the effect is almost immediate. As we know, STH stimulates the liver to produce and release somatomedins and insulin-like growth factors which in turn effect the desired results in the body. Since the liver can only produce a limited amount of these substances, we doubt that larger STH injections will induce the liver to produce instantaneously a larger quantity of somatomedins and insulin-like growth factors. It seems more likely that the liver will react more favorably to smaller dosages.

If the STH solution is injected subcutaneously several consecutive times at the same point of injection, a loss of fat tissue is possible. Therefore, the point of injection, or even better, the entire side of the body, should be continuously changed in order to avoid a loss of local fat tissue (lipoathrophy) in the injection cell. One thing has manifested itself over the years: The effect of STH is dosage-dependent. This means either invest a lot of money and do it right or do not even begin. Half-hearted attempts are condemned to failure. Minimum effective dosages seem to start at 4 I.U. per day. For comparison: the hypophysis of a healthy, adult releases 0.5–1.5 I.U. growth hormones daily. The duration of intake usually depends on the athlete's financial resources. Our experience is that STH is taken over a prolonged period, from at least six weeks to several months. It is interesting to note that the effect of STH does not stop after a few weeks; this usually allows for continued improvements at a steady dosage. Bodybuilders who have had positive results with STH have reported that the built-up strength and, in particular, the newly-gained muscle system were essentially maintained after discontinuance of the product. The American physician, Dr. William N. Taylor, confirms this statement in his book Anabolic Steroids and the Athlete, where on page 75 he writes: "Evidence for increased muscle number (hyperplasia) in athletes stems from their statements that the increased muscular size and strength remain after the HGH therapy has been discontinued. In fact, there may be further muscular size and strength gains as the training-induced hypertrophy continues in the month beyond."

It remains to be clarified what happens with the insulin and LT-3 thyroid hormone. Athletes who take STH in their build-up phase usually do not need exogenous insulin. It is recommended, in this case, that the athlete eats a complete meal every three hours, resulting in 6-7 meals daily. This causes the body to continuously release insulin so that the blood sugar level does not fall too low. The use of LT-3 thyroid hormones, in this phase, is carried out reluctantly by athletes. In any case, you must have a physician check the thyroid hormone level during the intake of STH. Simultaneous use of anabolic/androgenic steroids and/or Clenbuterol is usually appropriate. During the preparation for a competition the use of thyroid hormones steadily increases. Sometimes insulin is taken together with STH, as well as with steroids and Clenbuterol. Apart from the high damage potential that exogenous insulin can have in non-diabetics, incorrect use will simply and plainly make you FAT! Too much insulin activates certain enzymes which convert glucose into glycerol and finally into triglyceride. Too little insulin, especially during a diet, reduces the anabolic effect of STH. The solution to this dilemma? Visiting a qualified physician who advises the athlete during this undertaking and who, in the event of exogenous insulin supply, checks the blood sugar level and urine periodically. According to what we have heard so far, athletes usually inject intermediately-effective insulin having a maximum duration of effect of 24 hours once a day. Human insulin such as Depot-H-Insulin Hoechst is generally used. Briefly-effective insulin with a maximum duration of effect of eight hours is rarely used by athletes. Again a human insulin such as H-Insulin Hoechst is preferred.

The undesired effect of growth hormones, the so-called side effects, are also a very interesting and hotly-discussed issue. Above all it must be said: STH has none of the typical side effects of anabolic/androgenic steroids including reduced endogenous testosterone production, acne, hair loss, aggressiveness, elevated estrogen level, virilization symptoms in women, and increased water and salt retention. The main side effects that are possible with STH are an abnormally small concentration of glucose in the blood (hypoglycemia) and an inadequate thyroid function. In some cases antibodies against growth hormones are developed but are clinically irrelevant. What about the horror stories about acromegaly, bone deformation, heart enlargement, organ conditions, gigantism, and early death? In order to answer this question a clear differentiation must be made between humans before and after puberty. The growth plates in a person continue to grow in length until puberty. After puberty neither an endogenous hypersection of growth hormones nor an excessive exogenous supply of STH can cause additional growth in the length of the bones. Abnormal size (gigantism) initially goes hand in hand with remarkable body strength and muscular hardness in the afflicted; later, if left untreated, it ends in weakness and death. Again, this is only possible in pre-pubescent humans who also suffer from an inadequate gonadal function (hypogonadism). Humans who suffer from an endogenous hypersecretion after puberty and whose normal growth is completed can also suffer from acromegaly. Bones become wider but not longer. There is a progressive growth in the hands and feet, and enlargement of features due to the growth of the lower jaw and nose. Heart muscle and kidneys can also gain in weight and size. In the beginning all of this goes hand in hand with increased body strength and muscular hardness; it ends, however, in fatigue, weakness, diabetes, heart conditions, and early death.

What the authorities like to do now is to present extreme cases of athletes suffering from these malfunctions in order to discourage others and to drum into athletes the fact that with the exogenous supply of growth hormones they would suffer the same destiny. This, however, is very unlikely, as reality has proven. Among the numerous athletes using STH comparatively few are seven feet tall Neanderthalers with a protruded lower jaw, deformed skull, claw-like hands, thick lips, and prominent bone plates who walk around in size 25 shoes. In order to avoid any misunderstandings, we do not want to disguise the possible risks of exogenous STH use in adults and healthy humans, but one should at least try to be open-minded. Acromegaly, diabetes, thyroid insufficiency, heart muscle hypertrophy, high blood pressure, and enlargement of the kidneys are theoretically possible if STH is used excessively over prolonged periods of time; however, in reality and particularly when it comes to the external attributes, these are rarely present. Tests have shown no causal relation between treatment with somatropin and a possible higher risk of leukemia. Some athletes report headaches, nausea, vomiting, and visual disturbances during the first weeks of intake. These symptoms disappear in most cases even with continued intake. The most common problems with STH occur when the athlete intends to inject insulin in addition to STH. We know two competing German bodybuilders who, because of improper insulin injections, fell into comas lasting several weeks.

The substance somatropin is available as a dried powder and before injecting it must be mixed with the enclosed solution-containing ampule. The ready solution must be injected immediately or stored in the refrigerator for up to 24 hours. It is usually recommended that the compound be stored in the refrigerator. With the exception of the remedy Saizen the biological activity of growth hormones is usually not impaired when storing the dry substance at 15-25° C (room temperature); however, a cooler place (2-8° C) is preferable. On the black market the price for 4 I.U. each of the compounds Genotropin, Humatrope, Norditropin, and Saizen, in Europe is $80 - 120 for a prick-through vial including the solution ampule. As already mentioned, there are many fakes. It is noted that for the U.S.-American growth hormone compounds, the substance content is not given in I.U. (International Units) but in mg (milligrams). Since 1 mg corresponds to exactly 2.7 I.U. the 5 mg solution of the compound Humatrope by Lilly contains exactly 13.5 I.U. of Somatropin. The 10 mg solution of the Protropin compound by Genentech therefore contains 27 I.U. of Somatropin. In American powerlifting and bodybuilding circles Humatrope is usually preferred over Protropin. The reason is that Humatrope is synthesized from a chain of 191 amino acids and thus is identical to the amino acid sequence of the human growth hormone. Protropin, on the other hand, consists of 192 amino acids, one amino acid too many. This might be the explanation for why more antibodies are developed with Protropin than with Humatrope. Growth hormones are on the doping list but they are not yet detectable during doping tests.

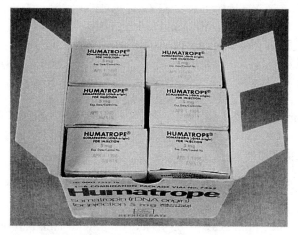

Humatrope by Lilly / U.S., 6 vials per box

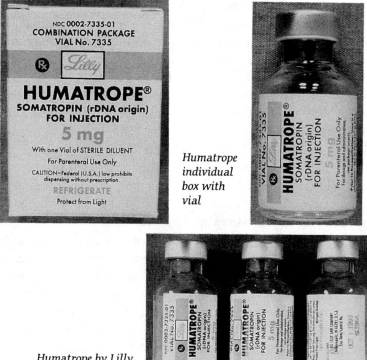

Humatrope individual box with vial

Humatrope by Lilly, U.S. version

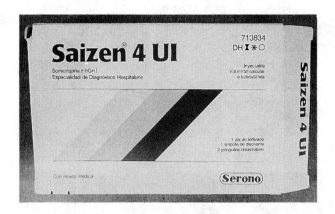

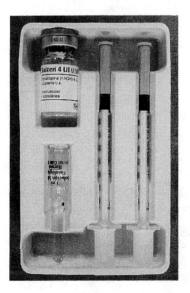

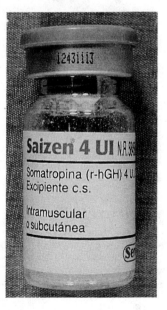

Saizen, growth hormone by Serono / Spain, 4 I.U.

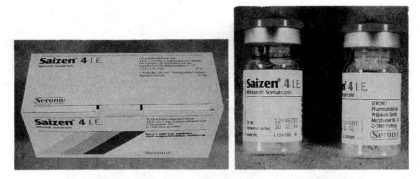

Saizen 4 I.U. by Serono / Germany, 10 vials per box

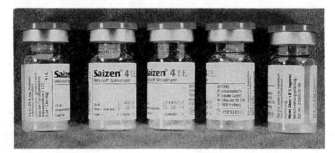

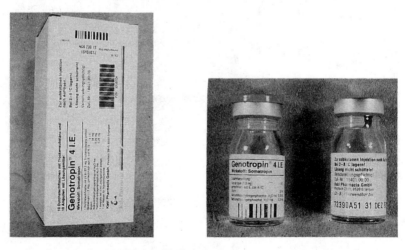

Genotropin 4 I.U. by Kabi Pharmacia / Germany, 10 vials per box

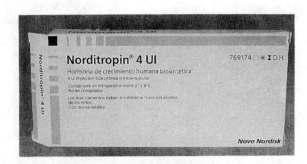

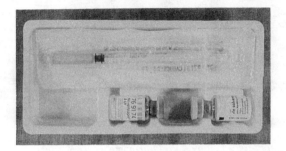

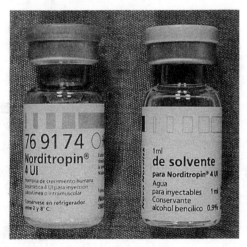

Norditropin 4 I.U. by Novo Nordisk / Spain

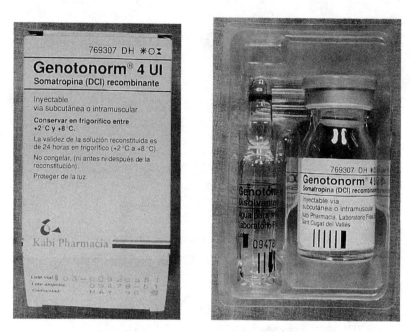

Genotonorm 4 I.U. by Kabi Pharmacia / Spain

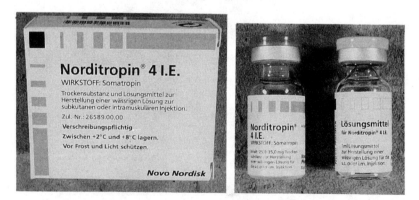

Norditropin 4 I.U. by Novo Nordisk / Germany

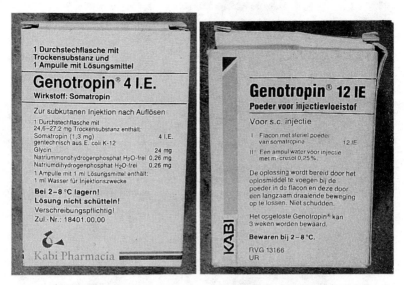

1 Durchstechflasche mit Trockensubstanz und 1 Ampulle mit Lösungsmittel

Genotropin® 4 I.E.

Wirkstoff: Somatropin

Zur subkutanen Injektion nach Auflösen

1 Durchstechflasche mit
24,6–27,2 mg Trockensubstanz enthält:
Somatropin (1,3 mg)   4 I.E.
gentechnisch aus E. coli K-12
Glycin   24 mg
Natriummonohydrogenphosphat H_2O-frei   0,26 mg
Natriumdihydrogenphosphat H_2O-frei   0,26 mg
1 Ampulle mit 1 ml Lösungsmittel enthält:
1 ml Wasser für Injektionszwecke

Bei 2–8 °C lagern!
Lösung nicht schütteln!
Verschreibungspflichtig!
Zul.-Nr.: 18401.00.00

Kabi Pharmacia

Genotropin® 12 IE

Poeder voor injectievloeistof

Voor s.c. injectie

I   Flacon met steriel poeder
van somatropine   12 IE

II   Een ampul water voor injectie
met m-cresol 0,25 %.

De oplossing wordt bereid door het
oplosmiddel te voegen bij de
poeder in de flacon en deze door
een langzaam draaiende beweging
op te lossen. Niet schudden.

Het opgeloste Genotropin® kan
3 weken worden bewaard.

Bewaren bij 2–8 °C.

RVG 13166
UR

KABI

Genotropin 4 I.U. from Germany

Genotropin 12 I.U. from the Netherlands

Russian growth hormone

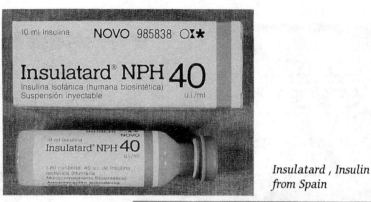

Insulatard , Insulin
from Spain

Depot-H-Insulin, often in
combination with HGH,
by Hoechst / Germany

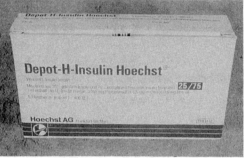

LASIX

Substance: furosemide

Trade names

Diural	5, 10, 20, 40, 250, 500 mg tab.;	DK, NO
Diurapid 40/500	40, 500 mg tab.;	Jenapharm G
Durafurid	40 mg tab.;	Durachemie G
Fumarenid (o.c.)	40 mg tab.;	Brenner-Efeka G
Furanthril	40, 500 mg tab.;	Medphano G
Furo-Puren (o.c.)	40 mg tab.;	Klinge-Natterm. Puren G
Furo-ratiopharm long (o.c.)	30 mg cap.;	ratiopharm G

Furomex	40 mg tab.;	Orion CZ
Furomin	40 mg tab.;	Merckle FI
Furon	40 mg tab.;	Merckle A, CZ
Furonet	40 mg tab;	Nettopharma DK
Furorese (o.c.)	40 mg, 500 mg tab.;	Hexal G
Furosemid	40 mg tab.;	Polfa PL
Furosemid DAK	5, 10, 20, 40, 500 mg tab.;	Nycomed dak DK
Furosemid "Genericon"	40 mg tab.;	Genericon Pharma A
Furosemid "Lannacher"	40 mg tab.;	Lannacher Heilmittel A
Furosemid NM Pharma	25, 40, 500 mg tab.;	NM Pharma S
Furosemid pharmagen	40 mg tab.;	Pharmavit HU
Furosemid slovakofarma	40, 250 mg tab.;	Slovakofarma CZ
Furosemid tab	20, 40, 500 mg tab.;	Orion NO
Furosemid 40 Heumann	40 mg tab.;	Heumann G
Furosemid 40 Stada (o.c.)	40 mg tab.;	Stadapharm G
Furosemid-ratiopharm (o.c.)	40, 500 mg tab.;	ratiopharm G
Furosemide	20, 40, 80 mg tab.;	Steris U.S.
Furosemide	20, 40, 80 mg tab.;	Schein U.S.
Furosemide	20, 40, 80 mg tab.;	Mylan U.S.
Furosemide (o.c.)	10, 20, 40, 80 mg tab.;	Huffman U.S.
Furosemide	10, 20, 40, 80 mg tab.;	Pharmed Group U.S.
Furosemide	20, 40, 80 mg tab.;	Lederle U.S.
Furosemide (o.c.)	20, 40, 80 mg tab.;	Pharmafair U.S.
Furosemide (o.c.)	20, 40, 80 mg tab.;	Warner Chilcott U.S.
Furosemide (o.c.)	20, 40, 80 mg tab.;	Barr Labs U.S.
Furosemide (o.c.)	20, 40, 80 mg tab.;	Martec U.S.
Furosemide (o.c.)	20, 40, 80 mg tab.;	Squibb U.S.
Furosifar	40 mg tab.;	Inpharzam CZ
Fursemid tbl	40 mg tab.;	Belupo CZ
Fusid	40 mg tab.;	Sanofi Winthrp G
Hydro-rapid Tablinen (o.c.)	40 mg tab.;	Sanorania G
Impugan	40, 500 mg tab.;	Dumex DK
Impugan	40 mg tab.;	Dumex NO, CH
Jenafusid (o.c.)	40 mg tab.;	Jenapharm G
Lasix	20 mg tab.;	Hoechst DK, BG, I, GB,U.S.; Mylan Pharm. U.S,Roxane Labs U.S.,Geneva

		U.S., Danbury U.S.
Lasix	25 mg tab.;	Hoechst I
Lasix	30 mg tab.;	Hoechst GR, B, S, DK, FI, A, NO
Lasix	40 mg tab.;	Hoechst G, B, S, DK, BG, FI, A, NO, NL, GR, U.S.; Quimica oechst Guatemala, Costa Rica, Nicaragua, Panama, Guatemala, El Salvador, Honduras, Dom. Rep; Mylan Pharm. U.S., Roxane Labs U.S. Geneva U.S., Danbury U.S.
Lasix	60 mg tab.;	Hoechst S, DK, FI, NL, NO
Lasix	80 mg tab.;	Hoechst A, U.S. Mylan Pharm. U.S. Roxane Labs U.S. Geneva U.S., Danbury U.S.
Lasix	500 mg tab.;	Hoechst G, I, CH, NL, GR, S,GB, A
Odemase (o.c.)	40 mg tab.;	Azupharma G
Seguril	40 mg tab.;	Hoechst ES
Semid	40 mg tab.;	Erfar GR
Sigasalur	40 mg tab.;	Siegfried G
Trofurit	40 mg tab.;	Chinoin CZ
Vesix	40 mg tab.;	Benzon FI
Vesix retard	30, 60, 120 mg tab.;	Benzon FI
Vesix special	500 mg tab.;	Benzon FI
Injection solutions:		
durafurid	20 mg/2 ml;	Durachemie G
Furanthril	20 mg/2 ml;	Medphano G
Furon	20 mg/2 ml;	Merckle A
Furorese (o.c.)	40 mg/4ml;	Hexal G
Furosemid biotika forte inj.	125 mg/10 ml;	Biotika CZ
Furosemid biotika inj.	20 mg/2 ml;	Biotika CZ

Furosemid inf kons	10 mg/1 ml;	Orion NO
Furosemid inj.	20 mg/2 ml;	Chinoin HU
Furosemid NM Pharma	10 mg/1 ml;	NM Pharma S
Furosemid-ratiopharm (o.c.)	20 mg/2 ml;	ratiopharm G
F. ratiopharm 250 inf	250 mg/25 ml;	Merckle CZ
Furosemid Stada (o.c.)	20 mg/2 ml;	Stadapharm G
Furosemide	20 mg/2ml, 40 mg/4 ml; 100 mg/10 ml;	Elkins-Sinn U.S.
Furosemide	20 mg/2 ml; 40 mg/4 ml; 80 mg/8 ml, 100 mg/10 ml;	Astra Pharm. U.S.
Furosemide	10 mg/1 ml, 20 mg/2 ml; 40 mg/4 ml;	Huffman U.S.
Furosemide (o.c.)	20 mg/2 ml, 40 mg/4 ml;	Warner Chilcott U.S.
Fusid	20 mg/2 ml;	Sanofi Winthrop G
Impugan	10 mg/1 ml;	Dumex DK, CH
Lasix	10 mg/1 ml;	Hoechst S, DK, NO, NL, U.S.
Lasix	20 mg/2 ml;	Hoechst G, A, CH, I, U.S.
Lasix	40 mg/4 ml;	Hoechst G, A, CH, U.S.
Lasix	250 mg/25 ml;	Hoechst G, I, GB, A
Lasix Oral Solution	10 mg/1 ml 60/120 ml;	Hoechst U.S.
Semid	20 mg/2 ml;	Erfar GR
Trofurit	20 mg/2 ml;	Chinoin CZ
Vesix	10 mg/1 ml;	Benzon FI

Note: The substance furosemide is also available as an infusion solution. There are also numerous other compounds in various forms of administration which, due to limited space, are not listed.

Lasix is not a hormone compound but a diuretic. It belongs to the group of saluretics and to be exact is a loop diuretic. Its effect consists of distinctly increased excretion of sodium, chloride, potassium, and water. A very important characteristic which must be absolutely monitored with loop diuretics is the reabsorbtion of potassium ions, sodium ions, and chloride ions. This causes a considerable disturbance of the electrolyte household. Due to its intense effect on water excretion Lasix is used for treatment of edemas and high blood pressure. Bodybuilders use Lasix shortly before a competition to excrete excessive, mostly subcutaneous, water so that they appear hard, defined, and ripped to the bone when in the limelight. The effect of tablets begins within an hour and continues for 3-4 hours. Depending on how much water is still in the athlete's body he must have more or less frequent access to a restroom. This can cause a considerable weight loss within a very short time. For this reason, athletes often use Lasix to lose weight and to compete in a lower weight class. Athletes usually prefer the oral form of the compound. Bodybuilders occasionally use the injectable and intravenous version the morning of the competition since it becomes immediately effective when the athlete, due to a more or less strongly remaining water film, begins to panic. This, however, can also produce the opposite effect. That is, the muscles become small and flat; the athlete loses vascularity, and has no pump during warm-up when during a very short time too much water and minerals are lost. It is thus possible that some pro or top amateur shortly before the beginning of a competition as a last countermeasure is seen with a bag of glucose solution being injected intravenously so that the blood volume rises again. In order to compensate for the potassium loss many athletes take potassium chloride tablets. This, however, involves a certain risk since an overdose of potassium can cause cardiac arrest. In our experience, Lasix is taken in the last two days before a competition.

The amount of the dosage, the duration of application, and the intervals of intake usually depend on the diuretic effect or the athlete's shape. Bodybuilders usually take a half or whole 40 mg tablet and wait to see what happens. Some repeat this procedure once or twice in an interval of a few hours. Lasix is the strongest diuretic and the most dangerous compound in bodybuilders' arsenal of medicine. Side effects can include circulatory disturbances, dizziness, dehydration, muscle cramps, vomiting, circulatory collapse, diarrhea, and fainting. In extreme cases cardiac arrest is possible. This also seems to have been the cause of death for Austrian bodybuilder Heinz Sallmayer, who passed away during the 1980's, and for Mohammed Benaziza, who died in October 1992. Extreme caution is advised when athletes who are already substantially drained and dehydrated continue their loop diuretic treatment with a "make it or die attitude," or even continue the intake altogether with a completely reduced liquid intake. ATTENTION: The 500 mg tablet version must not be used under any circumstances by persons with a normal kidney function. Loop diuretics are prescription drugs and are only available in pharmacies. The compound Lasix by Hoechst Company, for example, is sold in packages containing 20 tablets of 40 mg each and costs about $10.

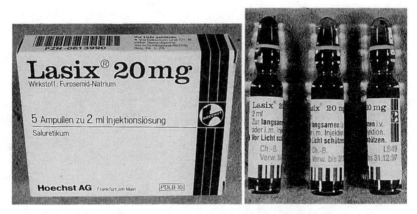

Lasix 20mg, 5 amp/box, by
Hoechst / Germany

Lasix ampules, 20mg

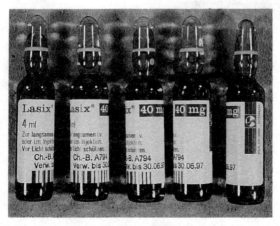

Lasix ampules 40mg from Germany

Lasix 500 tabs with blister from Germany

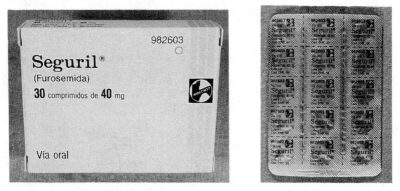

Seguril, furosemide from Spain, 40mg per tablet

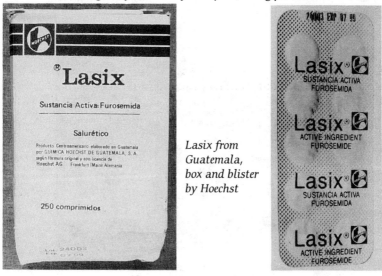

Lasix from
Guatemala,
box and blister
by Hoechst

LAURABOLIN

Substance: nandrolone laurate

Trade names

Fortabol	20 mg/ml; 10/50 ml	Parfam Mexico
Fortadex	25 mg/ml; 5 ml	Hydro G
Fortadex	50 mg/ml;	10/50 ml Hydro G
Laurabolin	25 mg/ml/ 5/10/50 ml	Vemie Veterinär Chemie GmbH G
Laurabolin	50 mg/ml/ 5/10/50 ml	Vemie Veterinär Chemie GmbH G
Laurabolin	50 mg/ml; 10/50 ml	Intervet Mexico
Laurabolin	50 mg/ml;	Werfft-Chemie A
Laurabolin V	50 mg/ml;	Intervet International NL

Laurabolin is an injectable steroid used in veterinary medicine. It is usually intended for canine use. Bodybuilders use Laurabolin since it has similarities to the other nandrolones Deca-Durabolin, Durabolin, and Anadur. The main difference between these steroids is in their durations of effect. Laurabolin is a long-term anabolic that stays active for almost four weeks. Theoretically one single injection per month would be sufficient but no athlete observes this, since such a low dosage would not have performance-enhancing characteristics. Bodybuilders inject Laurabolin at least once a week and report good results when sufficient dosages are injected. The generally observed dosage is 200-400 mg/week. The great disadvantage of Laurabolin is that this compound is only available in a strength of 50 mg/ml so that every week a total amount of 4-8 ml must be injected. Most athletes with whom we spoke usually inject 2 ml of solution twice weekly. The achieved results are similar to those found with Deca-Durabolin (see also Deca-Durabolin); the same is also true for potential side effects. Those who can get an original Deca should give Deca the preference over Laurabolin. The advantage of Laurabolin consists in its relatively low price and the fact that—unlike Deca—here are not yet any fakes. Laurabolin is available in 5, 10, and 50 ml glass vials, depending on the country of origin. The 50 ml glass vial costs between $200 and $250 on the black market. This corresponds to a price of $4 - 5 per 50 mg so that Laurabolin, in any case, is considerably cheaper than Deca. Original Laurabolin by Intervet Company of Mexico is available in a brown glass vial with 10 ml or 50 ml solution. The label has square corners and the expiration date and batch number are clearly visible and imprinted later. Since the substance included in Laurabolin is very inexpensive it is often used when manufacturing injectable fakes.

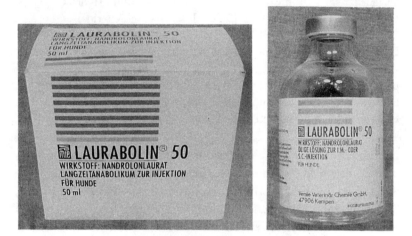

Laurabolin 50 from Germany, new box and vial

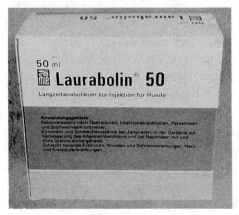

Laurabolin, old box from Germany

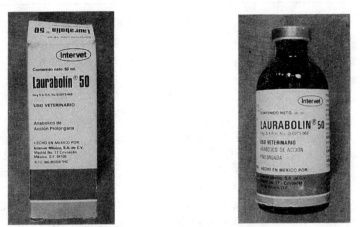

Laurabolin 50, box and vial by Intervet / Mexico

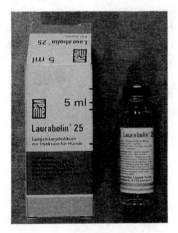

Laurabolin 25, box and vial by Vemie / Germany

L-THYROXINE

Substance: levothyroxine sodium

Trade names

Eferox	25, 50, 75, 100, 125, 150 mcg tab.;	Wyeth G
Eltroxin	25, 50, 75, 100, 125, 150 mcg tab.;	Glaxo Thailand
Euthroid (o.c)	25, 50, 75, 100, 125, 150 mcg tab.;	Warner Lambert U.S.
Euthroid (o.c)	25, 50, 75, 100, 125, 150 mcg tab.;	Warner Chilcott U.S.
Euthyrox	25, 50, 75 mcg tab.;	Merck G, BG
Euthyrox	50 mcg tab.;	Merck A, HU, CZ
Euthyrox	75 mcg tab.;	Merck A
Euthyrox	100, 125, 150 mcg tab.;	Merck D, A
Euthyrox	100 mcg tab.;	Merck BG, HU, CZ
Euthyrox	125 mcg tab.;	Merck BG
Euthyrox	150 mcg tab.;	Merck HU, CZ
Euthyrox	175, 200, 300 mcg tab.;	Merck G
Eutirox	50, 100 mcg tab.;	Bracco I
Levoid (o.c.)	100, 200 mcg tab.;	Nutrition U.S.
Levoroxine (o.c.)	50, 100, 200, 300mcg tab.;	Bariatric U.S.
Levothroid	50, 100 mcg tab.;	Rhone-Poulenc Rorer ES
Levothroid (o.c.)	25, 50, 75, 100, 125, 150 mcg tab.;	Rhone-Poulenc Rorer U.S.
Levothroid	25, 50, 75, 100, 125, 150 mcg tab.;	Forest Pharm. U.S.
Levothroid Inj.	500 mcg amp.;	Rhone ES
L-Thyroxin Henning	25, 50, 75, 100, 125, 150 mcg tab.;	Henning G
L-Thyroxin Henning	200, 1000 mcg tab.;	Henning G
L-Thyroxin Henn.inj.	500 mcg dry substance	Henning G
L-Thyroxin Henning	50, 100, 150 mcg tab.;	Henning A, CZ

L-Thyroxine Sodium	500 mcg/ml;	McGuff U.S.
L-Thyroxin	25, 50, 100 mcg tab.;	Berlin-Chemie G, CZ HU, BG
Levothyroxine	500 mcg/10ml;	Steris U.S.
Levothyroxine (o.c.)	200 mcg/10 ml, 500 mcg/10 ml;	Lyphomed U.S.
Levothyroxine	200 mcg/10 ml, 500 mcg/10 ml;	Fujisawa U.S.
Levothyroxine	25, 50, 75, 100, 125 mcg tab.; 150, 200, 300 mcg tab.;	Lederle U.S.
Levothyroxine (o.c.)	25, 50, 75, 100, 125 mcg tab.;	Quad U.S.
Levoxine (o.c.)	25, 50, 75, 100, 125 mcg tab.;	Daniels U.S.
Levoxine (o.c.)	175, 200, 300 mcg tab.;	Daniesl U.S.
Levoxyl	25, 50, 75, 100, 125, 150 mcg tab.;	Daniels U.S.
Levoxyl	175, 200, 300 mcg tab.;	Daniels U.S.
S.L.T. (o.c.)	100, 200 mcg tab.;	Western Res. U.S.
Synthroid	25, 50, 75, 88, 100, 112 mcg tab.;	Boots U.S.
Synthroid	125, 150, 175, 200, 300 mcg tab.;	Boots U.S.
T4 tabl	50, 75, 100, 125, 150 mcg tab.;	Unipharma GR
T4 tabl	175, 200 mcg tab.;	Unipharma GR
Tiroxino Leo	100 mcg tab.;	Leo ES
Thevier	50, 100 mcg tab.;	Glaxo G
Thyrax	15 mcg tab.;	Organon CZ, NL
Thyrax	25 mcg tab.;	Organon HU, ES, NL, CZ
Thyrax	100 mcg tab.;	Organon HU, ES, NL
Thyrex	50, 100, 160, 200 mcg tab.;	Sanabo A
Thyro-4	100, 200 mcg tab.;	Faran GR, BG
Thyro Hormone	100, 200 mcg tab.;	Ni-The GR
Thyroxin	100, 250 mcg tab.;	Orion FI
Thyroxin-natrium	50, 100 mcg tab.;	Nycomed NO

Note: There are numerous other compounds worldwide which contain the substance levothyroxine sodium. Due to limited space, however, they are not part of this list.

L-Thyroxine is a synthetically manufactured thyroid hormone. Its effect is similar to that of natural L-thyroxine (L-T4) in the thyroid gland. L-thyroxine is one of two hormones which is produced in the thyroid. The other one is L-triiodthyronine (L-T3, see Cytomel). L-thyroxine is clearly the weaker of the two hormones. For this reason it is often used for a longer time period than L-T3. Bodybuilders use L-Thyroxine to accelerate the metabolizing of carbohydrates, proteins, and fat. The body burns more calories than usual so that a lower fat content can be achieved or the athlete burns fat although he takes in more calories. In the past L-Thyroxine was often used by competing bodybuilders. Unfortunately, with increased dosages (more than 400 to 600 mcg/day) usually not only more fat but more carbohydrates and proteins are burned as well. The athlete no doubt becomes harder but he can also lose muscle mass if steroids are not administered simultaneously. L-Thyroxine is rarely used today since most athletes use Cytomel or Triacana. When used properly there are few side effects to L-Thyroxine. Dosages that are too high and, in particular, dosages that are increased too quickly and too early at the beginning of intake can cause trembling of the fingers, excessive perspiration, diarrhea, insomnia, nausea, increased heartbeat, inner unrest, and weight loss.

The dosages taken by athletes are usually in the range of 200-400 mcg/day. We advise that you begin with a small dose and increase it slowly and evenly over several days. L-Thyroxine is a prescription drug and available only in pharmacies. One hundred tablets of 150 mcg each of the compound Levothroid cost about $50 on the black market. One hundred tablets of 200 mcg each of Synthroid by the Boots Company usually cost about the same. Unlike Cytomel and Triacana, L-Thyroxine is rarely found on the black market.

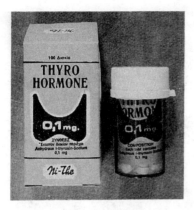

Thyro Hormone, 0.1mg / tab

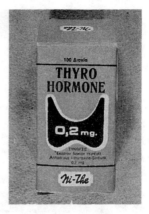

Thyro Hormone from Greece, 0.2mg / tab

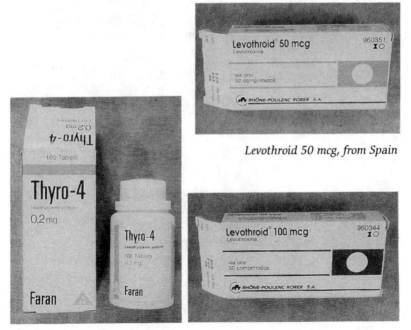

Levothroid 50 mcg, from Spain

Thyro-4, L-Thyroxine from Greece, 0.2mg/tab

Levothroid 100 mcg, from Spain

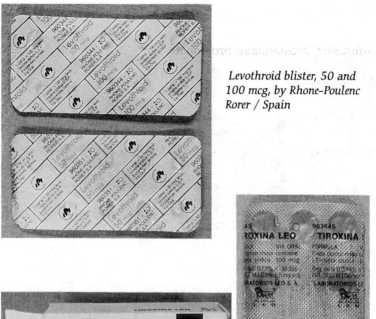

Levothroid blister, 50 and 100 mcg, by Rhone–Poulenc Rorer / Spain

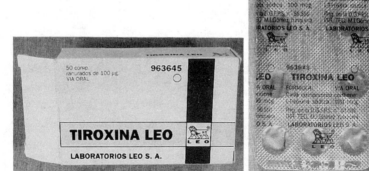

Tiroxina Leo, box and blister by Leo / Spain

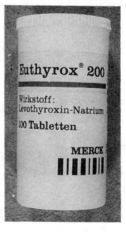

Euthyrox from Germany

MASTERON

Substance: drostanolone propionate

Trade names

Drolban (o.c.)	50 mg/1 ml;	Lilly U.S.
Masterid (o.c.)	100 mg/2 ml;	Grünenthal G
Masteril	100 mg/2 ml;	Syntex GB, BG
Masteron	100 mg/ 2 ml;	Sarva-Syntex B; Cilag PT
Mastisol	5% injection sol.;	Shionogi Japan
Metormon (o.c.)	100 mg/2 ml;	Syntex ES
Permastril (o.c.)	100 mg;2 ml;	Cassenne FR

Masteron is a steroid highly valued by competing bodybuilders. The great popularity of this injectable steroid in bodybuilder circles is due to the extraordinary characteristics of its included substance. Drostanolone propionate is a synthetic derivative of dihydrotestosterone. This causes the Masteron not to aromatize in any dosage and thus, it cannot be converted into estrogens. This distinctive feature is confirmed by the Belgian manufacturer, Sarva-Syntex, who on the enclosed package insert calls Masteron a steroid with strong, antiestrogenic characteristics. Since Masteron is a predominantly androgenic steroid, the athlete can increase his androgen level without also risking an increase in his estrogen level. This results in a dramatically improved hardness and sharpness of the muscles. One must, however, make a distinction here since Masteron does not automatically improve the quality of muscles in everyone. A prerequisite is that the athlete's fat content must already be very low. In this case Masteron can then be the decisive factor between a smooth, flat muscle or a hard and ripped look. For this purpose Masteron is often only used during the last four weeks before a competition so that the muscles get the last "kick." Masteron is especially effective in combination with steroids such as Winstrol, Parabolan, Primobolan, Oxandrolone and also Testosterone propionate.

The usual dosage taken by athletes is around 100 mg three times per week. Since the substance drostanolone propionate is quickly broken down in the body, frequent and regular injections are necessary. This fact makes Masteron a very interesting steroid when doping tests must be passed by a negative urine analysis. Since the propionate substance of drostanolone does not remain in the body very long in a sufficient, detectable amount, athletes inject the compound with great success up to two weeks before a test. However, since it also has anabolic characteristics and thus helps the buildup of a high-qualitative muscle system, the use of Masteron is not only limited to the preparation stage for a competition. Athletes who want to avoid water retention and who readily have a problem with an elevated estrogen level, likewise appreciate Masteron. Also in this case usually one ampule (100 mg) is injected every second day. In combination with Primobolan, Winstrol or Testosterone propionate no enormous strength and weight gains can be obtained, only high-quality and long-lasting results. Although women do not use Masteron very often some national and international competing female athletes do take it before a championship. The dosages observed are normally 100 mg every 4-5 days.

Masteron is not hepatoxic so liver damage is quite unlikely. High blood pressure and gynecomastia are not a problem since neither water nor salt retention occurs and the estrogen level remains low. The main problem are acne and a possible accelerated hair loss since dihydrotestosterone is highly affinitive to the skin's androgen receptors, in particular, to those on the scalp. Since Masteron, in most cases, is not administered in excessively high dosages and the intake, at the same time, is limited to a few weeks, the compatibility for the athlete is usually very good. The Belgian Masteron is packaged in a box containing two ampules of 2 ml each. The ampules have no imprint but are packaged with a paper label and included in a pull-out ampule bed. The manufacturer also includes two ampule saws. The Masteron package with two ampules costs between $30 and $40 on the black market. In the meantime several fakes of Masteron exist.

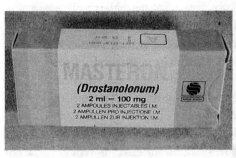

Masteron, box and ampules by Syntex /
Belgium

MEGAGRISEVIT-MONO

Substance: clostebole acetate

Trade names

Alfa-Trofodermin	0.5% gel;	Farmitalia I
Megagrisevit-mono	15 mg drag.;	Pharmacia G
Megagrisevit-mono	10 mg/1.5 ml;	Pharmacia G
Steranabol (o.c.)	40 mg/2 ml;	Farmitalia G

Megagrisevit is an unusual steriod which has several characteristics. In addition to the substance clostebole acetate it also contains
the two vitamins B6 and B12. The vitamin B12 is present as
cyanocobalamin in the amount of 100 mcg per dragee and 2500
mcg per 1.5 ml ampule. The chemical denomination for the vitamin
B6 is pyridoxinhydrochloride and is included in a dragee with a
strength of 50 mg while the 1.5 ml ampule contains only 10 mg. It
is also noted that in the injectable Megagrisevit both vitamins are
included separately so that the red 1.5 ml vitamin ampule must be
mixed with the 1.5 ml steroid injection vial prior to injection.

The main effect of Megagrisevit consists of stimulating the protein synthesis and leading to a positive nitrogen balance. It has a predominantly anabolic effect which is combined with a very weak and subliminal, androgenic residual effect. "This all sounds great," some of you will say but, unfortunately it must also be noted that the anabolic effect of this compound is also not very strong. No large strength and muscle gains can be obtained with Megagrisevit but one should not immediately discard this remedy since, when used properly, it is interesting for bodybuilders. The dragees are not recommended for bodybuilders since their effect is weak, so in the following we will exclusively discuss the injectable version. Also in this context we would like to recommend in the beginning that you do not use the red ampule with the vitamin cocktail. The vitamin injection might indeed increase the appetite and in some cases lead to an improved psychological well-being but it has the disadvantage that, together with a steroid injection, too large an injection volume will accumulate in the body if the athlete injects the required steroid amount. It must also be considered that a high amount of B12 and B6 will not necessarily improve performance. What remains then, is a 1.5 ml injection vial with a milky suspension that is really interesting. All those of you who have absolute confidence in the 20 mg Primobolanacetat ampules and bemoaned the day when they were taken off the market will find a potent substitute in this 1.5 ml injection vial. The substance clostebole acetate is dissolved in water, has a low half-life time, does not aromatize, does not retain water, and is non-toxic. It is, however, still an excellent steroid when preparing for a competition. Athletes normally use two 1.5 ml vials per day which can be combined into one large 3 ml injection, equal to a daily intake of 20 mg of clostebole acetate. Women also achieve remarkable results and inject the same amount every second day.

As the only steroid used during a diet phase Megagrisevit certainly is too weak; however, in combination with the stronger androgenic steroids such as Parabolan, Masteron, or Testosterone propionate it has effects similar to the old Primoacetat ampules. But there is more. Megagrisevit is not liver-toxic and in these dosages rarely has side effects. Even women have few virilization symptoms. It is also one of the few steroids which is still manufactured in Germany and available in German pharmacies with a prescription so that shortages are unlikely. Since most people do not know the benefits offered by Megagrisevit, the demand, in our experience, is so low that one wonÆt find it on the U.S. black market. Megagrisevit is available in German pharmacies in package sizes of 3 inj. vials (price approx. $30) and 10 inj. vials (price approx. $85) The prices are taken from the German Red List 1995. The largest disadvantage, as can be readily recognized, is the high cost one would have to pay if injecting two vials per day. There are currently no fakes of this compound.

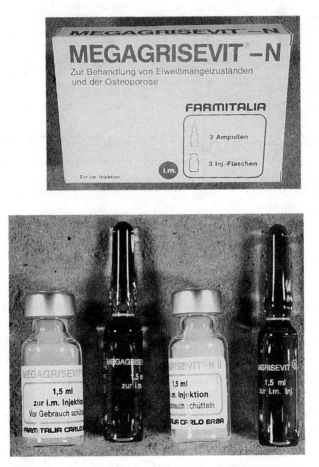

Megagrisevit-N for injections by Farmitalia from Germany

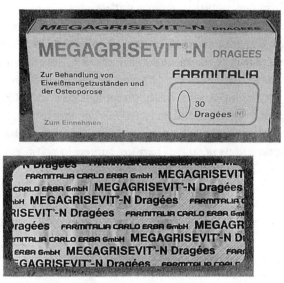

Megagrisevit–N–Dragees from Germany

METHANDRIOL

Substance: methylandrostenediol

Trade names

Methyldiol Aqueous (o.c.)   50 mg/ml;   Vortech U.S.

Methandriol was a popular steroid in the U.S. during the early 1980's and was used until a few years ago when it was taken off the market. It was a water-dissolved injectable compound which was available only in a strength of 50 mg/ml. Powerlifters and competing bodybuilders appreciated the strong androgenic effect and the extremely low half-life time. Since Methandriol was dissolved in water, daily injections were necessary. It had the advantage of not causing water retention and this, combined with the distinct androgenic component, allowed powerlifters a large strength gain without increasing the body weight, thus helping them obtain good muscle hardness and density. Since Methandriol was quickly effective after the injection some powerlifters used it as a "booster" before a workout or a competition to increase their aggressiveness. This steroid was usually taken only briefly, normally for 2-4 weeks, in a daily dose of 50 mg. Since the water-dissolved Methandriol was difficult to detect in doping tests, hammerthrowers, shotputters, javelin throwers, and sprinters were among its users. Women took it only rarely due to the possible masculinizing symptoms. Today the water-dissolved, injectable Menthandriol can be found neither as an original compound nor as a fake. Some remedies from veterinary medicine are known to contain methandriol. However these are exclusively combination compounds such as the German drug "Asthma-Tabletten." In addition to 5 mg methandriol, "Asthma-Tabletten" also includes 20 mg ephedrine HCL, 100 mg diprophylline, and 1 mg prednisolone. If you then take the effective dose of methandriol —assuming that at least 40 mg are taken orally— you are also taking 160 mg ephedrine HCL, 800 mg diprophylline, and 8 mg prednisolone at the same time. We strongly discourage you from taking such high amounts of broncholytic substances in order to take a sufficient dose of methandriol. The probability that such a compound will reach the black market for bodybuilders is next to nothing. We know of no fakes.

METHANDRIOL DIPROPIONATE

Substance: methylandrostenediol dipropionate

Trade names

Andris	10 mg tab.;	Chifar GR
Arbolic (o.c.)	50 mg/ml;	Burgin Arden U.S.
Crestabolic (o.c.)	50 mg/ml;	Nutrition U.S.
Durandrol (o.c.)	50 mg/ml;	Pharmex U.S.
Hybolin (o.c	50 mg/ml;	Hyrex U.S.
Methyldiol (o.c.)	2 mg tab.;	Vortech U.S.
Metylandrostendiol	10 mg tab.;	Polfa PL
Metylandrostendiol	25 mg tab.;	Polfa PL

| Novandrol | 10 mg drag.; | Galenika YU |
| Novandrol | 25 mg drag.; | Galenika YU |

Methandriol Dipropionate (M.D.) is a form of the water-dissolved Methandriol but it remains effective for a longer period of time. On the one hand, M.D. can be dissolved in oil for injection purposes and, on the other hand, it is produced in tablet form since it is also effective when taken orally. M.D. has a strong anabolic and androgenic component so that it is suitable for the buildup of strength and muscle mass. The effect can be compared to a cross between Deca-Durabolin and Testosterone enanthate. Like testosterone it contributes to a gain in both strength and muscle but does not retain more water than Deca-Durabolin. The best results can be obtained, however, if M.D. is not taken alone but in combination with another steroid. This is because M.D. is able to magnify the effects of other steroid compounds. It does this by increasingly sensitizing the androgenic receptors of the muscle cell, allowing a higher amount of the steroid molecules of the additionally taken steroids to be absorbed by the receptors. This also explains why injectable M.D. is only available today as a combination compound with an additional steroid substance. Injectable M.D. is only available in the Australian veterinary steroids Drive, Spectriol, Geldabol, and Filibol Forte so that procurement of the compound is difficult. The few athletes using this drug report good strength gains, a solid muscle gain, and low water retention. The combination steroids aromatize only slightly so, when taking only M.D., the use of antiestrogens is perhaps appropriate. The injectable form is only slightly toxic.

The usual dosage for athletes is 100 mg every 2-3 days. In Europe only the oral form of M.D. is available. Also in this case it is beneficial to combine M.D. with another steroid, preferably an injectable one. The normal daily dose is 40-60 mg and is usually taken in 2-3 individual doses spread over the day. The tablets are usually taken for only 4-6 weeks since the effect decreases quickly, thus requiring higher dosages. They are also 17-alpha alkylated so even a low dosage and a short intake can be damaging to the liver. Because of its androgenic effect women rarely use M.D. Possible side effects of the tablet form can be elevated levels of liver toxins, gastrointestinal pain, acne, gynecomastia, increased aggressiveness, and high blood pressure. Neither the injectable combination form nor the oral version of M.D. is normally found on the black market. Those who accidentally find Novandrol from the former Yugoslavia will notice that this compound is not available in tablet form but in dragees which are intended for subglossal intake.

METHYLTESTOSTERONE

Substance: methyltestosterone

Trade names

Afro	25 mg tab.;	Casel TK
Agovirin	10 mg drg.;	Leciva CZ
Android (o.c.)	5, 10, 25 mg tab.;	Brown U.S.
Android	5, 10, 25 mg tab.;	ICN Pharm. U.S.
Androral	10 mg	Galenika Richer HU
Arcosterone (o.c.)	10 mg sub.;	Acrum U.S.
Arcosterone (o.c	10, 25 mg tab.;	Acrum U.S.
Hormobin	5 mg tab.;	Sahin TK
Longivol	1 mg tab.;	Medical S.A. ES
Mediatric (o.c.)	10 mg tab.; cap.;	Wyeth-Ayerst U.S.
Mesteron	10 mg tab.;	Polfa PL
Metandren (o.c.)	5 mg lingual drg.;	Ciba U.S.
Metandren (o.c.)	10, 25 mg tab.;	Ciba U.S.
Methyltestosterone	10 mg tab.;	Goldline U.S.
Oreton Methyl (o.c.)	10 mg tab. buccal.;	Schering U.S.
Oreton Methyl	10 mg tab.;	Schering U.S.
Teston	25 mg tab.;	Remek GR
Testormon	10 mg tab.;	Unitas PT
Testosteron	5 mg tab.;	Berco G
T. Lingvalete	5 mg lingual drg.;	Galenika YU
Testovis	10 mg tab.;	SIT I
Testred	10 mg cap.;	ICN U.S.
Virilon	10 mg retard cap.;	Star U.S.

Methyltestosterone is an oral form of testosterone. Testosterone itself is ineffective when taken orally since the greatest part of the compound is metabolized and destroyed by the liver during the "first pass" so that at most 5-10% of the compound enters the blood and becomes effective. At a closer look methyltestosterone is a 17-alpha steroid molecule, which means that a methyl group is added to the C-17-alpha position of the molecule. Thus, methyltestosterone is not broken down and deactivated quite as fast by the liver as oral testosterone is. Still, it reaches the blood quickly and has only a low half-life time. Since methyltestosterone, in part, is reabsorbed through the mucous membrane in the mouth, this substance is also available for sublingual intake. Methyltestosterone is a very potent steroid since it has a distinct androgenic effect. In particular, it is used to increase aggressiveness. Powerlifters and weightlifters use it before a heavy workout or a competition since the increased androgenic effect can already be noted one hour after intake and the improved aggressiveness, the increased self-esteem, and the thrust of motivation taking place allow the athlete to lift heavier weights. In the U.S. Methyltest is often used as a stimulant by football players before a game. The use of methyltestosterone in bodybuilding is limited since it is not suitable for permanent strength and muscle gain. It is rarely used for this purpose since most bodybuilders prefer Dianabol which has a similar structure. Those, however, who would still like to try it will notice a quick and strong strength gain. The increase in body weight is within normal limits and is mostly due to water retention. Dianabol is clearly more effective to build up muscle tissue. Some bodybuilders use it in irregular intervals during a diet phase in order to increase their training willpower or they use Methyltest as a "training booster" in order to overcome a "dead point." The dosage is usually 25-50 mg/day. Methyltest is rarely taken—if at all—for more than four weeks and women usually do not use it.

Methyltestosterone is a very toxic steroid which can cause many side effects. It especially puts stress on the liver. A famous American powerlifter once said, "Methyltestosterone burns cute little holes in your liver." Since this steroid strongly aromatizes, gynecomastia is one of the most common side effects. The distinct water and salt retention can also increase blood pressure. The androgenic effect results in considerable virilization symptoms in women and acne and AGGRESSIVENESS in men. It is no joking matter to be around someone who works a lot with methyltestosterone. Effects include anti-social behavior, irritability, impatience, tantrums, and forgetfulness or light disturbances in consciousness. For example, it is possible that after training you cannot remember where you parked your car. These show that methyltestosterone really affects your brain in a negative manner. By the way, though a doping test was often assumed to exist, there is no such test for methyltestosterone that checks the testosterone/epitestosterone value. It is easily detectable in a test since Methyltesto breaks down on its own and specific metabolites can be easily tested in a urine analysis. Thus it does not make sense to take Methyltesto in small dosages hoping that in this way the permissible testosterone /epitestosterone level of 6:1 will not be exceeded.

Methyltestosterone is normally readily available on the black market. It is available in tablet, dragee, or capsule form for oral, sublingual or buccal intake; it is available under a variety of trade names and from a variety of manufacturers. The most common are the Hungarian Androral and the Greek Teston. Androral is sold in a small glass tube with a plastic cap containing 20 tablets of 20 mg each. There is a white paper label with rectangular corners on the tube. The expiration date is visible and imprinted later on the label. Since the tablets are not very large and fill only part of the glass tube, some cotton is added so that the tablets do not move. The Greek Teston is packaged in a small, white plastic box with a screw cap. It has a label with rounded corners which can be easily pulled off. The expiration date and the batch number are visible and punched into the label in red letters. Thirty 25 mg tablets are included in one box. The tablets are indented on one side. The manufacturer also offers the plastic box in a matching carton which, however, is rarely offered on the black market since it takes up too much room during smuggling. An unusual compound is the Spanish Longivol. These are large, pink-colored vitamin tablets which in addition include 1 mg of methyltestosterone. Methyltestosterone is a very low-priced and easily available substance. It is a welcome fact that the athlete does not have to pay much money for it. The 10 mg Androral tablets cost approx. $25 per 100 and the 25 mg version of Teston costs approx. $0.40 per tablet on the black market. The disadvantage is that methyltestosterone is the substance most often used in fakes.

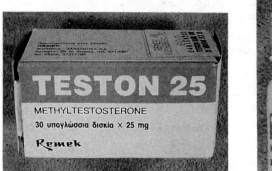
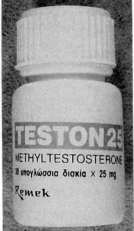

Teston 25 from Greece

Androral from Hungary

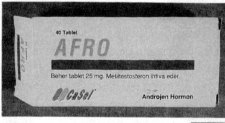

Afro, box and blister by Casel
from Turkey

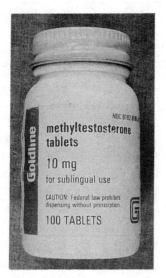

Methytestosterone tablets by Goldline / U.S.

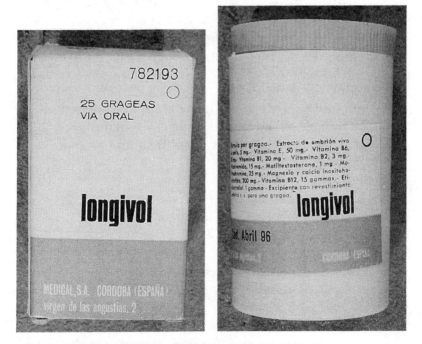

*Longivol, box and container by Medical S.A. Spain,
Methyltesto with vitamins*

MIOTOLAN

Substance: furazabol

Trade names

Miotolan   1 mg tab.;   Daiichi Seiyaku Japan

"The mysterious Ben Johnson favorite, Furazobol," Daniel Duchaine writes in his book Ask the Guru. He does not make this statement without a reason since, in this case, we are dealing with a completely unusual steroid. Furazobol, known by its tradename, Miotolan, is a synthetic derivative of dihydrotestosterone. Until 1990 this steroid was not detectable during any doping tests and could thus be taken by athletes even on the day of a competition. During the Olympic Games in Seoul it contributed largely to the many negative urine samples and, at the same time, to the fantastic performances presented to the television viewer. Field and track athletes, in particular, knew about this advantageous characteristic. Today Miotolan is on the list of detectable steroids but, in most cases, can still be taken up to 5 to 7 days before testing. When looking at the application of Miotolan you learn even more unusual things: This steroid is used as a lipid reducer. It is suitable for long-term treatment of arteriosclerosis and hypercholesterolemia. Miotolan reduces the cholestol level and increases the "good" HDL value. In Japan Miotolan is a standard treatment to lower cholesterol levels.

This steroid does not cause water and salt retention and does not aromatize. Since the tablets are effective for only a brief period of time they must be taken several times a day. Miotolan has a predominantly androgenic effect and only a very low repression of the body's own testosterone production. Although it is potentially hepatoxic a possible reduced liver function seems unlikely if the daily manufacturer-recommended dose of 2-6 mg is not exceeded. Since athletes use considerably higher dosages the risk of liver poisoning cannot be excluded. The usual question—What is a performance-improving dosage?—is difficult to answer. It is difficult because we do not know anybody who has ever taken this compound and because technical literature does not have anything to report in this regard either. The daily dosage should be at least 10-20 tablets, that is 10-20 mg/day. Due to its low substance amount per tablet and its high cost, this steroid will probably not be successful with body-builders. Not to mention that, so far, it is not available on the black market. We are therefore unable to offer price, photos, packaging, and tablet descriptions. (Possible doubts by readers that this steroid perhaps does not exist are inappropriate.) However, this steroid really does exist.

NILEVAR

Substance: norethandrolone

Trade names

Nilevar	10 mg tab.;	Searle FR, CH
Nilevar (o.c.)	10 mg tab.;	Searle U.S.

This is an oral steroid which is a derivative of nortesterone. It is interesting that Nilevar is produced by the same manufacturer who also introduced the well-known Anavar to the U.S. market. Nilevar, which was already sold in American pharmacies in 1956, was a precursor of Anavar which was introduced to the market in 1964 by Searle USA. It has since been voluntarily removed from the market. Thus it is not surprising that Nilevar has certain similarities to Anavar or Oxandrolone. Like Oxandrolone it has only a weak anabolic effect, whereas the androgenic component is distinctly stronger. Nilevar, even in low dosages, aromatizes easily so that the increased estrogen level could become a problem. The main effect of Nilevar, in par^t, is a considerable strength gain. This gain often goes hand in hand with a distinct water retention, especially if high dosages are taken, which also explains the gain in body weight of its users. The manufacturer of the French and Swiss Nilevar recommends a daily dose of 10-30 mg. Athletes using Nilevar—usually powerlifters—take 30-40 mg/day, divided into two to three equal dosages. It is mostly used for a short period, a maximum of 4-6 weeks. Women should not take Nilevar since it can cause considerable virilization symptoms. Nilevar is 17-alpha alkylated and therefore potentially hepatoxic which puts stress on the liver. Other possible side effects are acne, gynecomastia, aggressiveness, headaches, gastrointestinal pain, reduced production of the body's own hormones and high blood pressure. In the U.S. Nilevar cannot be found on the black market, whereas in Europe one can occasionally find the French Nilevar. In France Nilevar has been on the market since 1960. A package of thirty 10 mg tablets costs approx. $4 in the pharmacy. Because of its price it is an interesting compound, yet Nilevar is rarely used by bodybuilders in Europe since other steroids are readily available.

NOLVADEX

Substance: tamoxifen citrate

Trade names

Ceadon	10, 20 mg tab.;	Beta Argentina
Crioxifeno	20 mg tab.;	Cryo Pharma Mexico
Defarol	10 mg tab.;	Proel GR
Dignotamoxi (o.c.)	10, 20, 30, 40 mg tab.;	Dignos Chemie G
Duratamoxifen	10, 20, 30 mg tab.;	Durachemie G
Emblon	10, 20 mg tab.;	Berk GB
Jenoxifen	10, 20, 30 mg tab.;	Jenapharm G
Kessar	10, 20, 30, 40 mg tab.;	Pharmacia G
Kessar	10, 20, 30, 40 mg tab.;	Farmitalia A
Kessar	10, 20 mg tab.;	Farmitalia I; Farmitalia-Carlo Erba CH, FI, GR
Ledertam	10, 20 mg tab.;	Teva S
Mandofen	10, 20, 30, 40 mg tab.;	MW Pharma G
Mastofen	10 mg tab.;	Pentafarma PL
Noltam	10, 20 mg tab.;	Lederle GB

Nolvadex	10 mg tab.;	Zeneca G, Mexico, GB ICI Pharma, A, CH, B, DK, ES, FI,I, GR, NO, YU, NL, PL, S, FR,U.S., Panama, Guatemala, El Salvador, Honduras, Ecuador, Dom. Rep., Bolivia, Peru, Costa Rica, Nicaragua
Nolvadex	20, 30, 40 mg tab.;	Zeneca G ICI Pharma A, CH, DK, FR, NL, S, FI, ES, NO
Nolvadex D	20 mg tab.;	ICI B, ES, I, PL, GB, GR
Nolvadex forte	40 mg tab.;	ICI GB, B
Noncarcinon	10 mg tab.;	Fidelis PL
Nourytam	10, 20, 30, 40 mg tab.;	Nourypharma G
Oxeprax	20 mg tab.;	Wyeth-Orfi ES
Riboxifen (o.c.)	10, 20, 30, 40 mg tab.;	Ribopharm G
Tadex	10 mg tab.;	Atabay TK
Tadex	10, 20, 40 mg tab.;	Lääkefarmos FI
Tafoxen	10, 20 mg tab.;	Ciba-Geigy NL
Tamax	10, 20, 40 mg tab.;	Orion Corp. A
Tamaxin	10, 20, 40 mg tab.;	Lääkefarmos S; Orion DK
Tamcal	10, 20, 30, 40 mg tab.;	Pharmacal FI
Tamexin	10, 20, 30, 40 mg tab.;	Merckle FI
Tamifen	40 mg tab.;	Medochemie BG
Tamofen	10, 20, 40 mg tab.;	Leiras FI, Rhone-Poulenc DK, D, S; Tillotts GB; Huhtamaeki NO
Tamofene	10, 20 mg tab.;	Roger Bellon FR
Tamoplex	10 mg tab.;	Conforma B; Er-Kim TK
Tamoplex	30, 40 mg tab.;	Chefifarm, GR
Tamoplex	10, 20, 30 mg tab.;	Pharmachemie NL
Tamoxan	10, 20 mg tab.;	Tecnimede PL; Kener Mexico
Tamoxasta	10, 20 mg tab.;	Asta Medica G
Tamox-GRY	10, 20, 30, 40 mg tab.;	GRY G
Tamoxifen	10, 20, 40 mg tab.;	Farmitalia-Carlo Erba GB; Generics S
Tamox. AL (o.c.)	10, 20 mg tab.;	Aluid G
T. cell pharm	10, 20, 30, 40 mg tab.;	Cell pharm G
T. citrate	10, 20 mg tab.;	Chefifarm GR
Tamox. ct (o.c.)	10, 20, 30, 40 mg tab.;	CT Arzneimittel G
T. dumex	10, 20, 30, 40 mg tab.;	Dumex NL
Tamoxifen Ebewe	10, 20 mg tab.;	Ebewe A

F. Farmos	10, 20, 40 mg tab.;	Bristol-Myers CH; Orion CH
T. Fermenta	10, 20, 30, 40 mg tab.;	Fermenta S
Tamoxifen Hexal	10, 20, 30 mg tab.;	Durascan DK
T. Hexal (o.c.)	10, 20, 30, 40 mg tab.;	Hexal G
T. Heumann	10, 20, 30, 40 mg tab.;	Heumann G
T. Lachema	10 mg tab.;	CZ
Tamoxifen Leiras	10 mg tab.;	Leiras BG
Tamoxifen lederle	10, 20, 40 mg tab.;	Lederle NL
Tamoxifen medac	10, 20, 30, 40 mg tab.;	Medac G
Tamoxifen mp	10, 20 mg tab.;	MP LN
Tamoxifen NM	10, 20, 40 mg tab.;	NM Pharma S
Tamoxifen NM	10, 20, 30, 40 mg tab.;	Generics DK
T. Onkolan	10, 20, 30, 40 mg tab.;	Lannacher Heilmittel A
T.Pan Medica	10 mg tab.;	Pan-Medica FR
T.pharbita	10, 20 mg tab.;	Pharbita NL
T.-ratiopharm (o.c.)	10, 20, 30, 40 mg tab.;	Ratiopharm G
T. Sopharma	10 mg tab.;	The Chem. Pharm. & Res. Inst. Sofia BG
Tamoxifen Tabletts	10 mg tab.;	Bar Labs U.S.
Tamoxifeno	10 mg tab.;	Farmitalia-Carlo Erba ES
T. farmitalia	10, 20 mg tab.;	Farmitalia ES
Tamoxifeno Funk	10, 20 mg tab.;	Funk S.A. ES
Tamoxifeno Septa	20 mg tab.;	Septa ES
T. Wassermann	10 mg tab.;	Wassermann ES
Tamoxifenum	10, 20 mg tab.;	Centrafarm NL
Tamoxifenum gf	10, 20, 40 mg tab.;	GF NL
Tamoxifenum pch	10, 20, 30, 40 mg tab.;	PCH NL
Tamoxigenat (o.c.)	10, 20, 30, 40 mg tab.;	Azuchemie G
Tamox-Puren (o.c.)	10, 20, 30, 40 mg tab.;	Klinge-Nattermann-Puren G
Taxus	20 mg tab.;	Andromaco Mexico
Tecnofen	10, 20 mg tab.;	Tecnofarma Mexico
Zemide (o.c.)	10, 20, 30, 40 mg tab.;	Wyeth-Pharma G
Zitazonium (o.c.)	10 mg tab.;	Med Pharma G
Zitazonium	10 mg tab.;	Thiemann G; Egis HU

This remedy is somewhat different from others since it is not an anabolic/androgenic steroid. For male and female bodybuilders, however, it is a very useful and recommended compound which is confirmed by its widespread use and mostly positive results. Nolvadex belongs to the group of sex hormones and is a so-called antiestrogen. The normal application of Nolvadex is in the treatment of certain forms of breast cancer in female patients. With Nolvadex it is possible to reverse an existing growth process of deceased tissue and prevent further growth. The growth of certain tissues is stimulated by the body's own estrogen hormone. This is especially true for the breast glands in men and women since the body has a large number of estrogen receptors at these glands which can bond with the estrogens present in the blood. If the body's own estrogen level is unusually high an undesired growth of breast glands occurs. However, in healthy women and particularly in men this is not the case. Despite this, it is mostly male bodybuilders who use Nolvadex, and fewer women. At first sight this seems somewhat inconceivable but when taking a closer look, the reasons are clear. Bodybuilders who take Nolvadex also use anabolic steroids at the same time. Since most steroids aromatize more or less strongly, i.e. part of the substance is converted into estrogens, male bodybuilders can experience a significant elevation in the normally very low estrogen level. This can lead to feminization symptoms such as gynecomastia (growth of breast glands), increased fat deposits and higher water retention.

The antiestrogen Nolvadex works against this by blocking the estrogen receptors of the effected body tissue, thereby inhibiting a bonding of estrogens and receptor. It is, however, important to understand that Nolvadex does not prevent the aromatization but only acts as an estrogen antagonist. This means that it does not prevent testosterone and its synthetic derivatives (steroids) from converting into estrogens but only fights with them in a sort of "competition" for the estrogen receptors. This characteristic has the disadvantage that after the discontinuance of Nolvadex a "rebound effect" can occur which means that the suddendly freed estrogen receptors are now able to absorb the estrogen present in the blood. For this reason the combined intake of Proviron is suggested (see Proviron.) Nolvadex is also useful during a diet since it helps in the burning of fat. Although Nolvadex has no direct fatburning effect its antiestrogenic effect contributes to keeping the estrogen level as low as possible. Nolvadex should especially be taken together with the strong androgenic steroids Dianabol and Anadrol 50, and the various testosterone compounds. Athletes who have a tendency to retain water and who have a mammary dysfunction should take Nolvadex as a prevention during every steroid intake. Since Nolvadex is very effective in most cases it is no wonder that several athletes can take Anadrol 50 and Dianabol until the day of a competition, and in combination with a diruretic still appear totally ripped in the limelight. Those who already have a low body fat content will achieve a visibly improved muscle hardness with Nolvadex.

Several bodybuilders like to use Nolvadex at the end of a steroid cycle since it increases the body's own testosterone production—which will be discussed in more detail in the following—to counteract the side effects caused by the estrogens. These can occur after the discontinuance of steroids when the androgen level in relationship to the estrogen concentration is too low and estrogen becomes the dominant hormone. A very rare but all the more serious problem of Nolvadex is that in some cases it does not lower the estrogen level but can increase it. The Canadian physician, Dr. Mauro G. Di Pasquale, in his book *Drug Use and Detection in Amateur Sports, Update Five* confirms this possibility: "Recent studies have shown, however, that in a small number of people taking tamoxifen, the effect can be paradoxical. Instead of decreasing estrogen production, it can promote it; and instead of acting as an estrogen antagonist it can act as an agent. In these cases, for some unknown reason, adrenal DHEA production is dramatically increased. Since DHEA is a steroid precurser for peripheral estrogren (and testosterone) production, serum estrogen levels are increased and the higher serum levels overwhelm the tamoxifen which is binding to the central receptors. Apparently only a slight increase in the serum estrogen concentration is needed to overcome the anti-estrogen effects of tamoxifen."

Another disadvantage is that it can weaken the anabolic effect of some steroids. The reason is that Nolvadex, as we know, reduces the estrogen level. The fact is, however, that certain steroids —especially the various testosterone compounds—can only achieve their full effect if the estrogen level is sufficiently high. Daniel Duchaine in his book *Ask the Guru* bolsters this thesis: "But it (testosterone) is not anabolic in and of itself, because it requires the body to have a sufficient level of estrogen in order to achieve its fullest anabolic effect. This is why there is reduced anabolic activity from many steroids when Nolvadex (an estrogen antagonist, which is used primarily to prevent gynecomastia) is added to a steroid stack." Those who are used to the intake of larger amounts of various steroids do not have to worry about this. Athletes however, who predominantly use mild steroids such as Primobolan, Winstrol, Oxandrolone, and Deca-Durabolin should carefully consider whether or not they should take Nolvadex since, due to the compound's already moderate anabolic effect, an additional loss of effect could take place, leading to unsatisfying results.

A rarely observed but welcome characteristic of Nolvadex is that it has a direct influence on the hypothalamus and thus, by an increased release of gonadotropine, it stimulates the testosterone production in the testes. This does not result in a tremendous but still a measurable increase of the body's own testosterone. This effect, however, is not sufficient to significantly increase the testosterone production reduced by anabolic/androgenic steroids. Also the physician Dr. Mauro G. Di Pasquale whom we have mentioned several times writes in his book *Anabolic Steroid Side Effects-Fact, Fiction and Treatment* on page 29: "However these compounds seem to have little effect on preventing the suppression of the HPTH while anabolic steroids are being used, perhaps because of an over riding direct suppression exerted by the anabolic steroids on the HPTA." For natural bodybuilders, however, use of Nolvadex, in this context, should be worth considering.

The side effects of Nolvadex are usually low in dosages of up to 30 mg/day. In rare cases nausea, vomiting, hot flashes, numbness, and blurred vision can occur. In women irregular menstrual cycles can occur which manifest themselves in weaker menstrual bleeding or even complete missing of a period. Women should also be careful not to get pregnant while taking Nolvadex. It is important for female athletes that Nolvadex and the "pill" not be taken together since the antiestrogen Nolvadex and the estrogen-containing pill negatively countereffect each other. The normal daily dosage taken by athletes corresponds more or less to the dosage indications of the manufacturer and is 10-30 mg/day. To prevent estrogenic side effects normally 10 mg/day are sufficient, a dosage which also keeps low the risk of reducing the effect of simultaneously-taken steroids. Often it is sufficient if the athlete begins this preventive intake of Nolvadex only three to four weeks after the intake of anabolics. Athletes who have tendencies toward gynecomastia, strong water retention, and increased fat deposits with steroids such as Dianabol, Testosterone, Anadrol 50, and Deca-Durabolin usually take 20-30 mg/day. The combined application of Nolvadex 20-30 mg/day and Proviron 25-50 mg/day in these cases leads to excellent results. The same is true for athletes who are in competition, and for women. Women, however, should do without the intake of Proviron or at least reduce the dose to one 25 mg tablet per day. Unfortunately, in most cases, a very pronounced gynecomastia ("bitch tits") cannot be reduced by taking Nolvadex so that often surgery is required, surgery which is not paid for by health insurance. First signs of a possible gynecomastia are light pain when touching the nipples. The tablets are usually taken 1-2x daily, swallowed whole without chewing, with some liquid during meals.

Nolvadex unfortunately is a very expensive compound. Some examples: In Germany one hundred 20 mg tablets cost $192 (Red List 1995). Since the generic compounds (see list of various trade names) —usually at a lower price— are of the same quality than the trade name Nolvadex, athletes often prefer generics. The less expensive tamoxifen-citrate compound in Germany is Tamoxasta by Asta medica Company. One hundred 20 mg tablets, in comparison, cost $107 (Red List 1995). In Spain the prices are fixed by the government and it makes no difference whether it is an original Nolvadex or a generic compound. One hundred 20 mg tablets cost approx. $60 in Spain. In Greece the same quantity costs about $85. The athlete should look for the 20 mg version since, from its price, it is the most economical. On the black market mostly the foreign Nolvadex can be found costing about $2 - 3 per 20 mg tablet. Original Nolvadex tablets can be easily identified since, on the front, ICI (name of the manufacturer) is stamped and, on the back, the name "Nolvadex". Most of the time the tablet strength is also imprinted. Ten tablets are included in an unusually large push-through strip. The American Nolvadex can rarely be found on the black market. In the U.S. original Nolvadex is packaged by the manufacturer, ICI

Pharma, in small, white plastic boxes with a child-proof screw cap. So far, there are no fakes of Nolvadex and its generic products.

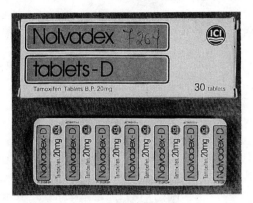

Nolvadex by ICI / Spain, 10mg tabs

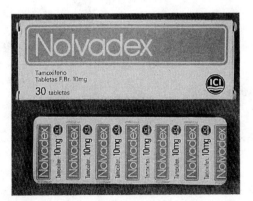

Nolvadex from Spain, 20mg tabs

New Spanish box

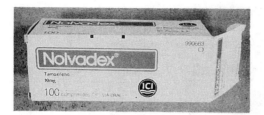

*Another Nolvadex
box from Spain*

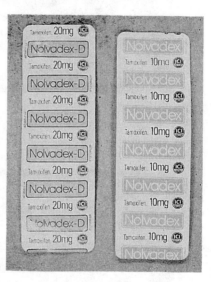

*Two Nolvadex
blisters from Spain*

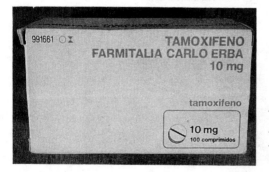

*Tamoxifeno by
Farmitalia / Spain,
30 tabs per box,
10mg*

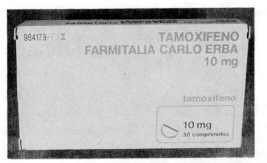

*Tamoxifeno by
Farmitalia / Spain,
100 tabs per box /
10mg*

*Tamoxifeno blister
from Spain*

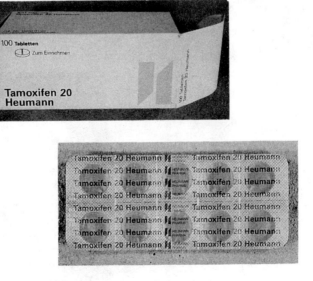

Tamoxifen 20 by Heuman / Germany, 100 tabs per box, 20mg

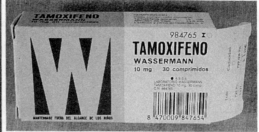

Tamoxifeno by Wassermann / Spain

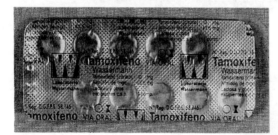

Tamoxifeno blister

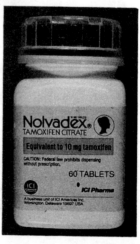

*American Nolvadex by
ICI Pharma*

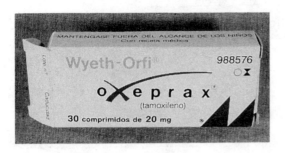

Oxeprax, tamoxifeno by Wyeth-Orfi / Spain, box and blister

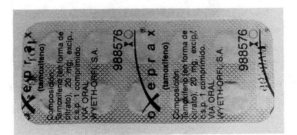

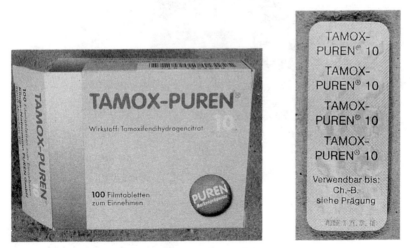

Tamox-Puren by Puren / Germany

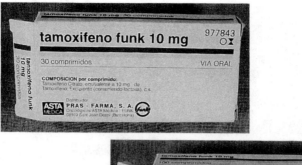

Two different boxes of Tamoxifeno Funk 10 mg, 30 and 100 tablets per box

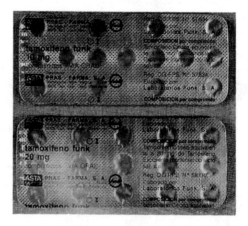

Two blisters, with 10mg and 20mg per tablets by Funk / Spain

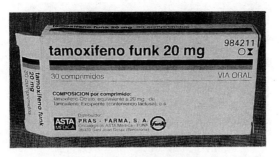

Two different boxes Tamoxifeno by Funk from Spain, 20mg/tab., 30 and 60 tablets per box

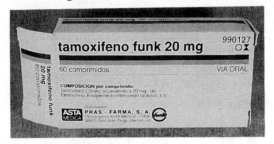

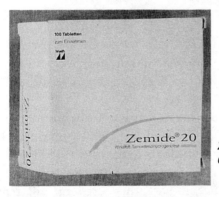

Zemide 20, Tamoxifen from Germany

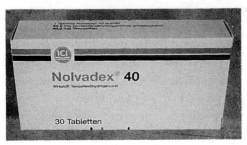

Nolvadex from Germany

Tamoxifen by Ratiopharm / Germany

OMNADREN 250

Substances:

Testosterone phenylproprionate	60 mg
Testosterone propionate	30 mg
Testosterone isohexanoate	60 mg
Testosterone hexanoate	100 mg

Trade names:

Omnadren 250 (o.c.)	250 mg/ml;	Polfa PL
Omnadren 250	250 mg/ml;	Jelfa PL

Omnadren is a four-component testosterone. The four different substances work together in such a timely manner that Omnadren remains in the body for a long time. For this reason many compare Omnadren to Sustanon 250. This comparison, however, is quite poor since, in part, there are large differences between the two compounds. Although both are "four-component testosterones" the individual substances of Omnadren and Sustanon are not completely identical. Both include testosterone phenylpropionate and testosterone propionate; however, the testosterone isocaproate in Sustanon is replaced by testosterone hexanoate and the testosterone decanoate in Omnadren is replaced by testosterone hexanoate in Sustanon (see also Sustanon.)

In bodybuilding and powerlifting Omnadren is exclusively used to build up strength and mass. The term "mass buildup" can be taken quite literally by the reader since the gain is not always the way expected by its user. In most athletes Omnadren leads to quite a rapid and pronounced increase in body weight, which usually goes hand in hand with a strong water retention. This results in watery and puffy muscles. Those who take "Omna" can often be recognized by this extreme water retention. The often-used term in Europe, "Omna skull," does not come from nowhere but because a fast and well-visible water retention occurs also in the face which is noticeable on cheeks, on the front of the face, and under the eyes. Some mockingly also talk about a hydrocephalus... The pronounced androgenic component of Omnadren goes hand in hand with a high anabolic effect which manifests itself in a high strength gain characterized by a liquid accumulation in the joints, an increased pump effect, increased appetite, and a possible improved regeneration of the athlete. Since Omnadren easily aromatizes, the intake of antiestrogens is suggested. This can also help reduce some of the water retention. Although Omnadren has a duration effect of a good 2-3 weeks it is usually injected at least once a week.

As for the dosage there is rarely an injectable steroid with a wide spectrum such as Omnadren's. The span reaches from athletes who inject one 250 mg injection every two weeks to extremes who use eight(!) "Omnas" a day (2000 mg/day). The reason is the low price of the compound. It therefore offers an economic alternative to the expensive Sustanon, Testosterone enanthate and -propionate; that explains why some take it in these exaggerated dosages. An acceptable and, for most, sufficient dosage is 250-1000mg/week. Omnadren is often combined with Dianabol, Anadrol 50, and Deca-Durabolin which accelerates the gain in strength, mass, and water retention. A pure "Eastern Block mixture" of Omnadren and the Russian Dianabol is very popular because, on the one hand, these two compounds are easily available on the black market and, on the other hand, strength and mass can be gained at a minimal cost. The gains achieved with Omnadren, as is the case with Testosterone, for the most part, usually subside very quickly after use of the compound is discontinued.

The side effects of Omnadren are similar to those of other testosterone compounds (see Testosterone enanthate). Next to the high water retention other negative effects that are noticed are a sometimes strong acne and a distinctly increased aggressiveness in some users. An aggressive behavior can mostly be explained by the fact that athletes simply use too high a dosage of Omnadren and too low a dosage of the other (and more expensive) testosterones. The very severe acne, however, is only caused by Omnadren. Often no purulent pustules but many small pimples appear so that the athlete looks as if he has an allergy. This is not intended to discourage anyone but it is a fact that many athletes after a brief time develop an acne on their lower arm, upper arm, shoulder, chest, back, and also in their face which, during an earlier intake of Sustanon or Testosterone enanthate, did not manifest itself. Women should not use Omnadren under any circumstances.

Another problem that should be considered is that possible impurities in the injection liquid cannot be excluded since the quality standards in Eastern European countries are not as high as in Western Europe and in the U.S. Thus it is possible that a 100% sterility and pureness does not exist. This could also be the reason for the unusually strong acne. In the German *Sportrevue*, October 1993 issue, magazine no. 298, the university professor Dr. med. F. Beuker in his series Alles über Doping, Teil 3, on page 137 confirms: "... the steroid acne is caused by impurities rather than by the products themselves..." Such impurities are often the main reason for a so-called "absess secondary to injection". In this context we still remember well one of our friends who, after an Omnadren injection, got an abscess on his behind which had to be removed surgically with a one and a half inch wide and two inches deep (!) cut.

Original Omnadren is offered by the manufacturer in a strength of 250 mg/ml ampule. Five ampules are included in a pink-colored box in which a removable paper carton (and later a white plastic one) protects them from touching each other (see photo). The ampules themselves are made of regular window glass and have a red and black imprint which can be removed with your finger. Often the imprint is no longer readable since it fades over time or gets lighter because of shipping. This fact is grist for the mill by fakers. It is quite simple to take off the Omnadren imprint and replace it with a Sustanon imprint, thus selling a "cheap" Omna as an "expensive" Susta. Since the imprint is very simple and unfortunately is not stamped into the glass, it can be replaced easily. So, for example, ampules containing only sesame oil quickly receive an "Omna" imprint. Omnadren usually costs $8 - 10 per ampule on the black market, where it is readily available. According to our experience there is no chance to buy Omnadren in a Polish pharmacy without a prescription so that a vacation in Poland with the intention of making a few cheap purchases does not pay off. Lately Omnadren fakes have appeared but they can be easily recognized. The imprint "Omnadren 250" is not placed on the lower border of the box as on the original but in the upper third. Furthermore, the other writing is in English while the original Omnadren packages are generally in Polish. It should also be mentioned that in the meantime the manufacturer is no longer Polfa but Jelfa.

Omnadren 250 by Polfa / Roland

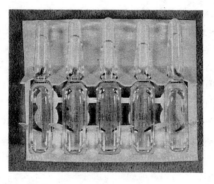

Omnadren ampules, 5 per box

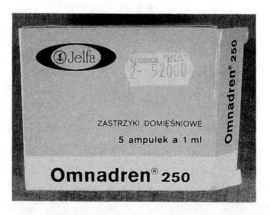

New box of Omnadren 250 by Jelfa / Poland

ORABOLIN

Substance: ethylestrenol

Trade names

Maxibolin (o.c.)	2 mg tab.;	Organon U.S.
Maxibolin Elixier (o.c.)	2 mg/5 ml;	Organon U.S.
Orabolin	2 mg tab.;	Organon B, GB
Orgabolin	2 mg tab.;	Organon NL; Santa TK
Orgabolin drops	2 mg;	Santa TK

Orabolin is an unusual steroid since its substance is a precursor of the female hormone progesterone. Technically it is a derivative of 19-nortestosterone. This also explains why during the early 1960's Organon introduced this remedy as Durabolin-Oral because Deca-Durabolin is also a precursor of 19-nortestosterone. Orabolin is a very weak, oral steroid which is not very suitable for the buildup of strength and muscle mass. It is a steroid with a mostly anabolic effect that has only very low androgenic characteristics. Athletes who have taken Orabolin as their only steroid were mostly disappointed by its effect. In combination with steroids such as Winstrol, Parabolan, Masteron and Orabolin it leads to a high-quality muscle gain which remains after discontinuing the use of the product. Orabolin, however, is more a steroid for female athletes. Virilization symptoms in dosages under 12-16 mg/day are rare and the fact that Orabolin is derived from the female hormone progesterone should also remove moral and ethical doubts. Since the tablets are not 17-alpha alkylated, liver toxicity is relatively low. However, in high dosages and over long intervals of intake it is possible that certain liver values will increase. Orabolin aromatizes only slightly so that estrogenic-caused side effects are rarely expected. Athletes report a minimal water retention. Some bodybuilders use Orabolin shortly before a championship since it slightly increases the blood pressure, resulting in a higher vascularity.

Orabolin requires a relatively high daily dosage since the substance is very poorly absorbed by the steroid receptors in the muscle cell.

Twenty or more tablets a day could have a certain effect but probably will also lead to several side effects. This is apart from the fact that such a large amount of tablets will cost the athlete quite a few dollars. You can turn this around as much as you like but male athletes only profit from taking Orabolin if the daily dosage is at least 20 to 40 mg. Since Orabolin is as expensive as Oxandrolone and the Winstrol tablets but less effective, almost nobody shows interest in this compound. This is also the reason why it is rarely found on the black market. Due to its low demand there are no fakes.

ORAL-TURINABOL

Substance: chlordehydromethyltestosterone

Trade names

Oral-Turinabol (o.c.)	1 mg tab.;	Jenapharm G
Oral-Turinabol (o.c.)	5 mg tab.;	Jenapharm G

"In GDR [the former East Germany] performance sports Oral-Turinabol (OT) in the past was the remedy of choice for anabolic assistance... Oral-Turinabol was the standard in all disciplines... The well-tried doping house brands such as Oral-Turinabol were directly ordered and picked up at the manufacturers, such as Jenapharm..." (from *Doping - Von der Forschung zum Betrug*, Brigitte Berendonk.)

Oral-Turinabol is an oral steroid which was developed during the early 1960's and introduced on the market in the former GDR. Next to its clinical application it was the number one doping drug of the GDR. In the West this anabolic was known only to very few insiders, mostly from the powerlifting and weightlifting scene. Also in bodybuilding, Oral-Turinabol was then, before Germany's reunification, still a wall flower. After all, East Germany had done a perfect job: everything was kept completely secret; reliable information did not get outside the country and there were no positive doping cases with OT. How could there be? The country's athletes were only allowed to leave the country or to participate in the Olympic Games, World and European Championships, international, and Grand-Prix meetings if the doping testing given in the GDR, given as preventative measure, showed a negative urine analysis. Only the dumb ones got caught.

With the fall of the Wall and the German reunification the situation changed drastically. The GDR doping practices came to light and, with the help of Brigitte Berendonk's book *Doping- Von der Forschung zum Betrug*, can be readily reconstructed in detail by anyone. The chances to procure the compound also changed for the better since the Jenapharm GmbH Company continued manufacturing Oral-Turinabol and the tablets were available without difficulty in German pharmacies with a prescription. And the black market was booming the most since, with the fall of the Wall, strict controls at the borders were eliminated and nothing was in the way of making a trip from the factory, east to west, with a trunk full of blue "Turis." With these small blue tablets one would have a very interesting, even unique, substance, a fact that quickly made the rounds in the bodybuilder and powerlifter community. The reasons for the enormous popularity of OT in sports using dumbbells are at hand. Continue reading.

OT has a predominantly anabolic effect which is combined with a relatively low androgenic component. On a scale of 1 to 100 the androgenic effect is very low —only a 6— and the anabolic effect is 53. (In comparison: the androgenic effect of Dianabol is 45 and its anabolic effect is 90.) Oral-Turinabol thus has milligram for milligram a lower effect than Dianabol. It is therefore not a steroid that causes a rapid gain in strength, weight, and muscle mass. Rather, the achievable results manifest themselves in a solid muscle gain and, if taken over several weeks, also in a good strength gain. The athlete will certainly not get a puffy look as is the case with Testosterone, Dianabol, and Anadrol 50. The maximum blood concentration of Oral-Turinabol when taking 10, 20 or 40 mg/day is 1.5 - 3.5 or 4.5 times the endogenous testosterone concentration (also see Dianabol). This clearly shows that the effectiveness of this compound strongly depends on the dosage. The success formula of the GDR (from *Doping - Von der Forschung zum Betrug*, page 142, Brigitte Berendonk) is

$$\frac{0.4 \times \text{pound (body weight)} \times \text{days}}{\text{mg / tablet}} = \text{number of tablets to take overall during the interval of intake}$$

which might not be sufficient in the minds of bodybuilders. Based on this formula an athlete weighing 200 pounds would take only 4 tablets of 5 mg (20mg/day.) In our experience bodybuilders take 8–10 tablets of 5 mg, that is 40-50 mg/day. Many enthusiastically report good results with this dosage: one builds a solid muscle mass, the strength gain is worthwhile seeing, the water retention is very low, and the estrogen-caused side effects are rare. Not without good reason OT is also popular among powerlifters and weightlifters who appreciate these characteristics. We know two athletes who in certain phases of their training take 20 tablets of 5mg daily, are massive and muscular and are able to bench press more than 450 pounds and squat over 650 pounds. Mind you, this is without additional intake of other steroids.

Due to its characteristics OT is also a suitable steroid both for men and women in competitions. A usually very effective stack for male bodybuilders consists of 50 mg OT/day, 228 mg Parabolan/week, and 150 mg Winstrol Depot/week. Those who have brought their body fat content to a low level by dieting and/or by using fatburning substances (e.g. Clenbuterol, Ephedrine, Salbutamol, Cytomel, Triacana), will find that the above steroid combination will manifest itself in hard, sharply-defined but still dense and full muscles. No enlarged breasts, no estrogen surplus, and no watery, puffy-looking muscle system. If OT were available on the U.S. black market for steroids, bodybuilders, powerlifters, and weightlifters would go crazy for this East German anabolic.

For a large number of athletes OT turned out to be a reliable guarantee of success when it became necessary to circumvent certain obstacles. We refer to persons who participate in championships with doping tests. Here OT enjoys a great popularity since it is quickly broken down by the body and the metabolites are excreted relatively quickly through the urine. The often-posed question regarding how many days before a test OT can be taken in order to be "clean" is difficult to answer specifically or in general. We know from a reliable source that athletes who only take OT as a steroid and who, in part, take dosages of 10-15 tablets/day, have discontinued the compound exactly five days before a doping test and tested negative. These indications are supported by the fact that even positive urine analyses have rarely mentioned the names Oral-Turinabol or chlordehydromethyl-testosterone. In the meantime we have talked to several competing athletes and are of the opinion that a period of 7-8 days is sufficient when OT is the only steroid that is being taken. The last few days can then be bridged over by taking, for example, Andriol, if that is discontinued 48 hours before a urine analysis. At doping tested IFBB European championships and IFBB world championships OT is a welcome help for German and East European athletes. With 10 "Turis" per day (discontinued seven days before the test), 8 Clenbuterol daily (discontinued 10 days before), the ephedrine-caffeine-aspirin cocktail (discontinued 4 days before), and thyroid hormones (preferably Cytomel or Thybon) and 4 - 12 I.U. Growth hormones/day (for those who can afford them)—the latter two mentioned hormones cannot be detected at all—not only can the athlete pass the doping test on the day of the championship but he will also obtain a competitive body condition.

During the 1980's a German work team of physicians and bioresearchers at the research institute for Körperkultur und Sport in Leipzig carried out a series of tests with the anabolic Oral-Turinabol on humans (remember humans, not rats) and came up with some interesting results. Those who want detailed information are referred to the book *Hormonelle Regulation und psychophysische Belastung* by R. Häcker/H. de Marees where results of the Oral Turinabol tests are described and illustrated. A summary of some results that seem important to us are readily presented to the reader here. The administration of even such a conservative dose as 20 mg OT/day, after only 10 days, results in a significant suppression of the endogenous testosterone production which, however, only five days after the discontinuance, is back to normal and in the following continues to increase even further. It is interesting that the production of the body's own testosterone only one week after discontinuance can be above the initial value before medication. In addition, researchers noted that the increased testosterone level is maintained over 8-10 days. This possible rebound effect must not be undervalued with regard to doping tests. The reason for the relatively quick rebound of the body's own testosterone level could be that, compared to other steroids, OT reduces the testosterone level "only" to 60-70% of its normal value while, for example, with the considerably more androgenic Dianabol this level decreases to 30-40% of its normal value.

Another interesting aspect was discovered by R.Häcker, B. Bernstein, and G. Rademacher in their study *Pharmakokinetische Vergleichsuntersuchung von Oral-Turinabol und Dianabol.* 20 mg Dianabol/day reduces the cortisone concentration in the blood after five days of intake by 50% and on the 15th day of intake it is even 74% lower compared to the initial level. With an intake of 20 mg OT/day, however, no significant suppression of the endogenic cortisone concentration was noticed. This might also be one of the reasons why administration of Dianabol usually results in faster and more drastic progress with respect to a gain in strength, weight, and possibly an improved regeneration, whereas the growth rates with Oral-Turinabol were slower and more even. The body's own testosterone production with OT does not decrease too much so that after its discontinuance it is quickly normalized. These are probably reasons why athletes, after discontinuing Oral-Turinabol tablets do not experience a dramatic performance breakdown, as is often the case with Dianabol. The organism reacts to the reduced cortisone production caused by Dianabol with a rebound effect, which means that the cortisone production exceeds the normal measure. The result is that the cortisone molecules will form a receptor-molecule complex with the steroid receptors of the muscle cells and force the muscle cell to break down protein. With Oral-Turinabol there is no such cortisone-rebound effect.

The substance chlordehydromethyltestosterone reaches its maximum concentration in the blood 1 to 3 hours after intake. The half-life time of OT is between 6.9 and 7.2 hours (The half-life time is an exponential decay law that describes the period which the body needs for half of the substance to be converted.) The logical consequence for the expert therefore is that the daily amount of tablets should not be taken all at once but divided equally into 3-4 daily doses so that a constant substance concentration in the blood is guaranteed. It is best when the tablets are taken during meals. According to the exponential decay law, 72 hours after the last application of OT no more anabolic equivalents can be found in the blood (not in urine!). Thus, exactly three days after the intake cycle of Oral-Turinabol is completed, the tablets are no longer effective. A higher training motivation was also noted among those tested when OT was administered. Oral-Turinabol activates the central nervous system through the bonding of the substance molecules with the steroid receptors in the brain. The East German research studies also mentioned that OT, together with an intense resistance training, helps to enforce the buildup of strength and muscles: with OT the resting urine value can also be considerably lowered which confirms the protein-anabolic effect of this remedy. OT stimulates the biosynthesis (formation) of cell proteins in the entire human organism.

The potential side effects of OT usually depend on the dosage level and are gender-specific. In women, depending on their predisposition, the usual virilization symptoms occur and increase when dosages of more than 20 mg per day are taken over a prolonged time. In men the already discussed reduced testosterone production can rarely be avoided. Gynecomastia occurs rarely with OT. Since the response of the water and electrolyte household is not overly distinct, athletes only rarely report water retention and high blood pressure. Acne, gastrointestinal pain, and uncontrolled aggressive behavior are also the exception rather than the rule with OT. An increased libido is reported in most cases by both sexes. Since the substance chlordehydromethyltestosterone is 17-alpha alkylated the manufacturer in its package insert recommends that the liver function be checked regularly since it can be negatively affected by high dosages and the risk of possible liver damage cannot be excluded.

Thus OT is also a steroid that can be taken without interruption for long intervals. Studies of male athletes who over a period of six weeks were given 10 mg OT/day did not show any indications of health-threatening effects: "Condition:The regularly recorded clinical and paraclinical diagnoses over the entire observation period showed no striking findings deviating from the norm." (from *Hormonelle Regulation und psychophysische Belastung im Leistungssport* by R. Häcker and H. de Marees.)

In the meantime the availability of OT is extremely poor. In July 1994 the only manufacturer, Jenapharm GmbH, took Oral-Turinabol off the market without prior notice. The further production of this anabolic was phased out and the tablets suddenly were no longer available in German pharmacies. More than a few power athletes were hit with a crushing blow by this message. The current situation reads as follows: Oral-Turinabol or the substance chlordehydro-methyltestosterone is not available from any pharmceutical group worldwide. There are only a few residual supplies of the 5 mg tablets by Jenapharm GmbH on the black market. The N1 package consists of a flat, oblong white cardboard box with a red, grey, and black imprint. The expiration date and the charge number are punched into the left lateral flap of the carton. The box contains one single push-through strip with 20 tablets of 5 mg each. The tablets are very small and have neither a breakage indent nor a stamp. Their small size and the blue color gave them the name "little blue men" among its users. The latest price of the original package with twenty 5 mg tablets was $9 in German pharmacies. Due to the high demand and the continuously decreasing supply the price for original "Turis" in Germany is usually around $0.90 - 1.20 per tablet. There is no chance finding an original Oral-Turinabol tablet in the U.S.

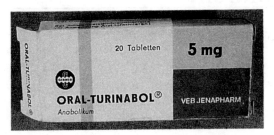

Oral-Turnabol by Jenapharm / Germany, old version

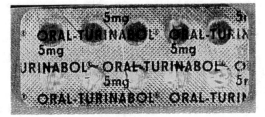

Blister by Jenapharm, old version

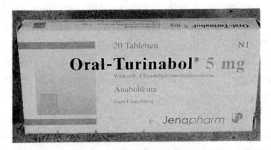

Oral-Turinabol by Jenapharm / Germany, new version but out of commerce

Oral-Turinabol blister

OXANDROLONE SPA

Substance: oxandrolone

Trade names

Anavar (o.c.)	2.5 mg tab.;	Searle U.S.
Anatrophill (o.c.)	2.5 mg tab.;	Searle FR
Lipidex	2.5 mg tab.;	Searle Brazil
Lonavar (o.c.)	2.5 mg tab.;	Searle Argentina
Lonavar	2 mg tab.;	Dainippon Japan
Oxandrolone SPA	2.5 mg tab.;	SPA I
Vasorome	0.5 mg tab.;	Kowa Japan
Vasorome	2 mg tab.;	Kowa Japan

Searle Company introduced the substance oxandrolone to the U.S. market in 1964 under the name Anavar and it enjoyed great popularity for over two decades until, on July 1, 1989, the production of Anavar was phased out. Today Anavar is manufactured under its various generic names in only a few countries (see above). The compound with the generic name Oxandrolone SPA by S.p.A. Milano Company (Società Prodotti Antibiotica) from Italy is the only original anabolic steroid available in Europe which contains the substance oxandrolone. There are 30 tablets in one box with two push-through strips of 15 tablets each. Oxandrolone is a weak steroid with only a slight androgenic component. It has been shown that Oxandrolone, when taken in reasonable dosages, rarely has any side effects. This is appreciated since Oxandrolone was developed mostly for women and children. Oxandrolone is one of the few steroids which does not cause an early stunting of growth in children since it does not prematurely close the epiphysial growth plates. For this reason Oxandrolone is mostly used in children to stimulate growth and in women to prevent osteoporosis. Oxandrolone causes very light virilization symptoms, if at all. This characteristic makes Oxandrolone a favored remedy for female athletes since, at a daily dose of 10–15 mg, masculinizing symptoms are observed only rarely.

Bodybuilders and powerlifters, in particular, like Oxandrolone for three reasons. First, Oxandrolone causes a strong strength gain by stimulating the phosphocreatine synthesis in the muscle cell without depositing liquid (water) in the joints and the muscles. Powerlifters and weightlifters who do not want to end up in a higher weight class take advantage of this since it allows them to get stronger without gaining body weight at the same time. The combination of Oxandrolone and 20 - 30 mg Holotestin daily has proven to be very effective since the muscles also look harder. Similarly good results can be achieved by a simultaneous intake of Oxandrolone and 120-140 mcg Clenbuterol per day. Although Oxandrolone itself does not cause a noticeable muscle growth it can clearly improve the muscle-developing effect of many steroids. Deca-Durabolin, Dianabol, and the various testosterone compounds, in particular, combine well with Oxandrolone to achieve a "mass buildup" because the strength gain caused by the intake of these highly tissue-developing and liquid-retaining substances results in an additional muscle mass. A stack of 200 mg Deca-Durabolin/week, 500 mg Testosterone enanthate (e.g. Testoviron Depot 250)/week, and 25 mg Oxandrolone/day leads to a good gain in strength and mass in most athletes. Deca-Durabolin has a distinct anabolic effect and stimulates the synthesis of protein; Oxandrolone improves the strength by a higher phosphocreatine synthesis; and Testosterone enanthate increases the aggressiveness for the workout and accelerates regeneration.

The second reason why Oxandrolone is so popular is that this compound does not aromatize in any dosage. As already mentioned, a certain part of the testosterone present in the body is converted into estrogen. This aromatization process, depending on the predisposition, can vary distinctly from one athlete to another. Oxandrolone is one of the few steroids which cannot aromatize to estrogen. This characteristic has various advantages for the athlete. With Oxandrolone the muscle system does not get the typical watery appearance as with many steroids, thus making it very interesting during the preparation for a competiton. In this phase it is especially important to keep the estrogen level as low as possible since estrogen programs the body to store water even if the diet is calorie-reduced. In combination with a diet, Oxandrolone helps to make the muscles hard and ripped. Although Oxandrolone itself does not break down fat, it plays an indirect role in this process because the substance often suppresses the athlete's appetite. Oxandrolone can also cause some bloating which in several athletes results in nausea and vomiting when the tablets are taken with meals. The package insert of the Italian Oxandrolone notes its effect on the activity of the gastrointestinal tract. Some athletes thus report continued diarrhea. Although these symptoms are not very pleasant they still help the athlete break down fat and become harder. Those who work out for a competition or are interested in gaining quality muscles should combine Oxandrolone with steroids such as Winstrol, Parabolan, Masteron, Primobolan, and Testosterone propionate. A stack of 50 mg Winstrol every two days, 50 mg Testosterone propionate every two days, and 25 mg Oxandrolone every day has proven effective. Another advantage of Oxandrolone's non-aromatization is that athletes who suffer from high blood pressure or develop gynecomastia of the thymus glands when taking stronger androgenic steroids will not have these side effects with this compound. The Oxandrolone/Deca-Durabolin stack is a welcome alternative for this group of athletes or for athletes showing signs of poor health during mass buildup with testosterone, Dianabol, or Anadrol 50. Athletes over forty should predominantly use Oxandrolone.

The third reason which speaks well for an intake of Oxandrolone is that even in a very high dosage this compound does not influence the body's own testosterone production. To make this clear: Oxandrolone does not suppress the body's own hormone production. The reason is that it does not have a negative feedback mechanism on the hypothalamohypophysial testicular axis, meaning that during the intake of Oxandrolone, unlike during the intake of most anabolic steroids, the testes signal the hypothalamus not to reduce or to stop the release of GnRH (gonadotropin releasing hormone) and LHRH (luteinizing hormon releasing hormone). This special feature of Oxandrolone can be explained by the fact that the substance is not converted into estrogen since, as Dr. Mauro G. Di Pasquale writes on page 23 of his book *Anabolic Steroid Side Effects - Facts, Fiction and Treatment*: "It is also thought that estrogens, produced from the aromatization of testosterone and other anabolic steroids in parts of the brain and hypothalamus, inhibit LH secretion, and thus decrease testosterone production." The American physician, Dr. Rober Kerr, confirmed this thesis in his book *The Practical Use of Anabolic Steroids with Athletes*, where on page 23 he states: "Oxandrolone (Anavar), when given to normal men in high doses does not reduce the seminal volume or count, nor can it be converted (aromatized) into estrogen, Goodman and Gilman have thus concluded that perhaps the feedback mechanism is not activated by the amount of testosterone as much as the estrogen level."

For this reason Oxandrolone combines very well with Andriol, since Andriol does not aromatize in a dosage of up to 240 mg daily and has only slight influence on the hormone production. The daily intake of 280 mg Andriol and 25 mg Oxandrolone results in a good gain in strength and, in steroid novices, also in muscle mass without excessive water retention and without a significant influence on testosterone production. As for the dosage of Oxandrolone, 8-12 tablets in men and 5-6 tablets in women seems to bring the best results. The rule of thumb to take 0.125 mg/pound of body weight daily has proven successful in clinical tests. The tablets are normally taken two to three times daily after meals thus assuring an optimal absorption of the substance. Those who get the already discussed gastrointestinal pain when taking Oxandrolone are better off taking the tablets one to two hours after a meal or switching to another compound.

Since Oxandrolone is only slightly toxic and usually shows few side effects it is used by several athletes over a prolonged period ot time. However Oxandrolone should not be taken for several consecutive months, since, as with almost all oral steroids it is 17-alpha alkylated and thus liver toxic. Oxandrolone is an all-purpose remedy which, depending on the athlete's goal, is very versatile. Women who react sensitively to the intake of anabolic steroids achieve good results when combining Oxandrolone/Primobolan Tabs and/or

Clenbuterol, without suffering from the usual virilization symptoms. Women, however, should not take more than 6 tablets daily. Otherwise, androgenic-caused side effects such as acne, deep voice, clitorial hypertrophy or increased growth of body hair can occur.

Probably the largest disadvantages that comes along with Oxandrolone are its high price and poor availability on the black market. A box with 30 tablets costs Lire 11,000 in an Italian pharmacy which is approximately $0.27 per tablet. Original Oxandrolone costs about $1 - 2 per tablet on the black market and is rarely available, if at all. For this reason the fake Oxandrolone is found more often than the original. The most widely distributed fake is a small white plastic container with a pull-off cap. It contains 100 tablets an —as could rarely be expected otherwise—has the name Oxandrolone SPA Milano, 100 Compresse. Contrary to popular opinion there is no injectable Oxandrolone, unless a smart businessman poors 50 ml sesame oil in a brown glass vial and attaches a label with the name "Oxandrolone Inject."

Original Oxandrolone from Italy with two different blisters

PARABOLAN

Substance: trenbolone hexahydrobencylcarbonate

Trade names

Parabolan   76 mg/1.5 ml;   Negma France

Parabolan is a relatively new steroid which was introduced on the French market in 1980 by Laboratoires Negma. Parabolan is still exclusively produced by this manufacturer and is officially available only in France. In bodybuilding and also in powerlifting Parabolan has become the most desired injectable steroid compound. This is not without reason since Parabolan is truly a phenomenal, unique product. Those who take a closer look at the name of the substance will immediately notice the similarities with the steroid Finaject which stopped being manufactured in 1987 (see chapter Finaject). The Finaject evolved from veterinary medicine and was the cult steroid of the 1980's. When Finaject was eventually taken off the market and ineffective fakes were circulating on the black market, the community of power athletes, in its search for a potent substitute, discovered the French Parabolan. Since trenbolone is the basic substance in both compounds there are strong similarities between "Fina" and "Para." To make this clear— Finaject is the trenbolone version for use in animals and Parabolan is the trenbolon version for use in humans.

Parabolan is a strong, androgenic steroid which also has a high anabolic effect. Whether a novice, hardgainer, powerlifter, or pro bodybuilder, everyone who uses Parabolan is enthusiastic about the results: a fast gain in solid, high-quality muscle mass accompanied by a considerable strength increase in the basic exercises. In addition, the regular application over a number of weeks results in a well-visible increased muscle hardness over the entire body without dieting at the same time. Frequently the following scenario takes place: bodybuilders who use steroids and for some time have been stagnate in their development suddenly make new progress with

Parabolan. Another characteristic is that Parabolan, unlike most highly-androgenic steroids, does not aromatize. The substance trenbolone does not convert into estrogens so that the athlete does not have to fight a higher estrogen level or feminization symptoms. Those who use Parabolan will also notice that there is no water retention in the tissue. To say it very clearly: Parbolan is the number one competition steroid. When a low fat content has been achieved by a low-calorie diet, Parabolan gives a dramatic increase in muscle hardness. In combination with a protein-rich diet it becomes especially effective in this phase since Parabolan speeds up the metabolism and accelerates the burning of fat. The high androgenic effect prevents a possible overtraining syndrome, accelerates the regeneration, and gives the muscles a full, vascular appearance but, at the same time, a ripped and shredded look.

Since Parabolan, unlike Finaject, is not the acetate version of trenbolone, theoretically less frequent injections are necessary. The manufacturer, Laboratoires Negma, in its package insert notes that Parabolan needs to be injected only once every 14 days; however, this is by no means an effective intake schedule for athletes. Most athletes inject Parbolan at least twice a week; some bodybuilders inject 1-2 ampules per day during the last three to four weeks before a competition. Normally a dosage of 228 mg/week is used, corresponding to a weekly amount of three ampules. It is our experience that good results can be achieved by injecting a 76 mg ampule every 2-3 days. Parabolan combined with Winstrol Depot works especially well and gives the athlete a distinct gain in solid and high-quality muscles together with an enormous strength gain. A very effective stack is 76 mg Parabolan every 2 days combined with 50 mg Winstrol every 2 days. Athletes who are interested in a fast mass gain often also use 30 mg Dianabol/day while those who are more interested in quality and strength like to add 25 mg + Oxandrolone/ day. Probably the most effective Parabolan combination consists of 228 mg Parabolan/week, 200 mg Winstrol Depot/week, and 40-50 mg Oral-Turinabol/day and usually results in a drastic gain in high-quality muscle mass together with a gigantic strength gain. Parabolon also seems to bring extraordinarily good results when used in combination with growth hormones.

Parabolan is not a steroid suitable for year-round treatment since it is quite toxic. The duration of intake should be limited to a maximum of 8 weeks. It has been proven that Parabolan, above all, puts stress on the kidneys, rather than the liver. Athletes who have taken it in high dosages over several weeks often report an unusually dark-colored urine. In extreme cases blood can be excreted through the urine, a clear sign of kidney damage. A former U.S. champion and pro bodybuilder once said to the point: "You know that the juice is working, when you start to piss blood." Those who use Parabolan should drink an additional gallon of fluid daily since it helps flush the kidneys. Since Parabolan does not cause water and salt retention the blood pressure rarely rises. Similar to Finaject, many athletes show an aggressive attitude which is attributed to the distinct androgenic effect. It is interesting that acne and hair loss only occur rarely which might be due to the fact that the substance is not converted into dihydrotestosterone (DHT). Some athletes report nausea, headaches, and loss of appetite when they inject more than one ampule (76 mg) per week. Since Parabolan considerably reduces the endogenic testosterone production, the use of testosterone-stimulating compounds at the end of intake is suggested. In older athletes there is an increased risk that Parabolan could induce growth of the male prostate gland. We recommend that male bodybuilders, during and after a treatment with Parabolan, have their physician check their prostate to be sure it is still small in size.

Steroid novices should not (yet) use Parabolan. The same is true for women; however, there are enough female athletes who do not care since the female organism reacts to the androgenic charge and the strong anabolic effect of Parabolan with distinct gains in muscles and strength, especially from a female point of view. Thus the entire body has a harder and more athletic look. Parabolan without a doubt is an enticing product for ambitous female athletes. In the end everything depends on your personal willingness to take risks, ladies. The fact is that the standards on the national and international competition scenes in female bodybuilding have achieved levels which cannot be reached without the administration of strongly androgenic steroid compounds. A combination well-liked by female boydbuilders consists of 76 mg Parabolan/week, 20 mg Winstrol tablets/day, and 100 mcg Clenbuterol/day. Women who do not inject more than one ampule of Parabolan per week and who limit the period of intake to 4-5 weeks can mostly avoid or minimize virilization symptoms. Female athletes who are overdoing it or who are sensitive to the androgenic part of trenbolone hexahydrobencylcarbonate can be confronted with some unpleasant surprises after several weeks of use: acne, androgenically-caused hair loss on the scalp, irregular menstrual cycles, missed periods, much higher libido, aggressiveness, deep voice, clitorial hypertrophy, and increased hair growth on face and on the legs. The last three side effects are mostly irreversible changes.

Some readers will say, "I don't really understand what they are writing here. I have tried Parabolan and, the effect, was not bad. However, I really cannot agree that this stuff is something special. It would be great to achieve an enormous strength gain, solid muscle buildup, and extreme muscle hardness. However I also did not have any side effects although I injected three ampules per week!" The reason why many athletes are unhappy with the effect of their 'Paras' is simple: It is almost impossible to find original Parabolan on the black market; however, there is an increasing selection of fakes. Let's say this clearly: The chance of finding real Parabolan on the black market is around 5%. That is the reason why we take a chance and claim that only very few of you who read this book will have ever held an original Parabolan in your hand, let alone injected one. Those who have not tried the originals simply cannot take part in this discussion. As to the effect, the difference beween the real French Parabolan and the fakes circulating on the black market is gigantic.

The original French Parabolan ampules (76 mg/1.5 ml) are always packaged individually, one to a box. The expiration date and charge number are attached on a label on the outer narrow longitudinal side of the package. Although this is also the case with most fakes there is, however, a noticeable difference. On many fakes the writing on the label is printed in black while the original prints this information in gray. Each original ampule is additionally packaged with an ampule saw in a plastic wrap which is open on the bottom side. Attention must be paid to the fact that the red print on the ampules is stamped into the glass and easily felt. It is not possible to scratch off the red imprint with your fingernail. It is also important that the expiration date on the ampule is given on the right side — that is vertically— and not, as with some fakes, in horizontal letters on the body of the ampule. Another clue is the injection solution itself. It contains exactly 1.5 ml peanut butter oil, directing one's attention to the exact quantity in millimeters. The injection solution has a diluted yellow color. An individual package with a 76 mg/1.5 ml ampule costs between $25 and $35 on the American black market. The current price in a French pharmacy is around 35.07 francs (approx. $7.) Parabolan, like all steroids in Europe must be prescribed by a physician and it is still on the market in France. Those who would like to purchase Parabolan on the black market should be very careful and skeptical toward the authenticity of the product offered.

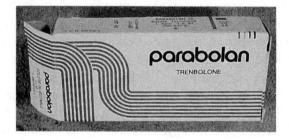

Parabolan by Negma / France, box and ampule

PRIMOBOLAN TABLETS

Substance: methenolone acetate

Trade names

Primobolan (o.c.)	5 mg tab.;	Schering G, A, B
Primobolan	5 mg tab.;	Schering Mexico, Costa Rica, Dom. Rep., Ecuador, El Salvador, Guatemala, Honduras, Nicaragua, Panama, Bolivia; Berlimed South Africa
Primobolan S	25 mg tab.;	Schering G, NL; Leiras FI; Berlimed South Africa
Primobolan (o.c.)	50 mg tab.;	Schering FR

Primobolan is one of the few anabolic steroids that was developed by a German company and is still being manufactured. During the early 1960's Schering AG in Berlin put Primobolan on the market in the form of various substances. On the one hand, this is a methenolone acetate and, on the other hand, it is a methenolone enanthate (see PRIMOBOLAN DEPOT). Until a few years ago the acetate form was still available as an injection and in various tablet strengths. The injectable Primobolan containing 20 mg of methenolone acetate per ampule in an oily solution, is especially and painfully missed in bodybuilding. Besides, in all European countries, the 5 mg tablets were taken off the market so that in Europe only the 25 mg strength tablet is available. The very popular 50 mg Primobolan tablets, which were available only in France, are no longer on the market, having been removed in June 1993. Although it does not make sense to write about compounds which are no longer manufactured, we would like to say a few words about the former 50 mg Primobolan tablets. We would like to clarify a widespread misunderstanding: The 50 mg Primobolan tablets were never intended for sublingual (1) intake but exclusively for normal oral intake. Since the French manufacturerer listed these tablets for buccal intake, non-French athletes came to this erroneous conclusion since "buccal" in English means "sublingual." In France, however, "buccal" is only another term for "oral." Since, with the exception of the American books by Daniel Duchaine, the bodybuilding literature pays no attention to this difference, many athletes tried to melt the 50 mg tablet in their mouths in the misdirected hope that they would obtain a better effect. Another problem with the 50 mg tablets was that they were almost identical to the common 5 mg tablets. Smart dealers on the black market often exchanged these two tablets or covered the glass vials containing the original 5 mg tablets, we must confess, a great-looking label. (See photo in chapter Fakes.) They were thus able to sell them as sublingual 50 mg Primobolan tablets at a huge profit. If today someone still offers you 50 mg Primo tablets either these are residual stock and you will pay an enormous price, or they are fakes. The probability of finding residual stock is almost zero, thus stay away from them.

Primobolan is an almost pure anabolic with an extremely low androgenic component. The ratio of the anabolic to the androgenic effect is indeed very favorable but, since the overall anabolic effect is only moderately strong, Primobolan tablets have only a limited effect in building up muscle mass and strength. With Primobolan neither fast weight gains nor explosive strength gains occur. Primobolan is therefore mostly taken over a prolonged period since it gives only a slow but also a high-quality muscle gain which mostly remains after use of the compound is discontinued. An effective daily dose observed in athletes is in the range of 50-150 mg so that the 25 mg tablets are preferred to the 5 mg tablets. As for the recommended dose, the athlete obtains interesting information from the German package insert by Schering AG for their compound Primobolan S: "Unless otherwise prescribed the following guidelines apply: The dosage should be 1 - 1,5 mg per pound of body weight/day, that is 4-6 tablets for 100 pound of bodyweight." A bodybuilder weighing 100 kg should therefore take 200-300 mg daily which would correspond to a dosage of eight to twelve 25 mg tablets per day. We believe that this dosage is too high; however, this example shows that a fairly large dosage of the oral acetate form is necessary. The reason is that the Primobolan acetate tablets are not 17-alpha alkylated and, during the first pass (2) in the liver, a large part of the substance is destroyed and thus deactivated leaving only a much smaller quantity of the substance to get into the blood.

If Primobolan is the only steroid that is taken, then with respect to strength and muscle buildup, it will usually lead to success in women and steroid novices. This, however, changes greatly when Primobolan is combined with steroids that are moderately to highly androgenic but which themselves do not aromatize or retain water. In such an environment the anabolic effect of Primobolan can develop to its optimum. Masteron, Parabolan, Equipoise, and Winstrol, are particularly suitable. The effect can be optimized by the additional intake of Oxandrolone. Steroid novices and the less advanced achieve a good strength and muscle gain by taking 50-100 mg Primobolan S/day and 150 mg Winstrol Depot/week, without retaining water. Even competing athletes report good quality gains with continuously "harder" muscles when taking 150 mg Primobolan S/day and 50 mg Winstrol Depot every two days, as well as 76 mg of Parabolan every two days.

The main uses of the Primobolan tablets, however, are in the preparation for a competition and in use by women. Since the acetate form does not aromatize into estrogens and does not cause water retention, the use of Primobolan during competitions is widespread. Acetate tablets are special in that they actively help burn fat. The Primobolan acetate tablets, however, must never be taken as the only steroid during a diet since, due to its extremely low androgenic effect, significant losses in muscle and strength can occur and there is a risk of overtraining. The abovementioned common steroid combinations are extremely effective when combined with a suitable diet during the preparation for a competition. Due to the fact that the acetate tablets burn fat but, at the same time, that in large part they are already deactivated in the liver, it would be most efficient to apply the compound locally, bringing the substance directly into the blood through the skin in the areas with undesired fat deposits. At first this seems a little adventurous, but it is possible with the DMSO compound. Dimethyl sulfoxide (DMSO) is one of few substances which are fully absorbed through the skin and distributed through the body. It is included in many ointments and gels which are used to treat sport injuries, contusions, swellings, and effusions in order to transport the easing substance through the skin. In addition, DMSO makes the skin permeable to other substances. Nobody else but the American steroid-guru Daniel Duchaine had this idea and he describes the intake procedure in his book Ask the Guru: "My recommendation: purchase a mortar and pestle (they cost about $8. from a lab supply store) and grind up 4 of the 5 mg tabs as finely as possible. Now pour 1/4 to 1/2 teaspoon of full strength (99%) DMSO into a bowl with the ground up tabs and swirl the mixture until it is almost completely dissolved. It will not fully dissolve because some of the tablet binders are insoluble. Now dilute this liquid with water to make a 50% solution (1:1, DMSO, Water). Then topically apply this liquid to your skin, concentrating on those stubborn areas which refuse to lose fat even while dieting. The steroid will sink right through the skin and then go into general circulation. With this method, the full 20 mg will reach the bloodstream and it will be the intact, fully effective version of Primo Acetate."

It is our experience that the preparation can be much simpler when you finely grind up one 25 mg Primobolan tablet with the grip of a knife on your kitchen board, mix it with half a teaspoon of DMSO gel and then apply a thin layer to your skin. It is important that you only apply it; do not rub it in. One or two applications is usually enough. Another way to avoid the liver and consequent destruction of the substance is to grind up the Primobolan tablets in a mortar and consume them together with heated vitamin E oil. The Primobolan/vitamin E mixture reaches the blood similar to Andriol, that is the absorption occurs through the lymph system and the solution does not reach the liver through the portal vessel. This idea is also Dan Duchaine's.

Since the Primobolan tablets are not 17-alpha alkylated but have a 17-beta hydroxy group they are almost non-toxic to the liver. In a high dosage, however, they can influence the liver values resulting in higher biliburin, GPT, GOT, and alkaline phosphatase. Primobolan generally does not cause any significant side effects since it does not aromatize, does not cause water retention, is not 17-alpha alkylated, and is only slightly androgenic. Blood pressure, liver values, cholesterol level, HDL and LDL values usually remain unaffected, making Primobolan well-liked by health-conscious older athletes. Primo is often an "entry drug" for novice users and, due to its rare side effects, encourages many steroid users to switch to "harder" stuff such as Dianabol, Anadrol 50, and testosterone. Since Primobolan is a precursor of dihydrotestosterone it can accelerate hair loss if such a predisposition exists.

As already mentioned the Primobolan S 25 mg tablets are particulary favored by women, not because of their outstanding effect but mostly because they are are well-tolerated. An often observed daily dosage in women is around 50-100 mg/day. Virilization symptoms, at least with Primo tablets, occur very rarely. Women, no doubt, do not experience an enormous strength increase but are usually able to gain two to four pounds of muscles in 6-8 weeks and obtain a visibly harder and tighter appearance at the same time. Female body-builders who are willing to take a higher risk like to combine 75 mg/day of Primobolan with 50 mg of Winstrol/week, and 50 mg of Testosterone propionate/week. Clenbuterol, Oxandrolone, and the 2 mg Winstrol tablets are also often taken together with Primobolan. The availability of Primobolan Acetate tablets on the black market is quite poor both in Europe and the U.S. The price for one 25 mg tablet on the black market is about $2. As a comparison: a glass vial with 50 tablets of 25 mg in German pharmacies costs about $53. The 5 mg version on the black market is mostly the South American version. Apart from the initially mentioned 50 mg tablets there are currently no fakes of Primobolan Acetate tablets available.

(1) Sublingual: With this form of intake the tablets are not swallowed but slowly dissolved under the tongue or in the cheek.
(2) First pass: All oral steroids (with the exception of Andriol), through the gastrointestinal tract, reach the liver where they are either partially destroyed or passed into the blood. Steroids which are 17-alpha alkylated, by attaching an alkyl group to the 17-alpha molecule, are protected against a fast breakdown by the liver.

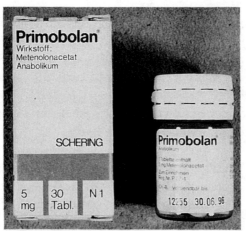

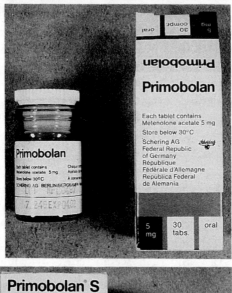

Primobolan tablets by Schering / Germany, 5mg/tab

Primobolan tablets by Schering / South America, 5mg/tab

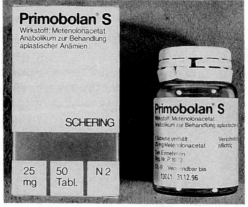

Primobolan S, 25mg/ tab, by Schering / Germany

PRIMOBOLAN DEPOT

Substance: methenolone enanthate

Trade names

Primobolan Depot	100 mg/ml;	Schering G, A, B, CH, ES, GR, I, PT, TK; Berlimed South Africa
Primobolan Depot (o.c.)	100 mg/ml;	Schering FR
Primobolan Depot	50 mg/ml;	Schering Mexico
Primobolan Depot mite	50 mg/ml;	Schering G

Much of what the reader has already heard about the Primobolan tablets in this book is also valid for Primobolan Depot. There are, however, a few differences between the two compounds so that a separate presentation makes sense. The most distinct difference is, of course, the various forms of administration since Primobolan Depot is injected intramuscularly and Primobolan tablets are taken orally. One important difference not immediately noticed lies in the different composition of Primobolan. The tablets are the acetate form of the substance methenolone while the injection is the enanthate form of methenolone. For many bodybuilders enanthate is simply the longer effective form of Primobolan. This is indeed true but inadequate as the only explanation. Primobolan Depot, due to the long duration of its effect needs to be injected only once a week. On the other hand, Primobolan tablets should be taken daily. When Primobolan Depot is taken in a dosage of 200 mg/week a low water retention stimulating the buildup of strength and muscles can occur. Since this is not so with the oral acetate form this could be one reason for the better effect of the Depot. Steroid novices can achieve good results by taking 200 mg/week. Within eight weeks they can gain 10 - 15 pounds without having to worry about losing them after discontinuing the use of the compound.

Primobolan Depot, although with a weaker effect than Deca-Durabolin, is a good basic steroid with a predominantly anabolic effect and, depending on the goal, can be effectively combined with almost any steroids. Those who would like to gain mass rapidly and do not have Deca available, can use Primo-Depot together with Sustanon 250 and Dianabol. Those who have more patience or are afraid of potential side effects will usually be very satisfied with a stack of Primobolan-Depot 200 mg/week and Deca-Durabolin 200-400 mg/week. We believe that the best combination is Primobolan Depot with Winstrol Depot. 200 - 400 mg/week is the normally used dosage of Primobolan Depot although there are enough athletes who inject a 100 mg ampule daily. Primobolan Depot, like the oral acetate form, is not converted into estrogen; however, low water retention can occur, which is the reason why during preparations for a competition the injections are usually preferred.

Side effects with Primobolan Depot are minimal and manifest themselves only rarely and in persons who are extremely sensitive. Due to the androgenic residual effect, side effects include light acne, deep voice or increased hair growth. Primobolan Depot has even less influence on the liver function than the oral form so that an increase of the liver's toxin values is extremely unlikely. The blood pressure, cholesterol level, HDL and LDL values, as with Primo tablets, usually remain unaffected. Primobolan Depot is generally the safest injectable steroid. Athletes whose liver values strongly increase when taking anabolic steroids but who still do not want to give up their use, under periodical supervision of these values, can go ahead and try a stack of Primobolan Depot, Deca-Durabolin, and Andriol. A well-known bodybuilder in Germany who had already won several national titles has admitted that his liver was damaged by his too frequent use of the 17-alpha alkylated steroids Dianabol, Anadrol 50 (at the time still Plenastril), and Oxandrolone. He was, however, able to bring his body back to national championship level by taking 200 mg Primobolan-Depot/week, 400 mg Deca-Durabolin/week, and 240 mg Andriol/day, without a negative effect on the liver values. Primobolan Depot, like the tablets, has only a very small influence on the hypothalamohypophysial testicular axis so that the body's own testosterone production is only reduced when very high dosages are taken over a prolonged period of time.

Women normally prefer the 25 mg tablets but there are several female athletes who inject 100-200 mg or more Primobolan Depot/week. 100 mg Primobolan Depot/week, combined with 50 mg Winstrol Depot/week, is usually an effective stack for many women and is tolerated well so that virilization symptoms are rarely observed. To avoid an undesired accumulation of androgens in the body women should pay attention that there are three to four days in between the relative injections. For competing female athletes this stack, however, is too weak. Primobolan Depot is often used in a dose of 100 mg/week to bridge over steroid breaks which, in our opinion, is not a good idea: The non-stop use of anabolic steroids has a strong negative influence on the body's own testosterone production and prevents the body from normalizing its functions. Dosages as low as 100 mg Primobolan Depot/week or 50 mg Deca-Durabolin/week (also often used for bridging) are non-toxic and mostly have no side effects. However, the effectiveness of such an intake must be strongly doubted since both compounds in this dosage are much too weak in order to effectively counteraffect the catabolic phase which begins in the steroid phases. Better results can usually be obtained with Clenbuterol without influencing the hormone system. Those who believe that in the "steroid free time" they must still take some "stuff" to bridge the usages should inject the long acting Testosterone enanthate (e.g. Testoviron Depot 250 mg/ml) every two to three weeks.

Primobolan Depot, unlike the tablets, is well distributed and readily available on the black market. The Spanish, Belgian, Greek, and German Primobolan Depot sell for approximately $15 per ampule. A Mexican version is also available but only in the 50 mg strength. Special attention must be paid to the fact that the injection solution of the original Spanish Primobolan is included in an ampule of brown glass with a red imprint burnt into the glass, and not in normal window glass as is common in other countries. The Mexican version is also in brown glass but the label is blue. When the package is opened a clear plastic bed is visible which, on the other side, is coated with aluminum foil and has the "Primobolan Depot" imprint on its surface. So far, according to our knowledge, there are no fakes yet. There are more or less good fakes of the other versions (see chapter "The Problem with Fake Steroids").

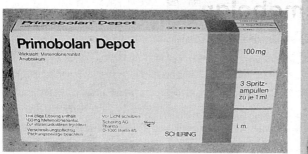

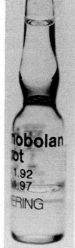

Primobolan Depot from Germany, box and ampule

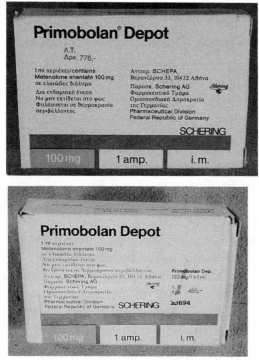

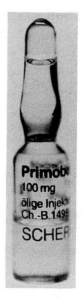

Two different boxes of Primobolan 100mg from Greece, the ampules are produced in Germany

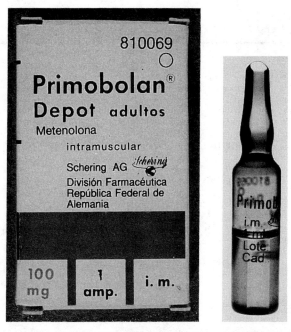

810069

Primobolan®

Depot adultos

Metenolona

intramuscular

Schering AG *Schering*

División Farmacéutica
República Federal de
Alemania

| 100 mg | 1 amp. | i. m. |

Spanish Primobolan, the ampule is made of brown glass

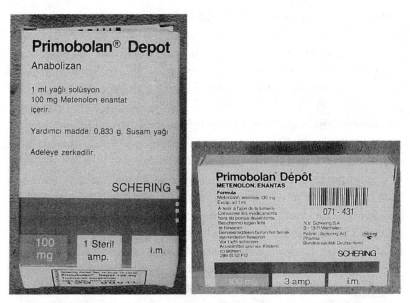

Primobolan® Depot

Anabolizan

1 ml yağlı solüsyon
100 mg Metenolon enantat
içerir.

Yardımcı madde: 0,833 g. Susam yağı

Adeleye zerkedilir.

SCHERING

| 100 mg | 1 Steril amp. | i.m. |

Primobolan Dépôt
METENOLON. ENANTAS

Formula
Metenolon enantas 100 mg
Excip. ad 1 ml
A teni à l'abri de la lumière
Conserver les médicaments
hors de portée desenfants
Beschermd tegen licht
te bewaren
Geneesmiddelen buiten het bereik
van kinderen bewaren
Vor Licht schützen
Arzneimittes sind vor Kindern
zu sichern
29Is IS 52 F12

071 - 431

N.V. Schering S.A.
B - 1831 Machelen
Fabric : Schering AG
Pharma
Bundesrepublik Deutschland

SCHERING

| 100 ml | 3 amp. | i.m. |

Primobolan from Turkey   *Primobolan from Belgium*

PROVIRON

Substance: mesterolone

Trade names

Mestoranum	25 mg tab.;	Schering DK, S, NO
Pluriviron	25 mg drg.;	Asche G
Proviron	10 mg tab.;	Schering TK
Proviron	10 mg tab.;	Leiras FI
Proviron	20 mg tab.;	Leiras FI
Proviron	25 mg tab.;	Schering G, A, B, CH, ES, FR, GB, GR, PL, NL, CZ, TK, Mexico, Dom. Rep., Panama, Guatemala, El Salvador, Honduras, Paraguay, Costa Rica, Nicaragua; Uruguay; Alkaloid YU
Proviron	50 mg tab.;	Schering I
Vistimon	25 mg tab.;	Jenapharm G

Proviron is a synthetic, orally effective androgen which does not have any anabolic characteristics. Proviron is used in school medicine to ease or cure disturbances caused by a deficiency of male sex hormones. Many athletes, for this reason, often use Proviron at the end of a steroid treatment in order to increase the reduced testosterone production. This, however, is not a good idea since Proviron has no effect on the body's own testosterone production but—as mentioned in the beginning—only reduces or completely eliminates the dysfunctions caused by the testosterone deficiency. These are, in particular, impotence which is mostly caused by an androgen deficiency that can occur after the discontinuance of steroids, and infertility which manifests itself in a reduced sperm count and a reduced sperm quality. Proviron is therefore taken during a steroid administration or after discontinuing the use of the steroids, to eliminate a possible impotency or a reduced sexual interest. This, however, does not contribute to the maintainance of strength and muscle mass after the treatment. There are other better suited compounds for this (see HCG, Clomid, and Teslac). For this reason Proviron is unfortunately considered by many to be a useless and unnecessary compound. (Daniel Duchaine *Underground Steroid Handbook 2*: "I can think of no legitimate use for Proviron in enhancing athletic performance.") Most, however, do not know the main use of Proviron in body-building.

You should be aware that Proviron is also an estrogen antagonist which prevents the aromatization of steroids. Unlike the antiestrogen Nolvadex which only blocks the estrogen receptors (see Nolvadex) Proviron already prevents the aromatizing of steroids. Therefore gynecomastia and increased water retention are successfully blocked. Since Proviron strongly suppresses the forming of estrogens no rebound effect occurs after discontinuation of use of the compound as is the case with, for example, Nolvadex where an aromatization of the steroids is not prevented. One can say that Nolvadex cures the problem of aromatization at its root while Nolvadex simply cures the symptoms. For this reason male athletes should prefer Proviron to Nolvadex. With Proviron the athlete obtains more muscle hardness since the androgen level is increased and the estrogen concentration remains low. This, in particular, is noted positively during the preparation for a competition when used in combination with a diet. Female athletes who naturally have a higher estrogen level often supplement their steroid intake with Proviron resulting in an increased muscle hardness. In the past it was common for bodybuilders to take a daily dose of one 25 mg tablet over several weeks, sometimes even months, in order to appear hard all year round. This was especially important for athletes' appearances at guest performances, seminars and photo sessions. Today Clenbuterol is usually taken over the entire year since possible virilization symptoms cannot occur which is not yet the case with Proviron. Since Proviron is very effective male athletes usually need only 50 mg/day which means that the athlete usually takes one 25 mg tablet in the morning and another 25 mg tablet in the evening. In some cases one 25 mg tablet per day is sufficient. When combining Proviron with Nolvadex (50 mg Proviron/day and 20 mg Nolvadex/day) this will lead to an almost complete suppression of estrogen. Even better results are achieved with 50 mg Proviron/day and 500 - 1000 mg Teslac/day. Since Teslac is a very expensive compound (see Teslac) most athletes do not consider this combination.

The side effects of Proviron in men are low at a dosage of 2-3 tablets/day so that Proviron, taken for example in combination with a steroid cycle, can be used comparatively without risk over several weeks. Since Proviron is well-tolerated by the liver, liver dysfunctions do not occur in the given dosages. For athletes who are used to acting under the motto "more is better" the intake of Proviron could have a paradoxical effect. The German manufacturer, Jenapharm, writes about its compound Vistimon in the package insert: "In high-dosage treatments an occasional retention of electrolytes and water, and edemas (accumulation of excessive water in tissues) can occur." Those taking less than 2-4 tablets daily do not have to worry about this. The most common side effect of Proviron—or in this case, secondary symptom— is in part a distinct sexual overstimulation and in some cases continuous penis erection. Since this condition can be painful and lead to possible damages, a lower dosage or discontinuing the compound are the only sensible solutions. Female athletes should use Proviron with caution since possible androgenic side effects cannot be excluded. Women who want to give Proviron a try should not take more than one 25 mg tablet per day. Higher dosages and periods of intake of more than four weeks considerably increase the risk of virilization symptoms. Female athletes who have no difficulties with Proviron obtain good results with 25 mg Proviron/day and 20 mg Nolvadex/day and, in combination with a diet, report an accelerated fat breakdown and continuously harder muscles.

Proviron is one of the very few steroid hormones which is still sufficiently available. The brand name Proviron costs about $35 in Germany and contains fifty 25 mg tablets. Vistimon by Jenapharm costs $14 per box and is packaged in two push-through strips of 10 tablets each. Pluriviron by Asche contains 30 dragees and costs $20. As one can see all German manufacturers charge about $.70 for one 25 mg Mesterolon tablet. This is similar to the generally observed price of $1 per tablet on the black market. Since the Spanish and Mexican Proviron are less expensive than the German Proviron (all compounds are by Schering) they are more readily available on the black market. The original price for 20 tablets in Spain, for example, is $3.60. Depending on the country of origin Proviron is packaged differently. The German Proviron is offered in small glass vials while the Spanish, Greek, and Mexican versions are included in push-through strips. However, all Proviron tablets have one thing in common: they are all indented and on the back have the stamp AX, surrounded by a hexagon. So far, there are no fakes available of either Proviron or its generic compounds.

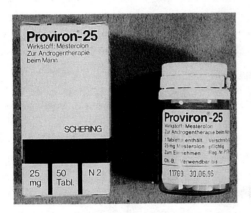

Proviron from Germany

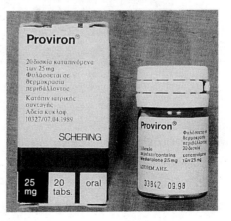

Proviron by Schering / Greece

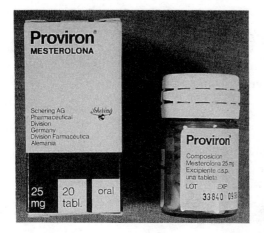

Proviron from Middle-
and South America

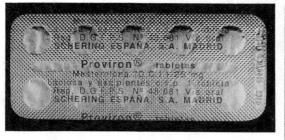

Spanish Proviron by Schering, blister and box

*Proviron from Turkey,
box and blister by
Schering*

*Vistimon by
Jenapharm, from
Germany, box and
blister*

Pluriviron from Germany

Pluriviron®
Zur Behandlung
von Potenzstörungen

ASCHE AG   **N1** 30 Dragees

SPIRONOLACTON COMP

Substance: spironolactone/furosemide

Trade names

Duraspiron 50-comp.	50 mg/20 mg tab.;	Durachemie G
Duraspiron 100 comp.	100 mg/20 mg tab.;	Durachemie G
Furo-Aldopur	50 mg/20 mg tab.;	Hormosan G
Furo-Aldopur-Forte	100 mg/20 mg tab.;	Hormosan G
Lasilacton	100 mg/20 mg tab.;	Hoechst A, CH
Lasilacton	50 mg/20 mg tab.;	Hoechst A, CH
Lasilactone	50 mg/20 mg tab.;	Hoechst GB
Osyrol 50-Lasix	50 mg/20 mg tab.;	Hoechst G
Osyrol 100-Lasix	100 mg/20 mg tab.;	Hoechst G
Spiro-50-D-Tablinen (o.c.)	50 mg/20 mg tab.;	Sanorania G
Spiro-100-D-Tablinen (o.c.)	100 mg/20 mg tab.;	Sanorania G
Spiro comp.-ratiopharm (o.c.)	50 mg/20 mg tab.;	ratiopharm G
Spiro comp.-forte-ratio (o.c.)	100 mg/20 mg tab.;	ratiopharm G
Spirolacton comp 50	50 mg/20 mg tab.;	Heumann G
Spirolacton comp 100	100 mg/20 mg tab.;	Heumann G

Note: In Europe there are also several other compounds which contain this compound combination. Due to a lack of space a further listing has been avoided. This remedy is unknown in the U.S. We were unable to locate a pharmaceutical manufacturer producing a drug containing these two substances.

This drug is a combination diuretic. It consists of a relatively mild potassium-sparing diuretic, spironolactone, (see also Aldactone) and the very strong loop diruetic, furosemide (see also Lasix). In body-building it is taken by both women and men shortly before a competition to excrete excessive water from the body. When everything goes well this results in hard, ripped and striated muscles. The diuretic effect of the tablets begins within an hour and is maintained over 3-4 hours. The extent of the diuresis depends on the athlete's body condition. A bodybuilder who is already hard and almost ôreadyô will lose only a small amount of liquid and feel the side effects, above all, muscle cramps; an athlete who holds a lot of water, however, will run to the restroom every few minutes. In addition to the often considerable water loss, a high excretion of sodium, calcium, and potassium also occurs so that the electrolyte househould is completely out of balance. The potassium excretion, however, can be balanced by the potassium-reabsorbing effect of spironolactone. For this reason no additional potassium-containing compounds must be consumed. The combination of these two substances has a synergetic effect so that both are needed in a lower dosage than when taken separately. Thus, with a low total dosage, not only can the side effects be reduced but similar results can also be achieved. Therefore, the tablet strength with 50 mg spironolactone and 20 mg furosemide is for many athletes an alternative to the strong 40 mg furosemide (Lasix) tablets. They are usually taken by athletes on the day of the competition and on the day before. Also in this case the athlete usually takes a 50 mg/20mg tablet and waits for the diuretic effect. Depending on how much undesired water is still accumulated between muscle and skin, male and female bodybuilders repeat this procedure 2-3 times every several hours.

The side effects depend greatly on the dosage and physical condition of the athlete (e.g. an already existing dehydration). It is possible that muscle cramps, weakness, dizziness, lower blood pressure, irregular heart beat, vomiting, diarrhea, reduced blood flow, numbness up to a possible circulatory collapse, and in extreme cases, even death occur. Male athletes, due to the anti-androgenic effect of spironolactone, can experience gynecomastia and impotence. However, because of the short period of intake this unpleasant side effect, occurs only rarely. With the use of furosemide-containing diuretics there is a small difference between absolute top shape by extreme dehydration and intensive care in the hospital. Those who manage to obtain a high level of dehydration without smaller or flatter muscles and who neither lose vascularity nor quit the competition because of severe cramps have a good chance of leaving the podium as the winner. The spironolactone/furosemide compounds are increasingly available on the black market in Europe. The tablets cost about $1 each. There are no fakes available.

Spiro comp forte by ratiopharm / Germany

SPIRONOTHIAZID

Substance: spironolactone/hydrochlorthiazide

Trade names

Aldactazide	25, 15 mg tab.;	SPA I
Aldactazide	25, 50 mg tab.;	Searle U.S.
Aldactazine	25, 15 mg tab.;	Searle PT, FR, B
Aldactazine	25, 15 mg tab.;	Vianex GR
Aldactide	25, 25 mg tab.;	Co-Flumactone GB
Aldactide	50, 50 mg tab.;	Co-Flumactone GB
Aldactine	25, 15 mg tab.;	Searle ES
Aldoleo	50, 50 mg tab.;	Leo ES

Risicordin	50, 50 mg tab.;	Heumann G
Risicordin mite	25, 25 mg tab.;	Heumann G
Spironazide	25, 25 mg tab.;	Schein U.S.
Spirono/Thiazide Generic (o.c.)		Lederle U.S., Warner Chillcott U.S., Barr Labs U.S.
Spirono/Thiazide Generic	25, 25 mg tab.;	Mylan U.S., Geneva U.S.
Spironothiazid	50, 50 mg tab.;	Henning Berlin G
Spironothiazid	100, 100 mg tab.;	Henning Berlin G
Spironothiazide	25, 25 mg tab.;	Mylan Pharm. U.S.
Spirozide	25, 25 mg tab.;	Rugby U.S.

Note: Worldwide there are several other compounds which contain the corresponding substance combination. Due to limited space they are not listed here.

Spironothiazide is a diuretic. It is a combination of a potassium-sparing diuretic, spironolactone (see also aldactone) and a thiazide. Thiazides, from their type, are similar to loop diuretics (see also Lasix). The main difference from loop diuretics is that thiazides lead to a lower release of calcium and have a less pronounced and less drastic dehydrating effect. Spironothiazide combines an aldosterone antagonist (see also Aldactone) with the stronger thiazid diuretic, making it a favorite and effective remedy for many competing body-builders to reduce excessive water. The advantage of this combination, on the one hand, is that potassium reabsorption by the spironolactone can be compensated by the thiazide. This usually leads to a suspension of the potassium-linked side effects. On the other hand, a good overall effect can also be obtained at lower dosages. Thus many use it as an alternative to the stronger and higher-risk furosemides (Lasix). Spironothiazide is usually taken by athletes during the last days before a competition. Generally a dosage of 2-3 tablets of 50 mg per day is taken and divided into 2-3 individual doses. The side effects are mostly caused by the expected inbalances in the fluids and electrolytes. These can manifest themselves in muscle cramps, irregular pulse rate (especially at an increased potassium level) and dizziness. In men, due to the antiandrogenic characteristics of spironolactone, gynecomastia and impotence are also possible but unlikely due to the short intake (see also Aldactone). As a preventive measure, the additional administration of potassium should be avoided and the period of intake should be as short as possible. Spironothiazide must be prescribed and is usually difficult to find on the black market since most athletes get prescriptions from their physicians. Fifty tablets of 50/50 mg cost approximately $40 on the black market. By comparison: Schein Company in the Medical Pharmaceutical & Surgical Supply Catalog offers 100 tablets of 25/25 mg for only $4.89.

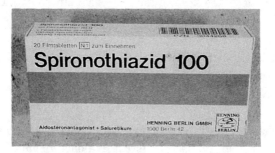

Spironothiazid 100 from Germany

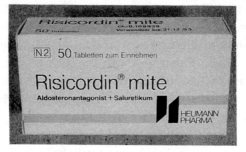

Risicordin mite from Germany

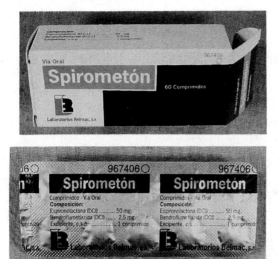

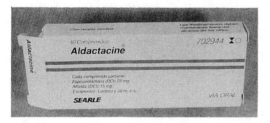

*Spirometón from Spain,
box and blister by
Laboratorios Belmac*

*Aldactacine by Searle /
Spain, box and blister*

STEN

Substance:	Testosterone propionate	25 mg
	Testosterone cypionate	75 mg
	Dihydrotestosterone	20 mg

Trade names

Sten	120 mg/2 ml;	Atlantis Mexico

This is another multi-component testosterone which is becoming increasingly popular. Although the substance combination is not the same, this remedy can definitely be compared to Sustanon. The total quantity of the substance corresponds to just slightly less than half of the quantity included in Sustanon and therefore, either more frequent or more voluminous injections of Sten are necessary. The characteristics of Sten will not be discussed in detail since the description would be almost identical to that found in the chapter "Sustanon." We currently do not know of any fakes of this compound. Sten is available for $30 on the black market. At this price, however, one receives 2 Redi-ject injections which seem to be worth the money. The 2 ml ampule has a brownish-red imprint which cannot be scratched off and is easily felt, having been burnt into the glass. Two ampules together with a 3 ml syringe and its needle are packaged in a plastic bed.

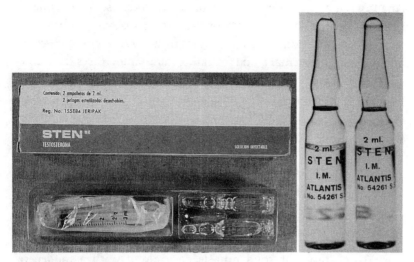

Sten by Atlantis from Mexico   *Sten ampules*

STENBOLONE

Substance: stenbolone acetate

Trade names

Anatrofin (o.c.)	25 mg/ml;	Syntex GB
Anatrofin (o.c.)	100 mg/ml;	Syntex Mexico
Stenbolone (o.c.)	25 mg/ml;	Farmacologico Latino ES
Stenbolone (o.c.)	50 mg/ml;	Syntex ES
Stenbolone (o.c.)	100 mg/ml;	Syntex ES

This steroid has not been manufactured since the late 1980's. However, we still would like to discuss it in a few sentences since it was such a popular steroid, with many potential customers even today. Stenbolone was introduced on the market in 1963 by Syntex, the same company that produced the popular steroids Anadrol, Oxitosona (o.c.), and Anapolon. It is therefore not surprising that Stenbolone has an application similar to the other three compounds. Syntex developed Stenbolone as a mild alternative to the toxic

Anadrol. And the company was successful because Stenbolone is neither liver-toxic nor does it aromatize, and it is only slightly androgenic. In addition, it has a similar effect to Anadrol in cases of anemia with abnormal blood formation since it increases the number of red blood cells. For this reason Stenbolone is especially suitable for competing athletes since it accelerates regeneration when dieting. Competing body builders in the weeks before a championship often experience a catabolic phase and a condition of overtraining. Stenbolone rapidly and reliably counters this and helps to obtain a good form since it does not draw water and does not increase the estrogen level. For the buildup of strength and mass, however, Stenbolone is by far not as suitable as Anadrol, although some erroneously call it an injectable Anadrol. Stenbolone has lower anabolic and androgenic effects than the oral version and it leads to a slow but solid muscle gain along with a moderate strength gain. For this purpose it is preferred by women and steroid novices, and by older athletes who obtain satisfying results without the fear of significant side effects. Despite this, Stenbolone is, above all, a competition steroid which is confirmed by the American "Steroid Guru" Daniel Duchaine in his book *Underground Steroid Handbook 2*: "This is an excellent steroid to use while dieting...."

Since the substance is in acetate form it has only a low half-life time so that frequent and regular injections are necessary in order to obtain sufficiently high and constant blood level values. For optimal results Stenbolone is normally taken daily and injected at least every 2 days. The usual weekly dose for athletes is 200–300 mg. For this reason the 50 mg strength is often preferred and the athlete either injects the entire one-milliliter ampule daily or limits the use to half of it. Women normally do well with 100–150 mg/week and should divide their weekly dosage into three equal parts. The potential side effects are low since the compound is well tolerated by the liver and edemas, gynecomastia, and high blood pressure do not occur. Cases of acne and increased aggressiveness in men are low and rare, as is a reduction in the body's own hormone production. Virilization symptoms in women also occur rarely and for the most part in very sensitive persons when high dosages are given or when the intake interval lasts over several weeks. There are no fakes on Stenbolone so neither the original compound nor an imitation can be found on the black market.

SUSTANON 250

Substance:	Testosterone propionate	30 mg
	Testosterone phenylpropionate	60 mg
	Testosterone isocaproate	60 mg
	Testosterone decanoate	100 mg

Trade names

Durandron (o.c.)	250 mg/ml;	Organon ES
Sostenon 250	250 mg/ml;	Organon Mexico, ES
Sustanon	250 mg/ml;	Ravasini I
Sustanon 250	250 mg/ml;	Organon GB, NL, FI, India, Russia, TK, CZ, BG
Sustanon '250'	250 mg/ml;	Organon Thailand
Sustenon 250	250 mg/ml;	Organon PT

Veterinary:
Deposterone   Gouglund Syntex Mexico

Sustanon is a very popular steroid which is highly appreciated by its users since it offers several advantages when compared to other testosterone compounds. Sustanon is a mixture of four different testosterones which, based on the well-timed composition, have a synergetic effect. This special feature has two positive characteristics for the athlete. First, based on the special combination effect of the compounds, Sustanon, milligram for milligram, has a better effect than Testosterone enanthate, cypionate, and propionate alone. Second, the effect of the four testosterones is time-released so that Sustanon goes rapidly into the sytem and remains effective in the body for several weeks. Due to the propionate also included in the steroid, Sustanon is effective after one day and, based on the mixed-in decanoates, remains active for 3-4 weeks. Sustanon has a distinct androgenic effect which is coupled with a strong anabolic effect. Therefore it is well suited to build up strength and mass. A rapid increase in body strength and an even increase in body weight occur. Athletes who use Sustanon report a solid muscle growth since it results in less water retention and also aromatizes less than either testosterone enanthate or cypionate. Indeed many bodybuilders who use testosterone and fight against distinct water retention and an elevated estrogen level prefer Sustanon over other long-acting depot testosterones.

It is further noticed that Sustanon is also effective when relatively low doses are given to well advanced athletes. It is interesting to note that when Sustanon is given to athletes who have already used this compound in the same or lower doses, it leads to similar good results as during the previous intake. Sustanon is usually injected at least once a week, which can be stretched up to 10 days. The dosage in bodybuilding and powerlifting ranges from 250 mg every 14 days up to 1000 mg or more per day. Since such high dosages are not recommended—and fortunately are also not taken in most cases—the rule is 250-1000 mg/week. A dosage of 500 mg/week is completely sufficient for most, and can often be reduced to 250 mg/week by combining Sustanon with an oral steroid. Sustanon is well-tolerated as a basic steroid during treatment which stimulates the regeneration, gives the athlete a sufficient "kick" for intense training units, and next to the already mentioned advantage—rapid strength increase and solid muscle gain—distinguishes itself also by its compatibility. In order to gain mass fast Sustanon is often combined with Deca-Durabolin, Dianabol or Anadrol while athletes who are more into quality prefer combining it with Parabolan, Winstrol, Oxandrolone or Primobolan.

Although Sustanon does not aromatize excessively when taken in a reasonable dosage many people, in addition, also take an antiestrogen such as Nolvadex and/or Proviron to prevent possible estrogen-linked side effects. Since Sustanon suppresses the endogenous testosterone production the intake of HCG and Clomid must be considered after six weeks or at the end of treatment. It is recommended that women not take depot testosterones since the androgen level would strongly increase and virilization symptoms could result. Despite this, it is not uncommon for female competing athletes in the higher weight classes to take testosterone since it helps in remaining "competitive." Women who use "Testo" or who would like to try it should limit its use to either only testosterone propionate or inject a maximum of 250 mg Sustanon every 10-14 days over a period of no longer than six weeks. At this point we would like to emphasize once more that steroid novices should stay away from all testosterone compounds since, at this time, they simply do not need them. The side effects of Sustanon are similar to those of Testosterone enanthate (see also Testosterone enanthate) only that they are usually less frequent and less severe. Depending on the predisposition and dosage, the user can experience the usual androgenic-linked side effects such as acne, aggressiveness, sexual overstimulation, oily skin, accelerated hair loss, and reduced production of the body's own hormones. Water retention and gynecomastia are usually within limits with the "Sustas" or are not as massive as with enanthate and cypionate. Liver damage is unlikely with Sustanon (see Testosterone enanthate); however, in very high dosages, elevated liver values can occur which, after discontinuing use of the compound, usually go back to normal. The fact that the liver is a very efficient organ and able to cope well with higher quantities of testosterone is confirmed in the book Doping-verbotene Arzneimittel im Sport by Dirk Clasing and Manfred Donike. On page 54 the authors state: "The liver is able to metabolize an almost unlimited amount of testosterone (2 g of rat liver are able to break down 100 mg/day of testosterone)."

Sustanon is well distributed on the black market and readily available. Unfortunately a large number of these compounds are more or less good fakes. When someone offers you ampules which do not have a paper label but a simple, usually red, imprint, these are certainly fakes. Mostly these are Polish Omnadren from which the original label was removed and replaced by a Sustanon imprint (see also Omnadren). Original Sustanon which almost exclusively is manufactured by Organon Company always has a paper label. It is more difficult to find the less frequently available original "Susta." On the black market mostly the Russian or Indian Sustanon 250 (see photos) is sold. The Indian Sustanon 250 is manufactured in Calcutta, India, by Organon and officially destined for export to Russia. Through Czechoslovakia, however, large quantities of this original Sustanon 250 are smuggled to Europe and the U.S. The Russian Sustanon 250 comes in a plastic film; printed in blue ink on the back are the name of the compound, the manufacturer, and the included substances (see photo). This imprint is either stamped on aluminum foil or on white paper. Five ampules are combined in one strip whereas each ampule is packaged individually. Original Sustanon 250 usually costs $12 - 18 per ampule on the black market and is certainly worth the price. In the meantime there are also several fakes of the Russian version which, however, can be easily identified by the rounded corners of the label. The originals always have a label with sharp corners.

Finally there are two more remedies from veterinary medicine we would like to mention which from time to time can be found on the black market. These two drugs reflect how difficult it is for some to find original compounds and what athletes have to go through since, ten years ago, nobody would have thought to inject such voluminous quantities of multicomponent testosterones as these. They are the two German remedies, Dobothylit, by Hydro Company, and Durateston, by Vemie Company.

Dobothylit includes per ml:	Testosterone propionate	6 mg
	Testosterone phenylpropionate	12 mg
	Testosterone isocaprinate	12 mg
	Testosterone caprinate	20 mg
Durateston includes per ml:	Testosterone propionate	6 mg
	Testosterone phenylpropionate	12 mg
	Testosterone methylpantanoate	12 mg
	Testosterone decanoate	20 mg

As one can see both preparations have almost the same substance combination as Sustanon. The complicating difference, as everyone can hardly overlook, consists of the milligram strength of the individual testosterone esters. In both compounds, unfortunately, only

1/5 of all substances of Sustanon is included which, in order to inject the correct substance, makes an injection a voluminous affair. The price for the 5 ml vial is $20. There are no fakes.

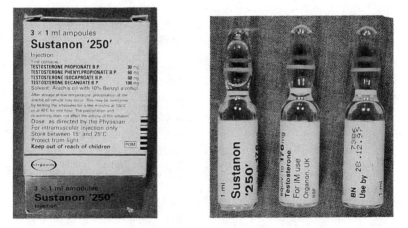

1 fiala da 1 ml

Sustanon

Preparato ad azione
androgena pronta e prolungata,
per via intramuscolare

1 ml della soluzione contiene:
Principi attivi:

Testosterone propionato	mg	30
Testosterone fenilpropionato	mg	60
Testosterone isocaproato	mg	60
Testosterone decanoato	mg	100

Eccipienti:

Alcool benzilico	ml	0,1
Olio di arachidi q.b. a	ml	1

Organon

Sustanon box from Italy

3 × 1 ml ampoules

Sustanon '250'

Injection

1 ml contains

TESTOSTERONE PROPIONATE B.P.	30 mg
TESTOSTERONE PHENYLPROPIONATE B.P.	60 mg
TESTOSTERONE ISOCAPROATE B.P.	60 mg
TESTOSTERONE DECANOATE B.P.	100 mg

Solvent: Arachis oil with 10% Benzyl alcohol

After storage at low temperature precipitation of the
arachis oil vehicle may occur. This may be overcome
by heating the ampoules for a few minutes at 100°C
or at 40°C for one hour. The precipitation and
re-warming does not affect the activity of the solution.

Dose: as directed by the Physician
For intramuscular injection only
Store between 15° and 25°C
Protect from light
Keep out of reach of children   POM

Organon

3 × 1 ml ampoules
Sustanon '250'
Injection

Sustanon '250' from UK, box and ampules

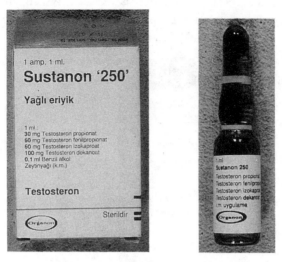

Sustanon from Turkey, box and ampule

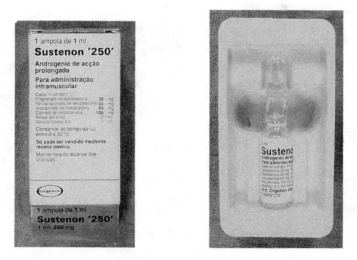

Sustenon '250' from Portugal, box with blister and ampule

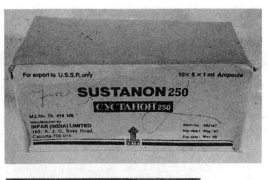

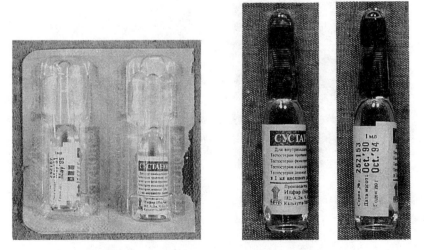

Russian Sustanon 250, produced in Calcutta / India by Infar.
5 ampules are in a foil strip, 10 strips per box.

Mexican rediject Sostenon 250 by Organon

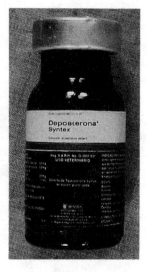

Deposterona by Syntex / Mexico, Veterinary "Susta," 60mg/ml, 5ml vial

TESLAC

Substance: Testolactone

Trade names

Fludestrin	100 mg/ml;	Bristol G
Fludestrin	50 mg/ml;	Bristol G
Teslac	50 mg tab.;	Squibb B, NL; Squibb Mark U.S.; Mead Johnson U.S.

Teslac belongs to the group of sex hormones and from a biochemical perspective, is a relative of the testosterones. Although this categorizes it as an androgenic steroid, from a technical point of view it is neither an androgenic nor an anabolic steroid. Teslac is very similar to the structure of androgenic steroids but it has only a very low androgenic and no anabolic effect. In school medicine this compound is used in the treatment of advanced mammary carcinomas in women. Before you discard Teslac as a completely useless drug and stop reading we want to tell you that Teslac does have his justified application in bodybuilding. Two reasons speak for an intake of Teslac: First, it is the most effective antiestrogen and second, it causes a distinct increase of the endogenic (body's own) testosterone production. Teslac is unique in its effectiveness as an antiestrogen. Like Proviron, it prevents the aromatizing process of the steroids from the basis. Thus, Teslac prevents almost completely the introduction of more estrogens into the blood and subsequent bonding with the estrogen receptors. Athletes who want to be absolutely certain combine Teslac with Proviron 50 mg/day and obtain a complete suppression of the estrogens. What makes Teslac different from Proviron, however, and so desirable is the characteristic that it can lead to an irreversible and permanent suppression of the estrogens in male athletes. Studies, in the meantime, have proven that Teslac makes male athletes resistant to an aromatization of steroids over a prolonged period. A water retention caused by the estrogens and gynecomastia is thus avoided in the long term. Another advantage of Teslac is that it directly influences the hypothalamus and upon its "signal" the hypophysis releases more gonadotropine, leading to a significant increase of the endogenic testosterone level. The strength of the testosterone-stimulating effect of Teslac can be compared with the one of HCG (see also HCG). Unlike HCG which after only a few hours results in an elevated plasmatestosterone level, Teslac does require a longer initial period. Thus a regular intake over several days is a preliminary. Although we have initially mentioned that Teslac does not have an anabolic effect, based on the increased testosterone level, a gain in muscles and strength can occur. This could lead to androgenically-linked side effects but they are very unlikely.

Side effects from Teslac are very rare. Since this compound, above all, was developed for women, it was extremely important to exclude the androgenic effect component as much as possible. This was successfully accomplished so that females very rarely experience masculinizing symptoms such as, for example, increased growth of body hair or deep voice. Possible side effects from Teslac are given on the package insert by the German manufacturer, Bristol Arzneimittel GmbH, for the remedy Fludestrin: "cutaneous eruptions (maculopapular erythema), high blood pressure, sensations such as itching and pricking (paresthesia), pain in the arms and legs and swelling, tongue infection, loss of appetite, nausea and vomiting." These side effects, as already mentioned, are extremely rare. The plasma calcium level of athletes should, however, be checked since Teslac could lead to hypercalcemia (increased calcium level).

Perhaps the greatest negative side effect of Teslac is its high price. A package of fifty 50 mg tablets costs about $200 on the black market. Every single tablet thus costs $4. The recommended daily dose of 10-20 tablets — that is 500-1000 mg/day! as indicated in technical publications in the German substance list— is completely unrealistic. Usually 4-5 tablets daily (200-250 mg/day) are sufficient. This corresponds to the daily dose indicated by the German manufacturer (Bristol Arzneimittel GmbH). However even such a dosage will discourage most athletes because of the high cost. An alternative would be to limit the intake of Teslac to two tablets per day and to supplement them with the similarly effective Proviron (50 mg/day). The only injectable drug that contains the substance testolactone (Fludestrin from Germany) is also very expensive and costs $20 per 100 mg ampule. Usually a lower daily dosage is required with the injectable form than with tablets so that 100 mg/day (one ampule) is sufficient. Also in this case, however, the cost is still way too high. For this reason Teslac is rarely found on the black market in the U.S. as Fludestrin is in Europe since an athlete is rarely willing to pay such an amount. If Teslac were to be found at a lower price this compound would certainly be the number one antiestrogen for athletes. So far, fakes of Teslac are not known.

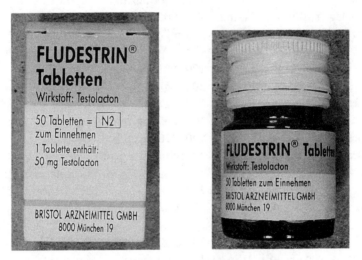

Fludestrin Tabletten by Bristol / Germany

TESTOSTERONE ENANTHATE

Substance: Testosterone enanthate

Trade names

Andropository	200 mg/ml;	Rugby U.S.
Andro 100 (o.c.)	100 mg/ml;	Forest U.S.
Andro L.A. 200	200 mg/ml;	Forest U.S.
Androtardyl	250 mg/ml;	Schering FR

Andryl 200 (o.c.)	200 mg/ml;	Keene U.S.
Arderone 100/200 (o.c.)	100, 200 mg/ml;	Burgin-Arden U.S.
Delatest (o.c.)	100 mg/ml;	Dunhall U.S.
Delatestryl (o.c.)	200 mg/ml;	Mead Johnson U.S.
Delatestryl	200 mg/ml;	Gynex U.S.
Dura-Testosterone (o.c.)	200 mg/ml;	Pharmex U.S.
Durathate-200 Injection (o.c.)	200 mg/ml;	Hauck U.S.
Durathate-200 Injection	200 mg/ml;	Roberts U.S.
Enarmon-Depot	125 mg/ml;	Teskoku Hormone Japan
Everone	100, 200 mg/ml;	Hyrex U.S.
Malogen 100/200 L.A. (o.c.)	100, 200 mg/ml;	Forest Pharm. U.S.
Primoteston Depot	250 mg/ml;	Schering GB, Mexico; Leiras FI
Primoteston Depot	100, 180 mg/ml;	Schering NO
Tesone L.A. (o.c.)	200 mg/ml;	Sig U.S.
Testanate No. 1 (o.c.)	100 mg/ml;	Kenyon U.S.
Testaval (o.c.)	100, 200 mg/ml;	Legere U.S.
Testo-Enant	100, 250 mg/ml;	Geymonat I
Testosteron-depo	50, 100, 250 mg/ml;	GalenikaYU; Hemofarm YU
Testosteron-Depot	250 mg/ml;	Jenapharm G, BG
Testosteron Depot	250 mg/ml;	Rotexmedica G
Test. prolongatum	100 mg/ml;	Polfa PL, BG
Testosterone Enanthate	100, 200 mg/ml;	Steris U.S.
Testosterone Enanthate (o.c.)	100, 200 mg/ml;	Quad U.S.
Testoviron Depot	100 mg/ml;	Schering B
Testoviron-Depot	250 mg/ml;	Schering G, A, B, CH, DK, ES GR, PL, S, Thailand, Columbia, Dom. Rep.;Paraguay, Uruguay
Testrin-P.A. (o.c.)	200 mg/ml;	Pasadena Res. U.S.

Veterinary:

Testosterona 200	200 mg/ml; 10 ml	Brovel Mexico

Note: Worldwide there are also several other compounds which contain the substance Testosterone enanthate. The trade names and manufacturers are not listed here since these products are normally not available on the black market.

"Testosterone enantate is an ester of the naturally occurring androgen, testosterone. It is responsible for the normal development of the male sex characteristics. In the event of insufficient testosterone production an almost complete balance of the functional, anatomic, and psychic deficiency symptoms can be achieved by substituting testosterone." (Excerpt from the package insert of the German pharmaceutical group, Jenapharm GmbH for its compound Testosteron-Depot.)

These lines clearly describe what an important and effective hormone testosterone is. One of the many testosterone substances is the testosterone enanthate. In a man it is normally used to treat hypogonadism resulting from androgen deficiency (1) and anemia (2). Surprisingly, in medical schools testosterone enanthate is also used in women and children. Boys and male youth take it as growth therapy (package insert, Testosteron-Depot, Jenapharm GmbH) and women take it as an "additive treatment for certain growth forms of the nipples during post-menopause" (package insert, Testoviron-Depot-250 Schering AG). In bodybuilding, however, it is THE "mass building steroid." No matter what you think of Dianabol, Parabolan, Anadrol 50, Finaject, and others, when it comes to strength, muscle mass, and rapid weight gains, testosterone is still the "King of the Road." Testosterone enanthate is the European counterpart to Testosterone cypionate which is predominantly available in the U.S. (see also Test. Cyp.). Testosterone enanthate, as most trade names already suggest, is a long-acting depot steroid. Depending on the metabolism and the body's initial hormone level it has a duration of effect of two to three weeks so that theoretically very long intervals between injections are possible. Although Testosterone enanthate is effective for several weeks, it is injected at least once a week in bodybuilding, powerlifting, and weightlifting. This, by all means, makes sense since Testosterone enanthate has a plasma half-life time in the blood of only one week (*Doping-verbotene Arzneimittel im Sport*, Dirk Clasing and Manfred Donike, p. 66.)

The decisive advantage of Testosterone enanthate, however, is that this substance has a very strong androgenic effect and is coupled with an intense anabolic component. This allows almost everyone, within a short time, to build up a lot of strength and mass. The rapid and strong weight gain is combined with distinct water retention since a retention of electrolytes and water occurs. A pleasant effect is that the enormous strength gain goes hand in hand with the water retention. Weightlifters and powerlifters, especially in the higher weight classes, appreciate this characteristic. In this group, Testosterone enanthate, Testosterone cypionate, and Sustanon (see also Sustanon) are the number one steroids; this is also clearly reflected in the dosages. Dosages of 500 mg, 1000 mg or even 2000 mg per day are no rarity—mind you, per day, not per week. Sports disciplines requiring a high degree of raw power, aggressiveness, and stamina offer an excellent application for Depot-Testosterone. *Muscle Mag International*, July 1992, page 71: "Pro football players are total androgen heads. Powerlifters take much heavier stacks. Professional wrestlers never come off the stuff. They have testicles the size of raisins." Daniel Duchaine, *Underground Steroid Handbook 2*: "...it is not uncommon to see very high doses in the 2000 mg - 4000 mg/week range used. Most powerlifters and football players are using these megadoses." The distinct water retention has also other advantages. Those who have problems with their joints, shoulder cartilages or whose intervertibral disks, due to years of heavy training, show the first signs of wear, can get temporary relief by taking testosterone.

For the bodybuilder, the water retention that goes hand in hand with Testosterone enanthate cuts both ways. Certainly, one gets rapidly massive and strong; however, one's reflected image after a few weeks often shows completely flat, watery, and puffy muscles. The muscles appear as if they have been pumped up with air to new dimensions, yet during flexing nothing happens. Those who do not believe this should bother to go visit the so-called "bodybuilding champions" during the OFF-season when these exaggerated quantities of "Testo" come in. A look at the now defunct bodybuilding magazine WBF makes it even clearer. An additional problem when taking Testosterone enanthate is that the conversion rate to estrogen is very high. This, on one hand, leads the body to store more fat; on the other hand, feminization symptoms (gynecomastia) are not unusual. However, it must be clearly stated that this depends on the athlete's predisposition. By all means, there are athletes who even with 1000 mg+/week do not show feminization symptoms or fat deposits and who suffer very low water retention. Others, however, develop pain in their nipples by simply looking at a Testoviron-Depot ampule. Yet the additional intake of Nolvadex and Proviron should be considered at a dosage level of 500 mg+/week. As already mentioned, Testo is effective for everyone, whether a beginner or Mr. Olympia. Testosterone enanthate also strongly promotes the regeneration process. This leads to distinctly shorter overcompensation phases, an increased feeling of well-being, and a distinct energy increase. This is also the reason why several athletes are able to work out twice daily for several hours six times a week and continue to build up mass and strength. Those who can work out again two hours after a hard leg workout know that Testo works. Athletes who take Testosterone enanthate report an excessively strong pump effect during training. This "steroid pump" is attributed to an increased blood volume with a higher oxygen supply and a higher quantity of red blood cells. Those who take megadoses of Testosterone enanthate will already feel an enormous pump in their upper thighs and calves when climbing stairs. Despite this we recommend that steroid novices stay away from all testosterone compounds. To make it very clear: Those who have never taken steroids do not yet need any testosterone and should wait until later when the "weaker" steroids begin to have little effect. For the more advanced, Testosterone enanthate can either be taken alone or in combination with other compounds.

For adding mass Testosterone enanthate combines very well with Anadrol 50, Dianabol, Deca-Durabolin, and Parabolan. As an example, a stack of 100 mg Anadrol 50/day, 200 mg Deca-Durabolin/week, and 500 mg Testosterone enanthate/week works well. After six weeks of intake the Anadrol 50, for example, could be replaced by 40 mg Dianabol/day. Principally, Testosterone enanthate can be combined with any steroid in order to gain mass. Apparently a synergetic effect between the androgen, Testosterone enanthate, and the anabolic steroids occurs which results in their bonding with several receptors. Those who draw too much water with Testosterone enanthate and Dianabol or Anadrol, or who are more interested in strength without gaining 20 pounds of body weight should take Testosterone enanthate together with Oxandrolone or Winstrol. The generally taken dose—as already mentioned—varies from 250 mg/week up to 2000 mg/day. In our opinion the most sensible dosage for most athletes is between 250-1000 mg/week. Normally a higher dosage should not be necessary. When taking up to 500 mg/week the dosage is normally taken all at once, thus 2 ml of solution are injected. A higher dosage should be divided into two injections per week. The quantity of the dose should be determined by the athlete's developmental stage, his goals, and the quantity of his previous steroid intake. The so called beach- and disco bodybuilders do not need 1000 mg of Testosterone enanthate/week. Our experience is that the Testosterone enanthate dosage for many, above all, depends on their financial resources. Since it is not, by any means, the most economic testosterone, most athletes do not take too much. Others switch to the cheaper Omnadren and because of the low price continue "shooting" Omnadren.

Testosterone enanthate has a strong influence on the hypothalamohypophysial testicular axis. The hypophysis is inhibited by a positive feedback. This leads to a negative influence on the endogenic testosterone production. Possible effects are described by the German Jenapharm GmbH in their package insert for the compound Testosteron Depot: " In a high-dosed treatment with testosterone compounds an often reversible interruption or reduction of the spermatogenesis in the testes is to be expected and consequently also a reduction of the testes size." Schering AG, the manufacturer of Testoviron-Depot-250, also suggests the same idea in its package insert: "A long-term and high-dosed application of Testoviron-Depot-250 will lead to a reversible interruption or reduction of the sperm count in the testes, thus a reduction of the testes size must be expected." Consequently, after reading these statements, additional intake of HCG should be considered. Those who take Testosterone enanthate should consider the intake of HCG every 6-8 weeks. An injection of 5000 I.U. every fifth day over a period of 10 days (a total of 3 injections) helps to reduce this problem. At the end of the testosterone treatment the administration of HCG, Clomid, Nolvadex and Clenbuterol is now quite common. To some extent the use of these compounds helps absorb the catabolic phase and helps elevate the endogenic testosterone level. By this method the strength and mass loss which occur in any event can be reduced. Those who go off Testosterone enanthate ôcold turkeyô after several weeks of use will wonder how rapidly their body weights and former voluminous muscles will decrease. Even a slow tapering-off phase, that is reducing the dosage step by step, will not prevent a noticeable reduction. The only options available to the athlete consist of taking testosterone-stimulating compounds (HCG, Clomid, Cyclofenil), anti-catabolic substances (Clenbuterol, Ephedrine), or the very expensive growth hormones, or of switching to milder steroids (Deca-Durabolin, Winstrol, Primobolan). Most can get massive and strong with Testosterone enanthate. However, only very few are able to retain their size after discontinuing the compound. This is also one of the reasons why really good bodybuilders, powerlifters, weightlighters, and others take the "stuff" all year long.

The side effects of Testosterone enanthate are mostly the distinct androgenic effect and the increased water retention. This is usually the reason for the frequent occurrence of hypertony (3). Those who have a predisposition for high blood pressure or whose blood pressure is elevated when they begin taking Testosterone enanthate should have it periodically checked by a physician. If necessary the intake of an antihypertensive drug (4) such as Catapresan is advisable. Many athletes experience a strong acne vulgaris with Testosterone enanthate which manifests itself on the back, chest, shoulders, and arms more than on the face. Athletes who take large quantities of Testo can often be easily recognized because of these characteristics. It is interesting to note that in some athletes these characteristics only occur after use of the compound has been discontinued, which implies a rebound effect. In severe cases the medicine Accutane can help. The already discussed feminization symptoms, especially gynecomastia, require the intake of an anti-estrogen. Sexual overstimulation with frequent erections at the beginning of intake is normal. In young athletes, "in addition to virilization,testosterone can also lead to an accelerated growth and bone maturation, to a premature epiphysial closing of the growth plates and thus a lower height" (Jenapharm GmbH, package insert for Testosteron-Depot). Since mostly taller athletes are successful in bodybuilding, young adults should reflect carefully before taking any anabolic/androgenic steroids, in particular, testosterone.

Other possible side effects are testicular atrophy, reduced spermatogenesis, and especially an increased aggressiveness. Those who transfer this aggressiveness to their training and not their environment do not have to worry. Unfortunately this is not the case in some athletes who take Testosterone enanthate. Testosterone and Finaject are both primary reasons for some eruptions. In particular, high doses are in part responsible for anti-social behavior among its users. One can talk here of a sort of "superman syndrome" that occurs in some users. Daniel Duchaine discusses this problem in his book *Underground Steroid Handbook 2* : "Men, though, with increased aggressiveness can become outright frightening and dangerous, as well as being general dickheads. Try riding in a car with a 300 pound, acne ridden, hungry testosterone respository during rush hour traffic." Although Testosterone enanthate is broken down through the liver, this compound is only slightly toxic when taken in a reasonable dose; therefore, changes of the liver values do not occur as often as with the oral 17-alpha alkylated steroids. Very interesting information as to the liver intoxication of testosterone can be found in the book Doping by Dirk Clasing written in collaboration with Manfred Donike et al. On page 60 one reads: "After earlier exams (Krüskemper 1975) guidelines for the evaluation of possible liver intoxication by steroids can be made (tab. 3). According to these guidelinges, testosterone and its esters seem to be non-toxic or very slightly toxic to the liver. This is clinically confirmed: even in cases with considerable pre-existing damage to the liver (alcoholic cirrhosis), testosterone was administered without additional liver damage." (Gluud 1988; Kley 1982). Further potential side effects can be deep voice and accelerated hair loss. "Some steroids can make your hair fall out. It is rarely an anabolic steroid that does this, but rather the androgens, notably the testosterones." (Daniel Duchaine, *Underground Steroid Handbook 2*, page 61.)

Women shoud normally avoid its intake since it could result in unpleasant androgen-linked side effects. Jenapharm GmbH describes these possible side effects of Testosterone enanthate in its package insert for the compound Testosteron-Depot: "The use of testosterone in women may cause symptoms of virilization such as acne vulgaris, hirsutism (5), androgenetic alopecia (6), voice changes, and occasional clitorial hypertrophy and an unnaturally perceived increase in libido. Changes in voice and alopecia must be classified as irreversible, hirsutism and clitorial hypertropy as in part reversible." Women who are not afraid of this are found at many competition scenes. In our opinion, 250 mg is the maximum quantity of Testosterone enanthate that a female athlete should take each 7-10 days. However in competition bodybuilding and especially in powerlifting much higher dosages and shorter injection intervals have been observed in women.

Another interesting side effect of Testosterone enanthate is mentioned in the bodybuilding magazine *Muscle Media 2000*, June-July 1993 on page 45. Judging whether this is positive or negative is left to the reader. "A few years ago, the *Lancet Medical Journal* of England reported that they found testosterone (the prototype anabolic steroid) to be a remarkably effective form of male birth control. Researchers conducted a 12 month study which included 270 men and determined that weekly injections of the hormone testosterone were 'safe, stable, and effective.' They discovered that weekly testosterone injections had a success rate of 99.2% as a birth control method. That makes it more effective than the birth control pill (97%) and much more effective than condoms (88%). The study also revealed that the effects of the contraceptive injections were entirely reversible upon discontinuing administration of the drug and that the testosterone injections produced minimal side effects."

Similar studies with identical data are also in progress at a German university clinic. Although this is not part of the actual subject of this book, these results stress at least the need for testosterone-stimulating compounds during and after the intake of Testosterone enanthate. Since it is effective for such a long period of time, Testosterone enanthate is always taken more frequently by athletes during their "steroid intervals." An injection of 250 mg every 2-3 weeks helps maintain strength and mass. Whether this application makes sense remains to be seen; the fact is that it works. Looking toward competitions with doping tests Testosterone enanthate is also an interesting substance. Since exogenous testosterone can only be detected through the testosterone/epitestosterone values, it is important not to exceed the critical 6:1 ratio. Daniel Duchaine, *Ask the Guru*: "Experimental military trials have shown that up to 300 mg a week of Testosterone cypionate or enanthate can be used while still maintaining the six to one ratio." However, we do not give any guarantee for the practical use of this information. The over bridging doping of the former GDR athletes with Testosterone enanthate and -propionate worked perfectly. The athlete can find more on this subject in the book *Doping* by Brigitte Berendonk. So far it is published only in German.

The Testosterone enanthate most frequently used by athletes is the compound Testoviron Depot 250 by Schering AG. Since the German compound is quite expensive — one injection ampule of Testoviron Depot 250 officially costs $18.50 (Red List 1995) — most athletes fall back on other European or on Mexican compounds. Above all others on the black market for steroids one will find the Spanish and Greek versions by Schering. On the Spanish Testoviron Depot one must check that the ampule is made of brown glass and not of white glass as is common in other countries. The price for Testoviron Depot 250 on the black market is around $10-15 per 1 ml ampule. Fortunately there are only a few fakes of the substance Testosterone enanthate.

(1) Inadequate function of the genital glands
(2) Anemia
(3) High blood pressure
(4) To reduce high blood pressure
(5) Increased hair growth in face and on legs
(6) Androgenic-linked loss of hair on the scalp.

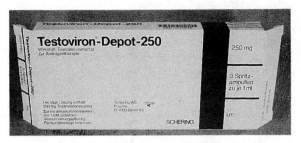

German Testoviron-Depot-250 rediject version

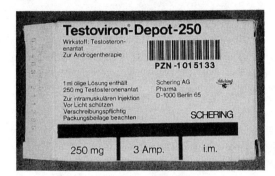

Testoviron-Depot-250 from Germany

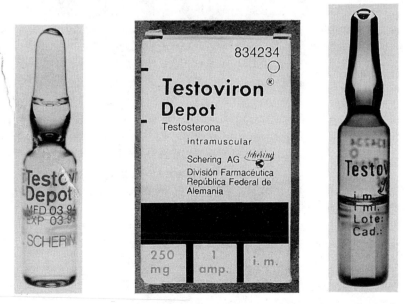

German Testoviron
by Schering

Testoviron Depot by Schering / Spain, box and ampule

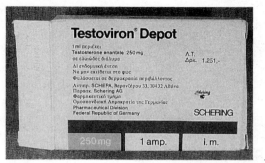

Testoviron Depot
from Greece

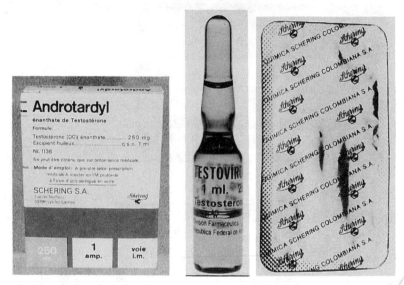

Androtardyl from France

Testoviron ampule and blister
from Columbia

Testoviron Depot from Columbia

Testoviron Depot from South
America

Testosteron Depo by Galeniga / Yugoslavia

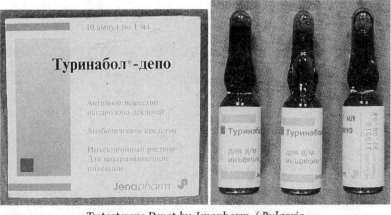

Testosterone Depot by Jenapharm / Bulgaria

Testosterone Depot by Jenapharm / Germany

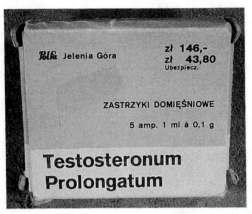

Polfa Jelenia Góra

zł 146,-
zł 43,80
Ubezpiecz.

ZASTRZYKI DOMIĘŚNIOWE

5 amp. 1 ml á 0,1 g

Testosteronum
Prolongatum

*Testosteronum
Prolongatum by Polfa /
Poland*

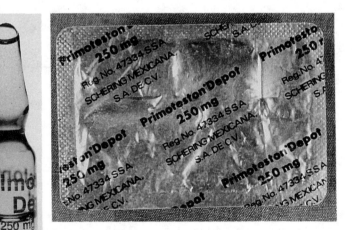

*Primoteston by Schering / Mexico,
blister and ampule, 250mg*

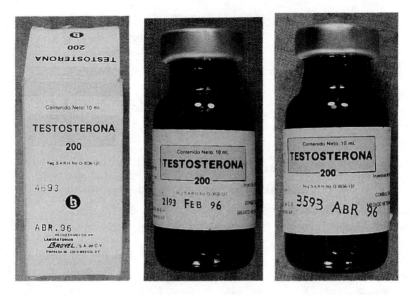

Testosterona 200, Veterinary Testosterone enanthate by Brovel / Mexico

TESTOSTERONE CYPIONATE

Substance: Testosterone cypionate

Trade names

Andro-Cyp (o.c.)	100 mg/ml, 200 mg/ml;	Keene U.S.
Andro-Cyp	100 mg/ml, 200 mg/ml;	Brown U.S.
Andronaq LA (o.c.)	100 mg/ml, 200 mg/ml;	Central U.S.
Andronate (o.c.)	100 mg/ml, 200 mg/ml;	Pasadena U.S.
D-Test 100/200 (o.c.)	100 mg/ml, 200 mg/ml;	Burgin-Aden U.S.
Dep-Test (o.c.)	100 mg/ml;	Sig u.S.
Dep-Testosterone (o.c.)	100 mg/ml, 200 mg/ml;	Rocky Mountain U.S.
Dep Andro-100-200	100 mg/ml, 200 mg/ml;	Forest U.S.
Depo-Testosterone	50 mg/ml;	Upjohn U.S.
Depo-Testosterone	100 mg/ml, 200 mg/ml;	Upjohn U.S.
Depotest	100 mg/ml, 200 mg/ml;	Hyrex U.S.; Kay U.S.

Duratest-100-200 (o.c.)	100 mg/ml, 200 mg/ml;	Hauck U.S.
Duratest-100-200	100 mg/ml, 200 mg/ml;	Roberts U.S.
Malogen Cyp (o.c.)	100 mg/ml, 200 mg/ml;	Forest U.S.
Testa-C	200 mg/ml;	Vortech U.S.
Testadiate-Depo	200 mg/ml;	Kay U.S.
Testex Leo prolongatum	100 mg/2ml, 250 mg/2ml;	Leo ES
Testoject (o.c.)	100 mg/ml;	Mayrand U.S.
Testoject-50 (o.c.)	50 mg/ml;	Mayrand U.S.
Testoject-LA (o.c.)	200 mg/ml;	Mayrand U.S.
Testosterone (o.c.)	50 mg/ml;	Huffman U.S.
Testosterone Cypionate	100 mg/ml, 200 mg/ml;	Huffman U.S.
Testosterone Cpyionate	200 mg/ml;	Legere U.S.
Testosterone Cpyionate	100 mg/ml, 200 mg/ml;	Goldline U.S., Steris U.S.
Testred Cypionate	200 mg/ml;	ICN U.S.

A glance at the trade names of Testosterone cypionate clearly shows that this compound is available almost exclusively in the U.S. It is the most popular and most used testosterone. Although Testosterone cypionate is also known in Europe its availability there is almost nonexistant. The only original and legitimate European compound "Testex Leo prolongatum" is manufactured by Leo Company and is available only in Spain. It is manufactured in two different strengths, 100 mg/ml and 250 mg/ml. Each ampule always incudes one milliliter (ml) of substance (see list). The price of the Spanish Testosterone cypionate on the black market in Europe is about $10 for one 250 mg/ml ampule. In Europe Testosterone cypionate is only rarely used by athletes, whereas in the U.S. the situation is completely reversed. Much more Testosterone cypionate is used than Testosterone enanthate. The reasons are at hand: As already mentioned above, Testosterone cypionate is manufactured almost exclusively in the U.S.; Testosterone enanthate, almost exclusively in Europe. Since the effects and side effects of both drugs are almost identical, this difference is explained only by the availability on the continents and not any advantages or disadvantages of the two testosterone esters. Cypionate, like enananthe, is an oil–dissolved injectable form of testosterone with strong androgenic and anabolic effects. It aromatizes quite easily which means that the conversion rate to estrogen, similar to enanthate's, is relatively high. Several athletes are of the opinion that cypionate stores more water in the body than enantathe does. The muscle buildup during the application along with the inevitable loss of strength and muscle mass after discontinuing use of one product, are the same with the other. Testosterone cypionate can be combined with many steroids and thus making it an excellent mass steroid. As with enanthate the dosage range is 250-1000 mg/week although several athletes inject megadoses (see Testosterone enanthate).

Almost everything written in this book about Testosterone enanthate can be applied to cypionate. In our opinion most athletes will not notice a difference between the two compounds. Daniel Duchaine confirms this in his book *Underground Steroid Handbook 2*: "Unless the athlete has a known sensitivity to the water retaining drugs, Enanthate and Cypionate are indistinguishable. So indistinguishable, that some counterfeit Enanthates are simply relabled Cypionates." Testosterone cypionate is one of the drugs which is most frequently faked. The products by Lemmon, Goldline, and International Pharmaceutical available on the black market are fakes and almost certainly contain no cypionate (see also chapter Fakes). Those who have access to the Spanish version can currently assume that they have purchased an original drug. The price situation is the same as with Testosterone enanthate. For 1 ml of 200 mg or 250 mg, $10 - 15 are being asked and also paid. By comparison, look at the price at the pharmaceutical dealer: Ten vials of generic testosterone cypionate, each in a strength of 200 mg/ml in a 10 ml multi-injection vial, cost $99.99. Thus for 1 ml one pays less than $1.(!) For further information as to the effects of Testosterone cypionate, see also Testosterone enanthate.

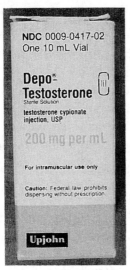

T. cyp. by Upjohn/U.S.

Testosterone cypionate by Leo / Spain, 100mg

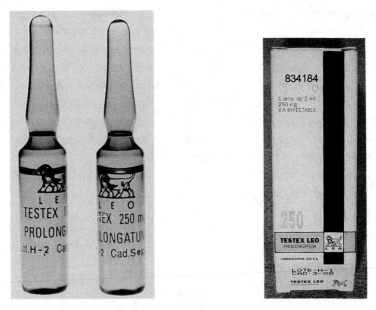

Testex Leo, T. Cypionate by Leo / Spain, 250mg/amp.

TESTOSTERONE PROPIONATE

Substance: Testosterone propionate

Trade names

Agovirin inj.	25 mg/ml;	Leciva CZ
Androfort-Richt.	10, 25 mg/ml;	Gedeon Richter HU
Androlan (o.c.)	50, 100 mg/ml;	Lannett U.S.
Hybolin Imp. (o.c.)	25, 50 mg/ml;	Hyrex U.S.
Neo-Hombreol	50 mg/ml;	Organon NL
Testex (o.c.)	50, 100 mg/ml;	Pasadena U.S.
Testex Leo	25 mg/ml;	Leo ES
Testosteron	5, 10 mg/ml;	Galenika YU; Hemofarm YU
Testosteron	25, 50 mg/ml;	Galenika YU; Hemofarm YU
Testosteron	10 mg/ml;	Sopharma BG
T. Berco Suppositorien	40 mg/S;	Funke G
T.-Prop. Disp.	10, 20 mg/ml;	Disperga A
T. Jenapharm (o.c.)	25 mg/ml;	Jenapharm G
T. Streuli	5, 10, 25, 50 mg/ml;	Streuli & CO.AG A
T.prop. Eifelfango	10, 25 mg/ml;	Eifelfango G
T.prop. Eifelfango	50 mg/ml;	Eifelfango G
T. Vitis (o.c.)	10, 25 mg/ml;	Neopharma G
T. propionicum	10, 25 mg/ml;	Polfa PL
Testosterone Prop. (o.c.)	50 mg/ml;	Quad U.S.,Lilly U.S.
Testosterone Prop.	100 mg/ml;	Steris U.S.
Testoviron	10, 25 mg/ml;	Schering I, ES
Testoviron	50 mg/ml;	Schering I, GR
Testovis	50, 100 mg/ml;	SIT I
Testovis Deposit.	50, 100 mg/ml;	SIT I
Triolandren	20 mg/ml;	Ciba Geigy CH
Virormone	25, 50 mg/ml;	Paines & Byrne GB
Virormone	100 mg/ml;	Paines & Byrne GB

Veterinary:

Ara-Test	25 mg/ml, 10 ml;	Aranda Laboratories Mexico

Testogan	25 mg/ml, 50 ml;	Laguinsa Costa Rica, Nicaragua, Panama, Guatemala, El Salvador, Honduras, Ecuador, Dom. Rep.
Testosterona 50	50 mg/ml, 10 ml;	Brovel Mexico

Testosterone propionate, after Testosterone cypionate and enanthate, is the third injectable testosterone ester that needs to be described in detail. This makes sense because, unlike cypionate and enanthate, both of which are widely used and well-spread in Europe, proprionate is little noticed by most athletes. The reader will now certainly pose the question of why the characteristics of an apparently rarely used substance are described in detail. At a first glance this might seem a little unusual but when looking at this substance more closely, there are several reasons that become clear. Testosterone propionate is used on so few occasions in weightlifting, powerlifting, and bodybuilding not because it is ineffective. On the contrary, most do not know about propionate and its application potential. One acts according to the mottos "what you don't know won't hurt you" and "If others don't use, it can't be any good." We do not want to go this far and call propionate the most effective testosterone ester; however, in certain applications it is superior to enanthate, cypionate, and also undecanoate because it has characteristics which the common testosterones do not have.

The main difference between propionate, cypionate, and enanthate is the respective duration of effect. In contrast to the long–acting enanthate and cypionate depot steroids, propionate has a distinctly lower duration of effect. The reader learns how long this time is from the package insert of the German Jenapharm GmbH for their compound "Testosteron Jenapharm" (see list with trade names): "Testosterone proprionate has a duration of effect of 1 to 2 days." In their book *Doping-verbotene Arzneimittel im Sport* Dr. Dirk Clasing and the well-known professor, Dr. Manfred Donike of the University for Sports Education, Köln state: "When injected intramuscularly the duration of effect of the testosterone esters depends on the type of esters (Testosterone enanthate and cypionate have longer effects than propionate and acetate) and on the amount of testosterone. With 50 mg Testosterone propionate i.m. elevated testosterone levels are observed for about 1-2 days; with 250 mg Testosterone enanthate i.m., about 1-2 weeks." It is a simplification to argue that propionate is only a quickly effective testosterone that must be injected more often. Based on the highly androgenic effect, propionate as well as enanthate and cypionate is very appropriate for the buildup of strength and muscle mass. An eye-catching difference, however, is that the athlete "draws" distinctly less water with propionate and visibly lower water retention occurs. Since propionate is quickly effective, often after only one or two days, the athlete experiences an increase of his training energy, a better pump, an increased appetite, and a slight strength gain. As an initial dose most athletes prefer a 50-100 mg injection. This offers two options: First, because of the rapid initial effect of the propionate-ester one can initiate a several-week-long steroid treatment with Testosterone enanthate. Those who cannot wait until the depot steroids become effective inject 250 mg of Testosterone enanthate and 50 mg of Testosterone propionate at the beginning of the treatment. After two days, when the effect of the propionates decreases, another 50 mg ampule is injected. Two days after that, the elevated testosterone level caused by the propionate begins to decrease. By that time, the effect of the enanthates in the body would be present, no further propionate injections would be necessary. Thus the athlete rapidly reaches and maintains a high testosterone level for a long time due to the depot testo. This, for example, is important for athletes who with Anadrol 50 over the six-week treatment have gained several pounds and would now like to switch to testosterone. Since Anadrol 50 begin its "breakdown" shortly after use of the compound is discontinued, a fast and elevated testosterone level is desirable.

The second option is to take propionate during the entire period of intake. This, however, requires a periodic injection every second day. Best results can be obtained with 50-100 mg per day or every second day. The athlete, as already mentioned, will experience visibly lower water retention than with the depot testosterones so that propionate is well-liked by bodybuilders who easily draw water with enanthate. A good stack for gaining musclemass would be, for example, 100 mg Testosterone propionate every 2 days, 50 mg Winstrol Depot every 2 days, and 30 mg Dianabol/day. Propionate is mainly used in the preparation for a competition and used by female athletes. And in this phase, dieting is often combined with testosterone to maintain muscle mass and muscle density at their maximum. Propionate has always proven effective in this regard since it fulfills these requirements while lowering possible water retention. This water retention can be tempered by using Nolvadex and Proviron. A combination of 100 mg Testosterone propionate every 2 days, either 50 mg Winstrol Depot/day or 76 mg Parabolon every 2 days, and 25 mg Oxandrolone/day help achieve this goal and are suitable for building up "quality muscles."

Women especially like propionate since, when applied properly, androgenic-caused side effects can be avoided more easily. The trick is to increase the time intervals between the various injections so that the testosterone level can fall again and so there is an accumulation of androgens in the female organism. Women therefore take propionate only every 5-7 days and obtain remarkable results with it. The androgenic effect included in the propionate allows better regeneration without virilization symptoms for hard-training women. The dosage is usually 25-50 mg/injection. Higher dosages and more frequent intervals of intake would certainly show even better results but are not recommended for women. The duration of intake should not exceed 8-10 weeks and can be supplemented by taking mild and mostly anabolic steroids such as, for example, Primobolan, Durabolin, and Anadur in order to promote the synthesis of protein. Men who do not fear the intake of testosterone or the possible side effects should go ahead and give propionate a try. The side effects of propionate are usually less frequent and are less pronounced. The reason is that the weekly dose of propionate is usually much lower than with depot testosterones. A daily injection of 50 mg amounts to a weekly dose of 350 mg while several depot injections easily launch the milligram content of testosterone into the four-figure range. When compared with enanthate and cypionate, propionate is also a "milder" substance and thus better tolerated in the body. Those who are convinced that they need daily testosterone injections should consider taking propionate. The reader receives interesting information from the package insert of the German Eifelfango Company for its compound Testosterone propionate. Under "Dosage Instructions and Form of Application" the following is written: "To promote the formation of red blood cells 300 to 750 mg (1000 mg per week, if necessary) of Testosteronpropionat-Eifelfango can be taken, divided into 2 to 3 injections per week." Athletes who want to incorporate the entire 1000 mg into only two injections can look forward to a 10 ml testo cocktail. In our opinion it makes sense to take the propionate once ore twice a week in larger quantities because the short duration of effect leads to high fluctuations of the testosterone level. This will result in unsatisfying results and create a hotbed for undesired side effects. The key to success with propionate lies in the regular intake of relatively small quantites (50-100 mg every 1-2 days.)

Several powerlifters and weightlifters often inject a larger quantity of Testosterone propionate on the day before the competition so that with high testosterone and androgen levels they can break new records the following day. In particular, the earlier East German weightlifters knew perfectly how to use this technique because they had known for some time that: "a high testosterone level, in the belief of the East German sports physicians, is absolutely necessary for top performances" (Berendonk, *Doping*, page 219). In competitions with doping tests the additional intake of epitestosterone guarantees a negative test result. Especially in the immediate preparation for a competition Testosterone propionate is excellent in overbridging so that doping tests can be passed. The use of the rapidly effective propionate can overbridge a possible performance breakdown caused by a premature discontinuance of the steroid compounds. In addition, propionate prevents a positive test result. The athlete thus kills two birds with one stone. This is possible because, after the injection of propionate, the T/E value in the urine decreases faster than the testosterone concentration in the blood does. The T/E value falls below the critical value of six while the performance level is maintained. All the different things propionate can do in this phase are described in detail by Brigitte Berendonk in her book *Doping-Von der Forschung zum Betrug*: "Clausnitzer, Höppner, and Häcker had already pointed out early (1982) that the T/E value of 6 was too high and that by cleverly timed injections or other forms of application of suitable testosterone esters (e.g. Testosterone propionate) one could exceed the normal range but still test under 6 (p.221). Thus several male and female athletes in critical training phases could adjust their performance levels without 'being detected'... When injecting Testosterone propionate, both the testosterone level in the blood (up to more than 250%) and the T/E value in the urine rise rapidly. After this single injection the T/E value decreases rapidly but the testosterone concentration in the blood falls more slowly. One should note that the T/E value stays at a level above six, the threshold value for a positive doping test, for more than three days after the injection... Clausnitzer et al. (1) (1982) found out... that with a lower dose of testosterone propionate (25 mg) the threshold value is exceeded only during the first few days."

Although the side effects of propionate are similar to the ones of enanthate and cypionate these, as already mentioned, occur less frequently. However, if there is a predisposition and very high dosages are taken, the known androgenic-linked side effects such as acne vulgaris, accelerated hair loss, increased growth of body hair and deep voice can occur. An increased libido is common both in men and women with the use of propionate. Despite the high conversion rate of propionate into estrogen gynecomastia is less common than with other testosterones. The same is true for possible water retention since the retention of electrolytes and water is less pronounced. The administration of testosterone-stimulating compounds such as HCG and Clomid can, however, also be advised with propionate use since it has a strong influence on the hypothalamohypophysial testicular axis, suppressing the endogenous hormone production. The toxic influence on the liver is minimal so that a liver damage is unlikely (see also Testosterone enanthate). What athletes dislike most about propionate are the frequent injections that are necessary.

As for frequent injections: The Testosterone Berco Suppositories by the German company Funke can help. This is quite an unusual testosterone compound since these are suppositories. The suppositories contain 40 mg Testosterone propionate and are introduced into the body through the rectum. This form of intake also has an additional advantage. The substance Testosterone propionate is reabsorbed very rapidly through the intestine. The official price in German pharmacies for a package with 18 suppositiories is around $9. The price on the black market is about $35.

The "Propis," as they are often called, are rarely found on the black market. The German compound Testosterone propionate "Eifelfango" is preferred by many athletes because of its excellent quality and low price. Ten 50 mg ampules, according to the "Rote Liste 1995" in Germany cost $22. On the black market one occasionally finds the institutional packages by Eifelfango containing fifty 50 mg ampules (see photo). The price per ampule should be approximately $6 on the black market.

(1) et al.: and collaborator

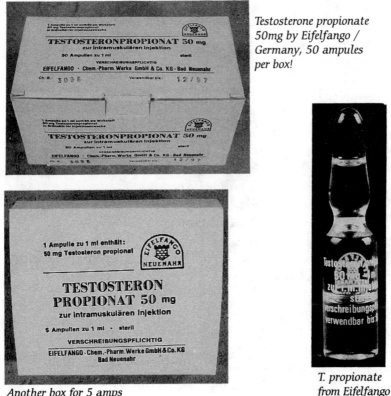

Testosterone propionate 50mg by Eifelfango / Germany, 50 ampules per box!

Another box for 5 amps

T. propionate from Eifelfango

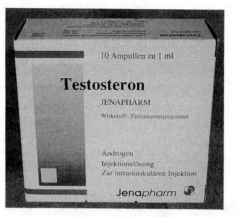

Testosterone propionate by Jenapharm / Germany

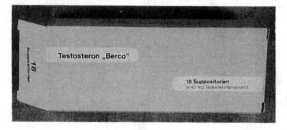

Testosterone suppositories by Berco / Germany, 40mg

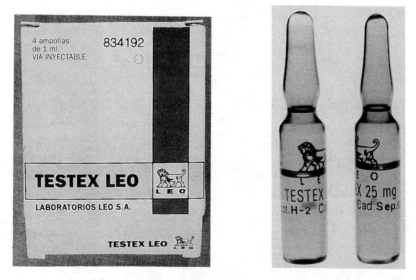

Spanish Testosterone propionate from Leo, 25mg/1ml amp.

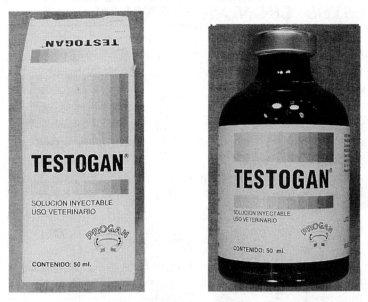

Testogan, Veterinary T. propionate by Progan / Rep. Dom.,
50ml vial, 25mg/ml

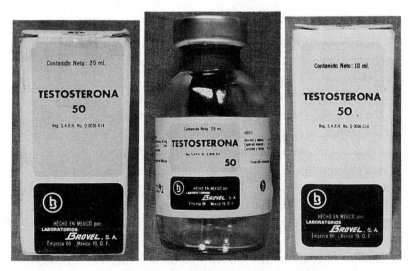

Testosterona 50, Veterinary Testosterone propionate by Brovel / Mexico,
50mg/ml, 10ml and 20ml vials

TESTOSTERONE SUSPENSION

Substance: Testosterone aqueous suspension

Trade names

Agovirin-Depot	50 mg/2 ml;	Biotika CZ
Androlan Aqueous (o.c.)	25, 50, 100 mg/1ml;	Lannet U.S.
Androlin (o.c.)	100 mg/1ml;	Lincoln U.S.
Andronaq-50 (o.c.)	50 mg/1ml;	Central U.S.
Histerone Injection (o.c.)	100 mg/1ml;	Hauck U.S.
Histerone Injection	100 mg/1 ml;	Roberts U.S.
Malogen (o.c.)	25, 50, 100 mg/1 ml;	Forest Pharm U.S.
Malotrone (o.c.)	25, 50 mg/1 ml;	Bluco U.S.
Tesamone (o.c.)	25, 50, 100 mg/1 ml;	Dunhall U.S.
Testolin (o.c.)	25, 50, 100 mg/1 ml;	Pasadena Res. U.S.
Testosterone-Aqueous	100 mg/1 ml;	Legere U.S.
Testosterone-Aqueous	50, 100 mg/1 ml;	Schein U.S., Steris U.S.

Another injectable testosterone compound which is used in powersports circles is Testosterone suspension. In the previous chapters, so far, as we have talked only about oil-dissolved testosterone we are now able to offer one of the oldest testosterone compounds. In the following we will describe the testerone dissolved in water. For athletes who readily and frequently work with the popular oily testosterone suspensions (Sustanon 250 or Testosterone Depot) this information might be something new. Besides, water-dissolved testosterone was actually the first injectable steroid. In Europe during the 1940's injectable testosterone was used in the German armed forces to increase aggressiveness and stamina, and also in the recovery of undernourished prisoners of war. This was nothing else but crystalline testosterone mixed with water. Russian weightlifters began experimenting with this testosterone compound during the late 1940's and broke one world record after another. Since, at the time, pure testosterone without additional esters was used, the substance remained in the body for only a few hours requiring daily injections, and often several per day. By first injecting the testosterone molecules with an ester, such as for example isobutyrate (in Agovirin), it was possible to prolong the duration of effect up to about one week.

Since testosterone is dissolved in water the substance reaches the blood after only 1-2 hours so that it is unnecessary to wait longer for results, a circumstance that is advantageous to powerlifters. In the last one or two weeks before a competition Testosterone suspension is injected daily, often resulting in amazing strength gains. Often Testo-suspension is even injected on the day of competition to increase the athlete's aggressiveness and self-esteem in order to approach the difficult tasks with the right attitude. For this purpose, this rapidly effective testosterone is considerably more effective than methyltestosterone (see chapter "Methyltestosterone"). Among East European powerlifters and competing bodybuilders Testo-suspension has always been a "last minute secret." Especially women can reliably change their estrogen/testosterone ratio to break down excessive water and to give softer muscles a visibly better hardness in a short time. Female bodybuilders usually have considerably greater difficulty in getting their calves and upper thighs in contest condition than their upper bodies. Often you see a female bodybuilder on the posing platform with striated pecs, delts and triceps, whereas her lower body appears flat and soft. For several reasons the estrogen level can be too high, leading to an increase in the hormone aldosterone. Since aldosterone regulates the body's own water househould—meaning the higher the aldosterone level, the more water is stored by the organism—it is important to keep the aldosterone level as low as possible. Finally it is known that women by nature store fat and water mostly in their upper thighs. An optimal form for a competition requires a high androgen level with a minimal estrogen level. Women who on the day of competition never obtain the right muscle hardness can usually achieve a significant performance enhancement by injecting 25-50 mg Testosterone suspension daily during the last 1-4 days before the competition.

However, men also use Testosterone supension during the last 10-14 days before a bodybuilding competition to make an all-out effort for optimal muscle hardness. Athletes report outstanding results when Testo-suspension is used together with the carbohydrate/loading technique. The athlete unloads his body by depriving it of carbohydrates for several days and begins loading carbohydrates three days before a competition with the goal of storing as much glycogen in the muscle cells as possible. He can optimize this process by taking 50-100 mg Testosterone suspension/day. Testosterone suspension considerably boosts the storing of glycogen in the muscle cells and, since dissolved in water, becomes effective almost immediately. As is known, glycogen also bonds with water in the muscle cells, which manifests itself in extremely tight and full muscles.

In the mass-gaining phase Testosterone suspension is only rarely used. With respect to strength and muscle mass the gains, as with all injectable testosterone esters, are very good; however, this testosterone compound requires frequent injections in order to reach a performance-enhancing dosage. With 100 mg every 1-2 days rapid muscle gains can usually be obtained and the strength increase can usually be felt from the first day. However a stale effect remains since the injection of testosterone dissolved in water is not only extremely unpleasant but the pain at the injection area remains for some time. To endure such martyrdom for several weeks is not to everone's liking. The gains disappear rapidly after use of the compound is discontinued.

As for side effects, the same is true for Testosterone suspension as it is for other testosterone esters. A considerable part of the compound is converted into dihydrotestosterone in the body so that acne and hair loss occur quite frequently. The endogenous testosterone production is already considerably lower after only a few days of use which during a several week long intake could result in testicular atrophy and temporary impotence. Women experience the usual virilization symptoms. An enormously increased sexual drive in both sexes is noted, often from the first day of intake. The same can be said about the influence of Testo suspensions on the aggression potential. Men are also at risk to develop a prostate condition or possible gynecomastia.

Testosterone suspension is usually difficult to find on the black market. In Europe there is only the 2 ml ampule of the Czech brand name Agovirin-Depot. This steroid contains only 25 mg testosterone isobutyrate/ml. In order to get the effective dosage quite voluminous injections are necessary. The ampule has a pink-colored label which can be scratched off or smeared. The price on the black market for a 2 ml ampule, according to reports by athletes, is around $6 - 10. Since steroid molecules do not easily bond with water (see also the chapter "Winstrol Depot"), Testosterone suspension must be well-shaken before the injection. Those who let the injection rest for more than 30 minutes without touching it will notice that the testosterone separates from the watery solution in form of a white, crystalline powder. After shaking, an opaque, white mixture is formed in the ampule. Fakes of the American versions are probable; however, no fakes of the Czech Agovirin-Depot have been found.

Agovirin Depot by Biotika / CZ   *Agoviron ampules*

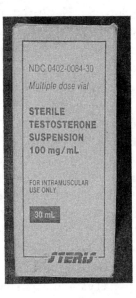

*Testosterone suspension by Steris / U.S.,
100mg/ml, 30ml vial*

TESTOSTERONE HEPTYLATE
THERAMEX

Substance: testosterone heptylate

Trade names

Testosterone Heptylate Theramex
   50 mg/ml, 100 mg/ml, 250 mg/ml;   Theramex France

Testosterone heptylate is another injectable testosterone ester. The French pharmaceutical Company Laboratoire Theramex is the only firm worldwide which manufactures this compound and has been selling it under the drug name Testosterone Heptylate Theramex since 1955. Testosterone Heptylate Theramex rates high among French, Belgian, and Dutch athletes since it is readily available, extremely economical, and very effective. The compound Testosterone heptylate, like every injectable testosterone, has a strong androgenic effect which goes hand in hand with a distinct anabolic component. Testosterone heptylate is excellent for the rapid buildup of strength and muscle mass. When looking at the gain rates of bodybuilders who use Testosterone Heptylate Theramex this steroid, milligram for milligram, seems to have a stronger effect than enanthate, cypionate, and propionate.

Testosterone Heptylate Theramex leads to a strong protein synthesis in the muscle cell and promotes recovery to a high degree. Athletes report an enormous pump effect during the workout and a noticeable appetite increase after only days of intake. The gains usually consist of solid muscle since the water retention that occurs during intake is usually lower than with enantathe and cypionate. Competing bodybuilders and athletes normaly become puffy because of the testosterone injections should give Testosterone Heptylate Theramex a try.

The French pharmaceutical reference guide *Dictionnaire Vidal* writes in its 1994 edition that Testosterone Heptylate Theramex has a duration of effect of 20 days. Although this theoretically allows long injection intervals athletes usually inject it at least once a week. Men usually prefer the 250 mg strength while women use the more conservative 50 mg or 100 mg version. With 250-750 mg/week most male bodybuilders get on well and make great progess. An effective combination in the buildup phase, for example, would be 500 mg Testosterone Heptylate Theramex/week, 200 mg Deca-Durabolin/week, and 30 mg Dianabol/day. Female bodybuilders, by taking 50 mg Testosterone Heptylate Theramex/week, 50 mg Deca-Durabolin, and 15 mg Oxandrolone/day can obtain good strength and muscle gains without fear of virilization symptoms.

The potential side effects of Testosterone heptylate are comparable to those of enantathe and cypionate. Since, when taking Testosterone Heptylate Termex, a certain percentage of the substance converts into estrogens in the body, athletes will also have to take antiestrogens. The administration of testosterone-stimulating substances such as HCG, Clomifen citrate or Cyclofenil could be indicated since the endogenous testosterone production is considerably reduced by Testosterone heptylate. Young bodybuilders should keep in mind that Testosterone heptylate could lead to an early stunting of growth since it prematurely closes the epiphysial growth plates. The manufacturer Laboratoire Theramex also seems to be aware that sick and fragile persons are not the only people interested in its compound. In the package insert, under "Special Remarks," one reads the following sentence: "Attention, athletes! The components of this compound could result in a positive doping test." Very attentive, don't you agree? This is called customer service.

As for the availability on the black market it can be noted that Testosterone Heptylate Theramex is not as widespread as cypionate and enanthate. The French, however, can purchase Testosterone Heptylate Theramex at a ridiculously low price in pharmacies. Following, please find the actual French pharmacy prices:

50 mg: 9.90 francs (approx. $2.05) per package
including two ampules;
100 mg: 12.50 francs (approx. $2.55) per package
including two ampules;
250 mg: 20.70 francs (approx. $4.25) per package
including two ampules.

The original French ampules have a dark-red imprint which cannot be scratched off and is easily felt when touched with the finger. There is no label. An eye-catching characteristic is the white ring on the neck of the ampule and is approximately 6 mm above the ampule cap. The injection liquid is of a light-yellow color. There are two ampules in a plastic bed. On the back side, the bed is welded to an aluminum foil pull-off. The package box is green on the front and has a removable, white paper label with the expiration date on the back. On the black market the 250 mg version usually costs $12 - 15. Unfortunately there are also several fakes of Testosterone Heptylate Theramex (see chapter "The Problem with Fake Steroids"). Those who want to be absolutely certain of buying an original should buy only ampules in a double pack, i.e. the ampules that are welded into the plastic bed and to the aluminum foil.

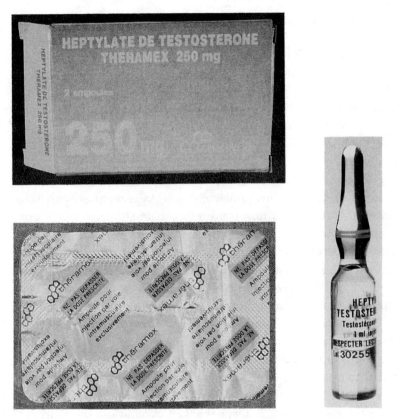

Testosterone Heptylate by Theramex / France, box, blister and ampule, 250mg

---

TESTOVIRON DEPOT 50, 100, 135, 250

Substance: Testosterone propionate, Testosterone enanthate

Trade names

Testoviron Depot 50	20 mg prop., 55 mg enant./ml;	Schering G, A, ES, I
Testoviron Depot 100	25 mg prop., 110 mg enant./ml;	Schering G, CH, A, ES,GR, I, NL, PT, Rep. Dom.

| Testoviron Depot 135 | 25 mg prop.; 110 mg enant./ml; | Schering DK, S |
| Testoviron Depot 250 | 50 mg prop.; 200 mg enant./ml; | Schering I |

This injectable testosterone compound is a mixture of two different testosterone esters. The Testosterone propionate leads to a quick effect which, due to the depot effect of Testosterone enanthate, remains for several days. Since it has an intense anabolic effect together with a strong androgenic effect, it is very suited for the buildup of strength and muscle mass. As is normal with testosterone, water retention occurs but in most cases is less pronounced than with pure enanthate. Theoretically, although long intervals between the injections are possible, athletes usually inject the drug at least once a week. The dosages are normally between 2 and 4 ml/week. Most often Testoviron Depot 100 is used since a favorable amount of the substance is present. For further information on its characteristics, see chapters on Testosterone enanthate and propionate. Although it should be a very interesting preparation for testo fans, it is much less used when compared to Sustanon, Omnadren and pure Testosterone enanthate. The reason is that the "Propionate-enanthate combi package" is rarely found on the U.S. black market. In addition, the other testosterone versions, milligram for milligram, are much cheaper. Testoviron Depot 100 in German pharmacies costs about $10 (Red List 1995). The price on the black market for TD 100, according to information from athletes, is around $10 - 15 per ampule. It must be observed that the ampules of the Spanish Testoviron Depot by Schering are made of brown glass. There are currently no fakes of this compound. During our interviews we noted that athletes who use this preparation do not buy it based on its special substance combination but because they are happy to be able to find an original injectable testosterone at all.

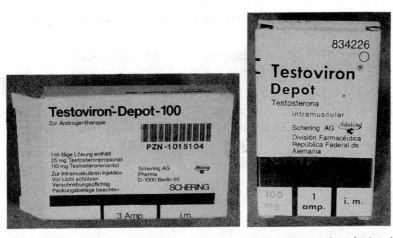

German Testoviron–Depot-100

Testoviron Depot by Schering / Spain, 100mg/ml

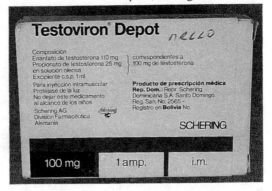

Testoviron Depot by Schering / Rep. Dom.

TRIACANA

Substance: tiratricol

Trade names

Nidolin	0.35 mg tab.;	Chelfar GR
Teatrois	0.35 mg tab.;	Theranol FR
Triacana (o.c.)	0.35 mg tab.;	Medgenix FR
Triacana (o.c.)	0.2 cream;	Medgenix FR

Triacana	0.35 mg tab.;	Marcofina FR, Sidus
		Argentina
Triacana	0.2 cream;	Marcofina FR

Triacana belongs to the group of thyroid hormone preparations. Its substance tiratricol is a precursor of the iodiferous thyroid hormone, L-triiodthyronine (L-T3). L-T3, together with another iodiferous thyroid hormone, L-T4 (L-thyroxine), is produced in the thyroid and is the dinstinctly stronger and more effective of these two hormones. School medicine use Triacana in the treatments of obesity and hyperthyroidism (e.g. Jod-Basedow phenomenon; goiter). Hyperthyroidism is an abnormal function of the thyroid gland in which the amount of secretion by the thyroid hormone is above average. The thyroid stimulating hormone (TSH) stimulates the thyroid gland to produce more L-T3 and L-T4. By the use of Triacana an excessive release of TSH can be avoided.

In the medical arsenal of bodybuilders Triacana has had a firm place since the late 1970's. After all, its lipolytic (fatburning) effect is sufficiently known. This is due to the hypermetabolic state, increased irritability, and especially higher body temperature (generation of heat) during the intake of Triacana. These are factors which help the competing bodybuilder break down fat more easily. By a caloric intake which is higher than usual it is still possible to obtain a lower bodyfat content together with good muscle hardness. Although Triacana enjoys the reputation among athletes as a strong and especially effective fatburning thyroid hormone preparation, this preparation is a rather mild, well-tolerated and relatively harmless compound. The often-made comparison with the two L-T3 thyroid gland hormone compounds, Cytomel and Thybon, is a poor comparison since Triacana, microgram for microgram, has a considerably lower effect. Even the more moderate L-T4 thyroid hormone drugs such as Synthroid or L-thyroxine are stronger than the substance tiratricol. The French pharmaceutical reference guide Vidal 1994 also confirms this on page 1416: "Pharmacologic examinations were able to verify that tiratricol compared to L-triiodthyronine (L-T3) and L-throxine (L-T4) has a lower biological effect."

In order to achieve a visible fat-reducing effect most athletes must usually take 10-14 tablets/day. Generally, two 0.35 mg tablets are taken on the first day of intake and with two tablets added each successive day until 10-14 tablets/day are taken. The half-life time of tiratricol is 5-7 hours, so Triacana is usually taken 3-4 times daily. This guarantees a constant quantity of the substance in the blood and thus a continued effect. Many athletes, in the meantime, are combining Triacana with Clenbuterol or Ephedrine and report considerably better fat breakdown than when Triacana alone is taken. Among competing female bodybuilders and participants at the Miss Fitness pageant, in particular, the simultaneous administration of 8-10 Triacana tablets/day and 80-100 mcg Clenbuterol/day is a favorite. A series of bodybuilders use Triacana in combination with growth hormones in order to meet the body's increased thyroid hormone need during STH treatment (see chapter "Growth Hormones"). The theoretical approach seems to be correct but Triacana is not an "ideal" thyroid hormone drug. The preparation Thyreocomb from the German Berlin-Chemie Company taken with a combination of the iodiferous L-T3 and L-T4 thyroid hormones would be more suitable.

As for the duration of application the opinions of athletes vary greatly. Some use Triacana for only 4 weeks, mostly because they are afraid of a thyroid dysfunction. Others take it over a period of months. When looking at the physiological characteristics of the substance tiratricol, it becomes easier to make more accurate indications as to a possible duration of intake and the potential health risks that go along with the use. When taken in a dosage of 0.6 mg/day the reduction in the body's own TSH release can be obtained; with increased dosages it can be completely suppressed. The fear that the TSH release will be continuously disturbed or suppressed after using the medication is without reason since this is a reversible, temporary process. "Already 2-3 weeks after the intake is discontinued the TSH release is completely normalized" (from Vidal 1994, page 1498). With this background knowledge and based on the experiences of several athletes we would choose an intake interval of 10-12 weeks.

Potential side effects such as palpitations, tremors, irregular heart-beat, dizziness, restlessness, nervousness, and excessive perspiration occur mostly during the first few days of intake. Those who increase their dosages slowly and evenly over several days as suggested usually have few problems with Triacana. Toward the end of the intake period a step by step reduction in the daily tablet dosage is better than abruptly discontinuing the substance. In summary one can say that Triacana is a (mild) alternative to the strong L-T3 thyroid hormone compounds such as Cytomel or Thybon with their strong side effects. It has only a lower lipolytic effect but can be taken over a prolonged period of time. Mistakes made during the intake are forgiven with Triacana rather than with Cytomel. Ambitious bodybuilders and athletes who are able to responsibly use strong medication choose Cytomel; persons who, however, fear side effects, who do not know much, or believe that "more is better," should select Triacana.

On the black market the French Triacana is usually found without difficulty. One hundred tablets are packaged in a box containing four push-through strips of 25 tablets each. The tablets are white and have neither an imprint nor a break indentation. The price on the black market is usually $60 - 80 per box while the French pharmacy price is approx. $12. There are currently no available fakes of Triacana. It must be observed, however, that the manufacturer is now a different company. The French Triacana is no longer manufactured by Medgenix Pharma Company but by Laboratoires Marcofina. The imprints on the box and on the back of the push-through strip are therefore slightly different (see photos).

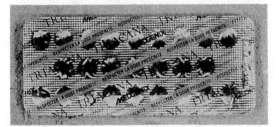

Triacana, box and blister by Medgenix from France

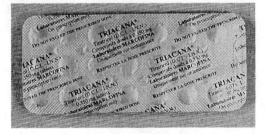

Triacana, box and blister by Marco-fina / France

WINSTROL DEPOT

Substance: stanozolol

Trade names

Winstrol Depot	50 mg/ml;	Zambon ES, I
Winstrol (o.c.)	50 mg/ml;	Winthrop GR
Strombaject (o.c.)	50 mg/ml;	Winthrop G, B
Stromba	50 mg/ml;	Sterling Research GB
Stromba (o.c.)	50 mg/ml;	Sterling-Winthrop S;
		Winthrop S

Veterinary:

Winstrol V	50 mg/ml;	Winthrop U.S.
Winstrol V	50 mg/ml;	Upjohn U.S.

"In my point of view the drug is absolutely useless in every respect. There are no appreciable side effects in conventional doses of Winstrol, but in any dose there is no appreciable gain in size nor strength. It is of no more use with woman or men. I don't even think that it's effect as a placebo is effective, a pink aspirin might be a better choice for a placebo drug." (*The Practical Use of Anabolic Steroids with Athletes* by Dr. Robert Kerr.)

"I do not find Winny V injection to be an effective steroid no matter how it is used." (*Underground Steroid Handbook 2* by Daniel Duchaine.)

"In Germany there are places where this medication is considered as poisonous as rat poison." (*Anabolic Handbook* by Michael Hagenbruch.)

"Stanozolol is an anabolic steroid which has been increasingly used since 1984 in high-performance sports. Up until 1984 Stanozolol was regarded as ineffected by several underground publications" (*Hormonelle Regulation und Psychophysische Belastung im Leistungssport* by R. Häcker and H.De Marees.)

These statements are in clear contrast to the well-spread use of Winstrol in several sports disciplines. Winstrol is one of the favorite steroids in general, as confirmed by many positive doping cases. Stanozolol, for example, was one of the substances which enabled Ben Johnson to achieve his magic sprints. It also gave this exceptional athlete a distinctly visible gain in hard and defined quality muscles, possibly making quite a few bodybuilders envious. During the first doping-tested professional bodybuilding championships, the Arnold's Classic 1990, the winner, Shawn Ray, and the enormously massive Canadian pro, Nimrod King, tested positive on Winstrol (stanozolol), (FLEX, July 1990). The Track and Field World Championships 1993 in Stuttgart also brought two positive "stanozolol cases" to light. To make a long story short: Winstrol is a very effective steroid when used correctly. It is important to distinguish between the two different forms of administration of stanozolol, since the injectable Winstrol Depot is distinctly more effective than the oral Winstrol. Thus it is preferred by most athletes.

What is special about the injectable Winstrol Depot is that its substance is not—as is common in almost all steroids—dissolved in oil; it is dissolved in water. Although almost every steroid-experienced bodybuilder knows this difference, the practical application of this knowledge rarely occurs: the injection-free intervals of the compound Winstrol Depot must be distinctly shorter than with the other common steroids. Simplified, this means that Winstrol Depot 50 mg/ml must be injected much more frequently than the oil-dissolved steroids (e.g. Primobolan, Deca-Durabolin, Sustanon 250, Parabolan, etc.). The reason for this is the relative low half-life time of steroids. Those dissolved in water must be injected at least every second day, and best results are observed at a daily injection of 50 mg. The substance stanozolol is a precursor to the dihydrotestosterone and consequently, it prevents Winstrol Depot from aromatizing into estrogens with water retention occuring only rarely. Based on these characteristics the main application of Winstrol Depot is clearly defined in bodybuilding: preparation for a competition. Together with a calorie-reduced diet which is rich in protein Winstrol Depot gives the muscles a continuously harder appearance. Winstrol Depot is usually not used as the only steroid during dieting since, based on its low androgenic component, it does not reliably protect the athlete from losing muscle tissue. The missing, pronounced, androgenic effect is often balanced by a combined intake with Parabolan. The combination of Winstrol Depot 50 mg/day and Finaject 30 mg/day, until a few years ago, was THE competition stack. Since original Finaject has been phased out for years Parabolon has taken over its place. Depending on the athlete's performance level, the athlete usually takes 50 mg Winstrol Depot every 1-2 days and Parabolan 76 mg/1.5 ml every 1-2 day. Although there is no scientific proof of a special combined action between Winstrol Depot and Parabolan, based on several practical examples, a synergetic effect seems likely. Other steroids which athletes successfully combine with Winstrol Depot during the preparation for a competition include Masteron, Equipoise, Halotestin, Oxandrolone, Testosterone propionate, Primobolan, and HGH.

Winstrol Depot, however, is not only especially suited during preparation for a competition but also in a gaining phase. Since it does not cause water retention rapid weight gains with Winstrol Depot are very rare. However, a solid muscle gain and an overproportionally strong strength increase occur, usually remaining after use of the compound is discontinued. Bodybuilders who want to build up strength and mass often combine Winstrol Depot with Dianabol, Anadrol 50, Testosterone, or Deca-Durabolin. With a stack of 100 mg Anadrol 50/day, 50 mg Winstrol Depot/day, and 400 mg Deca-Durabolin/week the user slowly gets into the dosage range of ambitious competing athletes. Older athletes and steroid novices can achieve good progress with either Winstrol Depot/Deca-Durabolin or Winstrol Depot/Primobolan Depot. They use quite a harmless stack which normally does not lead to noticeable side effects. This leaves steroid novices with enough room for the "harder" stuff which they do not yet need in this phase. Winstrol Depot is mainly an anabolic steroid with a moderate, androgenic effect which, however, can especially manifest itself in women dosing 50 mg/week and in men dosing higher quantities. Problems in female athletes usually occur when a quantity of 50 mg is injected twice weekly. The effect of Winstrol Depot decreases considerably after a few days and thus an injection at least twice weekly is justified. However, an undesired accumulation of androgens in the female organism can occur, resulting in masculinization symptoms. Some deep female voices certainly originated with the intake of Winstrol Depot. However, a dose of 50 mg Winstrol Depot every second day in ambitious female athletes is the rule rather than the exception. Other non-androgenic side effects can occur in men as well as in women, manifesting themselves in headaches, cramps, changes in the HDL and LDL values, and in rare cases, in high blood pressure. Possible liver damage can be estimated as very low when Winstrol is injected; however, in large doses an elevation in the liver values is possible. Since Winstrol Depot is dissolved in water the injections are usually more uncomfortable or more painful than is the case with oily solutions.

Although there are many fakes of the injectable Winstrol, the original "Winny" as it is lovingly called by its users, is easily recognized based on its unusual form of administration. At a first glance the content of the ampule is only a milky, white, watery solution which, however, has distinct characteristics. Original "Winny" is recognized because the substance separates from the watery injection fluid when the ampule is not shaken for some time. When the ampule is left flat in its ampule box or, for example, stands upright on a table, the substance accumulates as a distinctly visible white layer on the lower side of the glass and can only be mixed with the watery fluid if shaken several times or rolled forward and backward. An ampule containing 1 ml of suspension and its 50 mg dissolved stanozolol should normally separate a white layer in the size of almost a thumbnail. The athlete thus can easily determine whether his injectable Winstrol is actually stanozolol or is rather underdosed. Do not buy ampules or glass vials which contain more than 1 ml of suspension since an original injectable Winstrol is only available in one-milliliter glass ampules. The original Spanish ampules by Zambon have an unusually large round shape and a brown imprint. In the meantime there are several well-made fakes (see chapter *The Problem with Fake Steroids*).The Italian ampules by Zambon can also be easily recognized since this is a small push-through ampule which has a large round shape and comes with a blue imprint. The imprint on the Italian and Spanish Winnies can be felt well with your fingernail. Faked stanozolol usually comes in commercial, narrow ampules.

Since Winthrop Company discontinued the formerly well-distributed Strombaject, the international black steroid market carries the Spanish and Italian Winstrol Depot of Zambon Company almost exclusively. The price for a 50 mg Winstrol Depot ampule lies between $10 - 15 on the black market.

When injected daily Winstrol Depot can become a very expensive compound. It also has the disadvantage that, because of the frequent injections, the already-mentioned scar tissue will develop in the gluteal region (buttocks) which leads many athletes to inject Winstrol in their shoulders, arms, legs or even calves. Although this was originally intended as an expedient, injecting Winstrol Depot into certain muscles has become increasingly popular since athletes have noticed that this leads to an accelerated growth of the affected muscle. An American pro bodybuilder who is known for his cross-striated, horseshoe-shaped triceps owes this in considerable part to his regular "triceps Winstrol-Depot injections." A confusion with the also often used Esiclene is excluded. Athletes who want to avoid daily injections usually take 2-3ml Winstrol Depot twice a week. In the U.S. injectable stanozolol is manufactured only for veterinary medicine. It is distributed under the name Winstrol V by Winthrop and Upjohn Companies (see photos). Unfortunately there are several fakes of Winstrol Depot. In the meantime, the chances of finding the Spanish or Italian Winstrol in the U.S. are quite high.

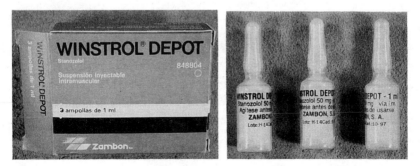

Winstrol by Zambon / Spain

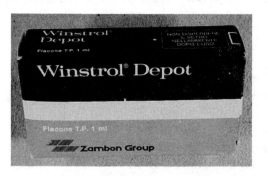

Winstrol Depot by Zambon / Italy

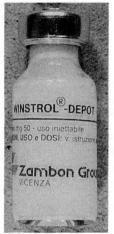

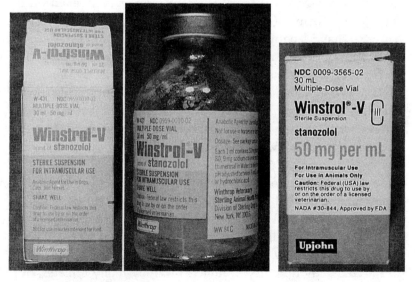

Winstrol-V, veterinary stanozolol by Winthrop/ U.S., 50mg/ml, 30ml vial

Winstrol-V by Upjohn/ U.S., veterinary stanozolol

WINSTROL TABLETS

Substance: stanozolol

Trade names

Stromba (o.c.)	5 mg tab.;	Winthrop CH, DK, NL, G, Sterling-Winthrop S, Sterling Research GB,Berger A
Stromba	5 mg tab.;	Winthrop B
Stromba	5 mg tab.;	Sterling-Health HU, CZ
Winstrol (o.c.)	2 mg tab.;	Winthrop GR, PT
Winstrol	2 mg tab.;	Winthrop Pharm. U.S., Upjohn U.S., Zambon ES, I

Much of what has been said about the injectable Winstrol is more or less also valid for the oral Winstrol. However, in addition to the various forms of administration there are some other differences so that a separate description—as with Primobolan—seems to make sense. For a majority of its users Winstrol tablets are noticeably less effective than the injections. We are, however, unable to give you a logical explanation or scientific evidence for this fact. Since the tablets are 17-alpha alkylated it is extremely unlikely that during the first pass in the liver a part of the substance will be deactivated, so we can exclude this possibility.

One of the reasons for the lowered effectiveness of the tablets, in our opinion, is that most athletes do not take a high enough quantity of Winstrol tablets. Considering the fact that the injectable Winstrol Depot is usually taken in a dosage of 50 mg/day or at least 50 mg every second day and when comparing this with the actual daily quantity of tablets taken by many athletes, our thesis is confirmed. Since, in the meantime, most athletes only get the 2 mg Winstrol tablets by Zambon one would have to take at least 12-25 tablets daily to obtain the quantity of the substance one receives when injecting. For two reasons, this, however, cannot be realized by most athletes. On the one hand, at a price of approximately $0.70 - $1 for one 2 mg tablet on the black market the cost for this compound is extremely high. On the other hand, after a longer intake such a high quantity of tablets can lead to gastrointestinal pain and an undesired increase in the liver values since the tablets —as already mentioned— are 17-alpha alkylated and thus are a considerable stress on the liver. Male athletes who have access to the injectable Winstrol Depot should therefore prefer this form of administration to the tablets. Women, however, often prefer the oral Winstrol This, by all means, makes sense since female athletes have a distinctly lower daily requirement of stanozolol, usually 10-16 mg/day. Thus the daily quantity of tablets is reduced to 5-8 so that gastrointestinal pain and increased liver values occur very rarely. Another reason for the oral intake in women is that the dosage to be taken can be divided into equal doses. This has the advantage that— unlike the 50 mg injections—it does not lead to a significant increase in the androgens and thus the androgenic-caused side effects (virilization symptoms) can be reduced. Athletes who have opted for the oral administration of Winstrol usually take their daily dose in two equal amounts mornings and evenings with some liquid during their meals. This assures a good absorption of the substance and, at the same time, minimizes possible gastrointestinal pain.

Stanozolol tablets are manufactured in the 5 mg version by only Winthrop Company in Belgium and by Sterling-Health in Hungary and in the Czech Republic. Even on the European black market these tablets are found only on rare occasions. Usually the Spanish and Italian Winstrol by Zambon show up. Their tablets are manufactured exclusively in push-through strips of ten or twenty pieces and can be easily identified since they are pink and indented. The Spanish Winstrol tablets also have a "W" punched in on their back and are packaged in push-through strips of 20 pieces each while the Italian version by Zambon contains only 10 tablets in a push-through strip and has no engraving such as "W". The American Winstrol tablets by Winthrop and Upjohn also contain 2 mg stanozolol tablets; however, they are not in push-through strips but in glass vials. Fake stanozolol tablets come in push-through strips of ten or twenty tablets each and apparently contain 5 mg of stanozolol. A well-distributed fake is a small brown glass vial with the label Stromba (stanozolol) Anabolic Steroid, 100 tablets 5 mg, Winthrop USA (see chapter on Fakes.)

Winstrol tabs by Zambon / Spain, box and blister

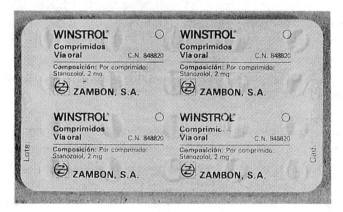

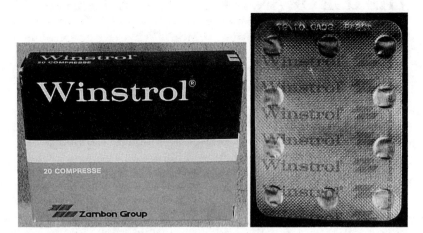

Winstrol tabs by Zambon / Italy

*Stromba, 5mg tabs
from Belgium, made
by Sanofi/Winthrop*

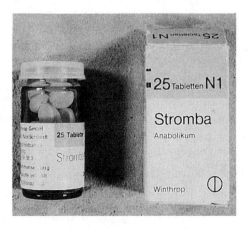

*Stromba, 5mg tabs by
Winthrop / Germany,
out of commerce*

THE USE OF ANABOLIC/ANDROGENIC STEROIDS

There is no doubt that steroids are most effective when they are administered in a sensible and logical manner. This requires that the athlete observe certain rules. A basic requirement is that the steroid intake be divided into cycles. By a steroid cycle most mean a 10-12 week application of a single compound or a combination of two to three different steroids, followed by an interval of discontinuance of the same length. As is often shown, such a type of administration does not make much sense for a continuous and lasting progress since a considerable part of the strength and muscle mass that was gained gets lost during the long interval of discontinuance. The reasons why athletes choose such an intake schedule are attributed to the fact that there are those who continuously emphasize that steroids are principally only effective after a period of several weeks and injections more than twice a year considerably increase the risk of damage to the organs. With regard to the apparently limited effect it must be said that, if that was true, today's pro bodybuilding would be at the same performance level as thirty years ago. As to the second contention, the risk of damage to the body, let us tell you that if that was true there would be no more bodybuilding pros because all would be dead. The fact is non-stop use of steroids in ambitious athletes is the norm, resulting in continuously higher performance levels as can easily be recognized when looking at the photos in the various "muscle magazines." If, for example, an athlete becomes a world champion at the age of 24, this not only shows his perfect genetics for this sport but also a period several years long of almost non-stop steroid consumption.

By a sensible cyclic application of anabolic/androgenic steroids we mean several timed intake schedules which, on the one hand, observe the basic rules for the intake of steroids and, on the other hand, are coordinated with the goal of the individual athlete and particularly the characteristics of the relative steroids that are taken. Principally, one should begin with a relatively low dosage and gradually and evenly increase it in order to maintain the positive nitrogen balance in the muscle cell. Since oral steroids begin to show their effect within several days and result in quite a rapid saturation of the receptors, their intake is limited to 6-8 weeks. Following that, the use of steroids is discontinued or the athlete switches to another (oral) steroid. It is also shown that the combination of two to three steroids in moderate dosages is much more effective and also guarantees a longer duration of effect than when only one steroid is taken in a high dosage. With the right combinations one will be able to obtain a synergetic effect if the athlete pays attention to selecting steroids which have different influences on the factors of strength, tissue buildup, and recovery. A stack which fulfills these requirements, for example, would be Deca-Durabolin as an anabolic basic steroid with depot character, Sustanon to promote recovery and general mass buildup, and Oxandrolone to increase body strength. The stimulation of various receptor types over a limited period leads to the best results. The buildup effect can be maintained over several months if the steroid combination is completely changed no later than every eight weeks, if the athletes alternate the stronger and mostly androgenic cycles with the weaker and predominantly anabolic cycles and when the dosages are continuously graduated. A long and even reduction of the doses at the end of the cycle helps in normalizing the body functions and preparing the organism for a suspension of the intake. The following listed programs are examples of how in our experience athletes use steroids while considering these factors. The reader should not take these as recommendations or as suggestions, nor as indications for the use of anabolic/androgenic steroids. The following examples are only to be considered informative.

Example 1

Week	Dianabol 5 mg tab.	Deca 100 mg/ml	HCG 5000 i.u.	Nol./Prov. 10/25 mg tab.	Primobolan Depot 100mg/ml	Winstrol Depot 50 mg/ml
1	15 mg/d	200 mg/w				
2	20 mg/d	200 mg/w				
3	25 mg/d	200 mg/w				
4	30 mg/d	300 mg/w				
5	30 mg/d	400 mg/w		10/25 mg/d		
6	25 mg/d	300 mg/w		10/25 mg/d		
7	20 mg/d	200 mg/w		10/25 mg/d		
8	15 mg/d	100 mg/w	7000 i.u./w	10/25 mg/d		
9			7000 i.u./w	10/25 mg/d		
10			7000 i.u./w	10/25 mg/d		
11					200 mg/w	100 mg/w
12					200 mg/w	150 mg/w
13					300 mg/w	150 mg/w
14					300 mg/w	150 mg/w
15					200 mg/w	100 mg/w
16					100 mg/w	50 mg/w
17			7000 i.u./w			
18			7000 i.u./w			

d = day   w = week

This program includes two extremely popular steroid combinations. The Dianabol/Deca-Durabolin stack has proven effective for the rapid buildup of strength and muscle mass. In order to avoid an increased estrogen level and excessive water retention the combined intake of Nolvadex and Proviron, both antiestrogens, is sensible. HCG will normalize the probably reduced testosterone production. The following Primobolan/Winstrol stack will not increase the body weight and the strength but will help to harden the newly-gained muscle mass. If the athlete suspends this program with the Dianabol/Deca intake a considerable performance breakdown is very likely to follow. Due to the cyclic application of the various steroids the saturation of the receptors is minimized. The two-week suspension of intake (weeks 9 and 10) helps bring back the endogenous testosterone production and gives the steroid receptors time to regenerate so that the following Primo/Winstrol stack can be effective. Beginning in week 17 the intake of anti-catabolic substances such as Clenbuterol should also be considered in order to absorb the beginning catabolic phase and to maintain a maximum of strength and muscle mass. Athletes use Clenbuterol for this purpose in a dosage of 120 mcg/ day over a period of 4-8 weeks. Those who would like to make fast progress limit the intake of Clenbuterol to only four weeks until the next steroid cycle while athletes with more patience continue over the entire eight weeks. The suspension of the intake during the ninth and tenth weeks by some is also overbridged with Clenbuterol instead of HCG. Example one is usually suitable for steroid novices; however, lower dosages must be used.

Example 2

Week	Dianabol 5 mg tab.	Deca 100 mg/ml	Testosterone Enanthate 250 mg/ml	HCG 5000 i.u.	Clenbuterol 0.02 mg tab.
1	15 mg/d	200 mg/w			
2	20 mg/d	200 mg/w			
3	25 mg/d	200 mg/w			
4	30 mg/d	200 mg/w			
5	35 mg/d	200 mg/w			
6	40 mg/d	200 mg/w		7000 i.u./w	
7		400 mg/w	500 mg/w	7000 i.u./w	
8		400 mg/w	500 mg/w		
9		400 mg/w	500 mg/w		
10		200 mg/w	500 mg/w		
11		200 mg/w	500 mg/w		
12		100 mg/w	250 mg/w	7000 i.u./w	
13		50 mg/w		7000 i.u./w	80 mgc/d
14-20				7000 i.u./w	120 mcg/d

With this program considerable gains in strength and muscle mass can be obtained. Deca is used as a strong anabolic steroid which promotes protein synthesis but is only moderately androgenic and is non-toxic over the entire 12 weeks. The intake of Dianabol is limited to six weeks since the gains with Dianabol occur more rapidly but often slow down after about six weeks. The athlete therefore takes optimal advantage of its effect. Since Dianabol is 17-alpha alkylated and thus potentially liver-toxic, the short time of intake is appropriate in this regard. The intake of Testosterone enanthate as the strongest of the three, together with its pronounced androgenic effect, gives another distinct performance improvement. By stimulating the various steroid receptors considerably better results can be obtained than if the athletes had taken Dianabol and Deca over the entire 12 weeks. HCG and Clenbuterol help to increase the testosterone production or to reduce the catabolic phase after use of the compound is discontinued. Also in this case the interval of the subsequent intake of Clenbuterol depends on the goals of the individual athlete. Experience has shown that an interval of four weeks is sufficient to create the basis for a further steroid cycle. The athlete should also consider the intake of Nolvadex/Proviron.

Example 3

Week	Anadrol 50 mg tab.	Sustanon 250 mg/ml	Dianabol 5 mg tab.	Parabolan 76 mg/1.5ml	Deca 100 mg/ml	HCG 5000 i.u.	Clenbuterol 0.02 mg tab.
1	50 mg/d						
2	100 mg/d						
3	150 mg/d	250 mg/w					
4		500 mg/w					
5		500 mg/w	20 mg/d				
6			25 mg/d				
7			30 mg/d	152 mg/w			
8				228 mg/w			
9				228 mg/w	400 mg/w		
10					400 mg/w		
11					400 mg/w		
12					200 mg/w	7000 i.u./w	
13						7000 i.u./w	80 mcg
14						7000 i.u./w	120 mcg
15-20							120 mcg

This is one of the favorite steroid cycles. Every steroid is used for only three weeks. The idea behind this is that the individual steroid cannot lead to a saturation of the receptors as is the case if one or two steroids is taken over the entire period. This leads not only to good overall results but also to a continuous effect. Possible lower dosages also result in lower side effects. Usually one begins with the strongest, most effective steroid and then, step by step, changes to the less androgenic and less toxic steroids. The intake of Nolvadex/Proviron should be considered especially during weeks 3-7 and 12-14. Example 3 is not for steroid novices.

Example 4

Week	Oxandrolone 2.5 mg tab.	Winstrol Depot 50 mg/ml	Parabolan 76 mg/1.5ml	Masteron 100 mg/2ml	Clenbuterol 0.02 mg tab.	Cytomel 25 mcg tab.
1	20 mg/d	100 mg/w	76 mg/w		80 mcg/d	
2	20 mg/d	150 mg/w	152 mg/w		120 mcg/d	
3	25 mg/d	150 mg/w	152 mg/w		120 mcg/d	
4	25 mg/d	150 mg/w	152 mg/w		120 mcg/d	
5	25 mg/d	150 mg/w	152 mg/w		120 mcg/d	
6	30 mg/d	150 mg/w	228 mg/w		120 mcg/d	
7	30 mg/d	150 mg/w	228 mg/w		120 mcg/d	
8	30 mg/d	150 mg/w	228 mg/w		120 mcg/d	
9	30 mg/d	150 mg/w		300 mg/w	120 mcg/d	25 mcg/d
10	30 mg/d	150 mg/w		300 mg/w	120 mcg/d	50 mcg/d
11	30 mg/d	150 mg/w		300 mg/w	120 mcg/d	75 mcg/d
10	30 mg/d	150 mg/w		300 mg/w	120 mcg/d	100 mcg/d

This example is a commonly used program for the preparation of a competition. The listed steroids normally do not aromatize and do not draw water. Parabolan maintains an elevated androgen level and prevents an overtraining syndrome. Since Parabolan is quite toxic many athletes switch to the similar effective but "milder" Masteron after a few weeks. The other option is to use Masteron during the first four weeks and to begin the intake of Parabolan only in the fifth week. The intake of Nolvadex and Proviron is possible but not really necessary. Clenbuterol accelerates the burning of fat which during the later weeks is further increased by the additive intake of Cytomel. Many athletes often use Example 4 to build up a high-quality muscle system. The strength gain that goes with it is considerable. The use of Clenbuterol and Cytomel is not applicable in this case and the dosages are usually reduced in the last 3-4 weeks. Steroid novices should not take this steroid treatment.

Example 5

Week	Anadrol 50 mg tab.	Sustanon 250 mg/ml	Winstrol Depot 50 mg/ml	Parabolan 76 mg/1.5ml	Dianabol 5 mg tab.	Deca 100 mg/ml
1	50 mg/d	250 mg/w				
2	100 mg/d	250 mg/w				
3	100 mg/d	500 mg/w				
4	100 mg/d	500 mg/w				
5	100 mg/d	250 mg/w				
6	50 mg/d	250 mg/w				
7			100 mg/w	152 mg/w		
8			150 mg/w	152 mg/w		
9			150 mg/w	152 mg/w		
10			150 mg/w	152 mg/w		
11			150 mg/w	152 mg/w		
12			100 mg/w	152 mg/w		
13					20 mg/d	200 mg/w
14					25 mg/d	300 mg/w
15					30 mg/d	400 mg/w
16					25 mg/d	300 mg/w
17					20 mg/d	200 mg/w

Athletes who use steroids over several months without suspension —there are many of those—often combine two steroids, mostly one oral and one injectable, hoping that a synergetic effect will occur. In order to assure a continued effect over a prolonged period of time without increasing the dosages to boundless quantities, steroid users often switch to a completely different combination after six weeks. Several athletes often suspend the intake for two weeks and overbridge this time by taking HCG and/or Clenbuterol. It is not uncommon for bodybuilders in the eighteenth week to start over again or continue the intake with a new combination. The use of testosterone-stimulating compounds (HCG, Clomid) and antiestrogens (Nolvadex, Proviron) should be considered in certain phases. The non-stop use of anabolic/androgenic steroids is customary, particularly with ambitious (competing) athletes. In the Winstrol/Parabolan combination some replace Parabolan with Primobolan Depot. The goal sought by switching these two compounds is the creation of a pattern of a strongly androgenic potentially toxic cycle (Anadrol, Sustanon) followed by a predominantly anabolic, less toxic cycle (Winstrol, Primobolan), followed by another more androgenic cycle (Dianabol, Deca). By doing this not only are serious side effects avoided but the androgenic receptors in the muscle cell also have time to recover. Empirical data confirms that continuous progress can be made by taking steroids over several months when two to three compounds are combined in moderate dosages over a relatively short period.

Example 6

Week	Oxandrolone 2.5 mg	Andriol 40 mg caps.	Deca-Durabolin 100 mg/ml	Clenbuterol 0.02 mg tab.
1	10 mg/d	200 mg/d	100 mg/w	
2	15 mg/d	200 mg/d	200 mg/w	
3	20 mg/d	240 mg/d	200 mg/w	
4	20 mg/d	240 mg/d	200 mg/w	
5	20 mg/d	240 mg/d	200 mg/w	
6	20 mg/d	240 mg/d	200 mg/w	
7	20 mg/d	240 mg/d	200 mg/w	
8	20 mg/d	240 mg/d	200 mg/w	
9	15 mg/d	240 mg/d	200 mg/w	
10	10 mg/d	200 mg/d	200 mg/w	
11		160 mg/d	100 mg/w	
12			50 mg/w	
13				80 mcg/d
14				120 mcg/d

This is a relatively "mild" steroid program that brings good results with only few side effects. Oxandrolone leads to an increase in strength, does not aromatize, does not suppress the body's own testosterone production and is only lightly androgenic. Since Oxandrolone, in the meantime, is difficult to find some use the 2 mg Winstrol tablets instead. Deca accelerates protein synthesis and is not potentially liver-toxic. The Andriol included in the Testosterone undecanoate promotes regeneration, does not aromatize, is not 17-alpha alkylated and has no distinct, inhibiting effect on the gonadal regulatory cycle. Athletes who experience changes in their liver values or fear a liver dysfunction should not take Oxandrolone. Some take Clenbuterol instead. The additional use of HCG, Nolvadex and Proviron is usually not required. Since Clenbuterol works well during the steroid-free time athletes take it after such a treatment. The reason for a twelve-week uninterrupted interval of intake is that this cycle does not cause rapid gains. Instead, it needs a certain initial time to allow even, continuous improvements over several weeks. Discontinuing or changing to another compound after 4-6 weeks would be counterproductive in this case.

Example 7

Week	Oxandrolone 2.5 mg	Deca 50 mg/ml	Testo Prop. 50 mg/ml	Clenbuterol 0.02 mg tab.	Dianabol 5 mg tab.	Primo bolan S 25 mg tab.	Winstrol Depot 50 mg/ml
1	10 mg/d	50 mg/w	50 mg/w				
2	12.5 mg/d	50 mg/w	50 mg/w				
3	15 mg/d	50 mg/w	50 mg/w				
4	15 mg/d	50 mg/w	50 mg/w				
5	12.5 mg/d	50 mg/w	50 mg/w				
6	10 mg/d	50 mg/w					
7-10				80 mcg/d			
11					10 mg/d		
12					10 mg/d		
13					10 mg/d		
14						50 mg/d	50 mg/w
15						75 mg/d	50 mg/w
16						50 mg/d	50 mg/w
17-24				80 mcg/d			

This steroid program is used by women. Oxandrolone gives a distinct strength gain and is only minimally androgenic. Because of its predominantly anabolic effect Deca helps transform the gained strength into solid body tissue. Use of the shorter effective Durabolin should be given a preference; however, due to its poor availability this is almost impossible. Deca is much more readily available. Testosterone propionate promotes regeneration; however, based on its possible androgenic-caused side effects it should not be taken for more than four weeks. Propionate and Deca are injected in intervals of 3-4 days. Women who have problems with this take Deca and Propionate alternately once every two weeks. The short duration of intake, a maximum of six weeks, is important as is the following four-week suspension of the steroid. Although 10 mg Dianabol are as androgenic as the daily testosterone production in a man, most women can usually make remarkable progress in a short time. The Primo tablets are not 17-alpha alkylated, only slightly androgenic and work quite well when combined with the injectable Winnies. The use of 20 mg Nolvadex/day should be considered in the first four weeks and possibly in weeks 11-13. This can reduce possible side effects; at the same time, however, the effectiveness of this program is reduced as well.

Example 8

Week	Anadrol 50 mg tab.	Sustanon 250 mg/ml	Parabolan 76 mg/1.5ml	Dianabol 5 mg tab.	HCG 5000 i.u.	Clenbuterol 0.02. mg tab.
1	50 mg/d	250 mg/w	76 mg/w			
2	100 mg/d	500 mg/w	152 mg/w			
3	150 mg/d	500 mg/w	152 mg/w			
4	150 mg/d	500 mg/w	152 mg/w			
5		500 mg/w	152 mg/w	40 mg/	7000 i.u./w	
6		500 mg/w	152 mg/w	35 mg/d	7000 i.u./w	
7		500 mg/w	152 mg/w	30 mg/d		
8		500 mg/w	76 mg/w	25 mg/d		
9		250 mg/w		20 mg/d		
10		250 mg/w		15 mg/d		
11				10 mg/d	7000 i.u./w	
12					7000 i.u./w	80 mcg/d
13					7000 i.u./w	120 mcg/d
14-20						120 mcg/d

With this program athletes usually achieve an enormous improvement in strength and muscle mass. Anadrol works very quickly and stores a high amount of water. Since it is very liver-toxic and has many side effects, athletes often change to Dianabol after four weeks. Further, the gain obtained by taking Anadrol usually subsides considerably after this time. The strong androgenic steroids Sustanon and Parabolan also continue to promote the growth, considerably accelerate regeneration, and strongly increase aggressiveness. The side effects, in part, can be considerable. Most athletes also use Nolvadex and/or Proviron. Despite all these safety measures in the suspension phase (HCG, Clomid, Clenbuterol, and possibly Cytadren) a distinct breakdown cannot be avoided. Since Parabolan is difficult to obtain, some use Deca instead (200–400 mg/week). For health reasons, in particular, Anadrol and Parabolan should not be taken for a prolonged period of time. Athletes who do not have much experience with steroids should not use this program.

Example 9

Week	Dianabl 5 mg tab.	Deca 100 mg/ml	Testosterone Enanthate 250 mg/ml	Oral-Turinabol 5 mg tab.	HCG 5000 i.u.
1	20 mg/d				
2	25 mg/d	200 mg/w			
3	30 mg/d	300 mg/w	250 mg/w		
4		400 mg/w	500 mg/w	30 mg/d	
5			750 mg/w	35 mg/d	
6				40 mg/d	7000 i.u./w
7	30 mg/d				7000 i.u./w
8	25 mg/d	400 mg/w			
9	20 mg/d	300 mg/w	750 mg/w		
10		200 mg/w	500 mg/w	40 mg/d	
11			250 mg/w	35 mg/d	
12				30 mg/d	7000 i.u./w
13					7000 i.u./w
14					7000 i.u./w

This program is quite similar to Example 3 except that three instead of two compounds are taken. In this program the athlete takes increasing dosages during the first six weeks and in the following six weeks continues the program with lower dosages. It is interesting to note during the second half of the intake the athlete continues to achieve further, distinct gains. Another significant performance improvement can be noticed during weeks 9 and 10. Because of the various graduated dosages and different steroid combinations receptor saturation is avoided and growth is continuously forced. In weeks 3-5 and 9-10 the intake of antiestrogens might be indicated. In order to maintain the achieved results Clenbuterol is often used beginning in week 13. Steroid novices should not use such a program.

Example 10

Week	Dianabol 5 mg tab.	Winstrol Depot 50 mg/ml	Testosterone Propionate 50 mg/ml	Clenbuterol 0.02 mg tab.
1	15 mg/d	50 mg/w	50 mg/w	
2	20 mg/d	100 mg/w	100 mg/w	
3	25 mg/d	150 mg/w	150 mg/w	
4	30 mg/d	150 mg/w	150 mg/w	
5	30 mg/d	150 mg/w	150 mg/w	
6	25 mg/d	150 mg/w	150 mg/w	
7	20 mg/d	150 mg/w	150 mg/w	
8	15 mg/d	100 mg/w	150 mg/w	
9		50 mg/w	100 mg/w	
10			50 mg/w	80 mcg/d
11-20				120 mcg/d

This program is included in athletes' most frequently used system. One combines two or three steroids over a period of 8–12 weeks. An oral compound is usually combined with an injectable compound. The dosage is first increased, then maintained for some time, and finally reduced. Some also use antiestrogens such as HCG and/or Clenbuterol at the end of the treatment.

These programs are only some examples of how athletes can take steroids. Based on the large number of various steroid compounds there are numerous other intake schedules. As for the indicated dosages there are also many differences. Some will only smile at these schedules while others might go ahead and try them. Others will not even have the financial resources for such a program. For some it will not be feasible because they   are unable to find the desired steroids. Some have an aversion to injections or for health reasons or a predisposition (e.g. in women) cannot use every compound. The athlete should not go ahead and choose one of these examples without criticism. Just because something is written in a book or because someone has tried it does not mean that it is suitable for you. Try to learn from this information and perhaps accept one or the other for your needs. Despite all this, the use of anabolic/androgenic steroids is a matter of "trial and error." Some find the right compounds, combinations, and dosages for them quite rapidly and continue using these compounds successfully while others are continuously on a (desperate) search of the magic method.

THE SIDE EFFECTS OF STEROIDS

In general, and especially through the mass media, anabol/androgenic steroids are usually frowned upon. Steroids are not only accused of causing many severe side effects, but also there are ethical and moral doubts involved. The mass media's sensational news coverage has contributed greatly to this negative information. During the anti-steroid campaign, the press deliberately used those cases of illness that occurred during steroid intake and were documented in the scientific literature to warn and scare everyone taking these drugs. Due to a possible negative publicity it was not mentioned, however, that in most of the cases the patients already had severe diseases and health problems prior to steroid therapy. Steroids are basically prescription drugs that influence various physiological processes and consequently, have potential side effects. When diagnosing these side effects one must tell the toxic from the hormone-induced side effects. This important difference is usually omitted by the official authorities, in part, due to pure ignorance but also on purpose, since only in this way the spread of lies and false information is possible.

In the category of the toxic side effects of anabolic/androgenic steroids, the potential effects on the liver are most apparent. These can manifest themselves in various dysfunctions of the liver. In the literature, cases have been mentioned where it came to a cholastasis (bile obstruction in the liver), a peliosis hepatis (bloodfilled cavities in the liver tissue, cysts), or liver cancer with the use of anabolic/androgenic steroids. It is of great importance that these manifestations could almost exclusively be seen in those patients who previously had undergone a long-term steroid therapy and already had extensive liver damage or suffered from other internal diseases prior to the intake of steroids. It is of further interest that the administered steroid medication consisted almost exclusively of the 17-alpha alkylated, oral androgenic steroids. Especially the potentially liver-toxic substances methyltestosterne and oxymetholone were given in the course of therapy without suspension for several years. Evidence that steroids cause similar liver damage in healthy athletes could only be found in one or two rare cases, which is neither of statistic relevance nor allows for the preconception to expect liver damage by consumption of anabolic/androgenic steroids. "Insofar as a connection between steroid intake and tumor development could be established, until now, there is no evidence where testosterone or a testosterone ester is responsible for liver cancer. The reason had always been the androgen/anabolic with an alkyl substitute on the C-17 alpha of the steroid molecule... Accordingly it seems that test-osterone and its esters are not (or are slightly) liver-toxic... Toxic liver damage: this, as mentioned above, is only expected with 17-alpha alkyl derivatives... With a proper choice of the drug, there is no danger here." (From: *Doping - verbotene Arzneimittel im Sport*, Dirk Clasing, Manfred Donike, et al, pages 60 and 63). At this time it once again must be stressed that nearly all the liver-damaging results have been found in patients whose physicians prescribed steroids for the treatment of already existing, serious diseases. Although one cannot exclude the possibility of liver damage and delayed reaction in the future, empirical data shows that even with repeated, excessive, and prolonged intake of the potentially liver-toxic 17-alpha alkylated steroids by athletes, these symptoms rarely occur. In order to avoid any possible risks, one should forego the use of 17-alpha alkylated steroids. Since a total abandonment of these steroids is impossible for most athletes one should follow strict guidelines regarding the duration of intake and the dosage. Far-sighted athletes will therefore interrupt their steroid regimes in regular intervals by either stopping steroid intake alltogether or switching to a (potentially) non-toxic steroid (usually injectable). In many cases the problematic steroid will be combined with one or more "milder" steroids which interact in order to keep the dosage of the first at a moderate rate level without diminishing the effectiveness. In conclusion, one can say that the toxic, critical side effects on the liver occur mostly in those patients who have previously been ill and have received 17-alpha alkylated steroids as their treatment over longer periods of time.

It is recommended that athletes using oral steroids have their liver function routinely checked by a qualified physician.

The second category of possible undesirable side effects arising during the use of anabolic/androgenic steroids will be summarized under the term "hormone-induced side effects." Simplified, these are the side effects experienced (in various stages) by healthy athletes. Here, once again, one must also distinguish according to age and sex, since children, young adults, and women react more intensely to the exogenous ingestion of hormones than male adults. Since some side effects have been noticed in both men and women and young adults, we have dispensed with a gender and age-specific classification. The following information describes some of the most common hormone-induced side effects that may occur in association with the steroid consumption by athletes.

INHIBITION OF THE GONAD CYCLE:

Anabolic/androgenic steroids exert an inhibiting effect on the hypothalomohypophysial testicular axis (see chapter: The Significance and Function of Testosterone). This results in a suppression of the normal testicular function which may further result in a reduced testosterone production, a decreased spermatogenesis, and a testicular atrophy. The degree of suppression depends on the duration of the steroid intake, the administered steroid, and the dosage of the steroid. During the beginning of steroid administration one may often notice an increase in libido which, in time can fall below normal standards. With the intermittent use of testosterone-stimulating substances, e.g. HCG, these problems may, in some cases, be avoided or at least reduced. Upon completion of the steroid regime, HCG is given to reactivate the testicular function. It should be mentioned that all these side effects are completely reversible. "... in all the cases, after the androgens/anabolics were discontinued, a restitutio ad integrum (a complete recovery to the original condition) occurred with regard to gonadotropins, size of testes, synthesis of the endogenous testosterones, and even spermatogenesis (!).

Conclusion: The effect of androgens/anabolics on the gonad cycle is reversible. Infertility is not always noticeable. The fear that athletes may be childless after the use of anabolics is ungrounded." (From: Doping - verbotene Arzneimittel im Sport, Dirk Clasing, Manfred Donike, et al, p. 61.)

WATER AND SALT RETENTION:

Most steroids cause a water and electrolyte imbalance in the body. This results in an increased storage of water and sodium which further results in a swelling of tissue (edema). This process is desirable to a certain degree since the muscle cell, the joints, and connective tissue profit from it. The results are a quick and distinct increase of muscle size and volume, a strength gain, due to a better leverage ratio, a stronger connective tissue, and a "lubrication" of the joints which often guarantees injury-free training. The drawback is an increased water retention in the skin and blood. With the first it is more a cosmetic problem because the tissue especially under the eyes and the cheeks becomes puffy thus giving the athlete the typical bloated "off-seasonal full-moon steroid face". The second deposit is more serious because health problems may arise. Since the organ is overloaded with additional water, the heart and blood vessels must transport more fluid than normal through the body, thus possibly resulting in an elevated blood pressure. The degree of the water and salt retention depends, for the most part, on the type and dosage of the given steroid and on the predisposition of the individual. This factor is noticeable in both males and females.

FEMINIZATION:

Feminization can occur in male athletes in the form of breast swelling (gynecomastia), increased tendency toward fatty deposits, and extremely soft muscles. These symptoms are largely due to aromatization, meaning the partial conversion of a steroid into the female sex hormones (estrogen). The development of female characteristics may take place when the estrogen level increases significantly. Especially after discontinuing the steroid regime one finds this problem most aggravating since the athlete's androgen level is low but, at the same time, the estrogen level is elevated. In conjunction with this, it is interesting that estradiol (an estrogen) has an inhibiting effect on the male gonad cycle (see chapter: The Importance and Function of Testosterone). One can determine that an elevated estrogen level reduces the body's own testosterone production. The elevation of the estrogen level and the extent of feminization depend on the dosage and the type of steroids given. The determining factor, however, seems to be the constitution of each individual, since some show no gynecomastia while others already notice pain and swelling of the mammary gland with a dose of only 10 mg Dianabol/day. The additive intake of anti-estrogens like Nolvadex, Proviron, or Fludestrin can be helpful in most cases. In general, after the steroids have been discontinued, the gynecomastia will slowly regress by itself. Since many are on the drugs year round, an operative removal of the undesired mammary tissue is no rarity. An elevated estrogen level is the "mortal enemy" of every competitive athlete because even with an extremely low fatty content, one never really becomes hard. An excessive estrogen portion can directly negatively influence the psyche of the male athletes (see psychic changes).

CHANGES IN THE SKIN:

For the most part this is noticed with the developing of acne. An already existing acne may get worse or a non-existing acne may be evoked. Male athletes are less affected than female athletes. The development of acne and its extent here also depends largely upon the individual's constitution, the consumed steroids, and the dosage. The receptors of the sebaceous glands have a high affinity to DHT so that one must assume that steroids, which are partially transformed into DHT in the body, are the main cause. This may also be the reason why the injectable testosterone, followed by Anadrol and Dianabol, are the number one cause of acne. With the increased sebaceous gland production oily skin occurs and, in combination with bacteria and dead skin, the pores become clogged. This can further, depending on one's disposition, lead to blackheads, pimples, pustules (filled with pus), or even cystes. Males experience the acne mainly on the back, shoulders and chest, less in the face, whereas female athletes are mainly affected in the face and on back and shoulder. Not only is there damage to the body's largest organ, the skin, but the noticeable acne is, even for an outsider, a distinct sign of steroid use. For many, acne can also be a psychic strain, presenting problems especially then, when small scars and holes remain in the face. An acne which is localized to the face only, can be minimized with the local application of e.g. benzoyl peroxide or ointments containing antibiotics. If larger body areas are involved, UV radiation (tanning studios) or the oral use of prescription drugs such as Tetracycline (antibiotic) or Accutane may be helpful. One must observe that oral antibiotics have an antianabolic effect and should, also, not be used in connection with sun exposure or UV radiation. Females may permanently lose their normal, soft skintone since the skin can become large-pored and uneven due to the continued use of androgenic steroids, antiestrogens, and excessive sun exposure. Stretch marks and skin fissures in the shoulder/chest area, on the inside of the upper arm, and on the buttocks, are often seen in athletes using steroids. This usually results from too quick a weight increase since the skin cannot adapt quickly enough or stretch.

PSYCHIC CHANGES:

Men and women , especially with the use of androgenic steroids, high dosages and long-term consumption, can develop aggressive behavior. The advantage of this is that one can train harder and more intensely. The disadvantage is that some cannot properly cope with this, thus letting their aggressions out on others. They become easily irritated, impatient, and inclined toward quick temper and anger outbursts. In extreme cases this can lead to an increase in the use of violence which has caused the breakup of relationships and marriages. Remarkable is that some male athletes using steroids (can) become depressive. The cause for this may be the fact that these athletes tend to transform a considerable amount of the consumed steroids into estrogens. One can explain the mood swings and depressions with the known fact that the male hypothalamus reacts to the female hormone estradiol. The supposition that steroids would make athletes psychically dependent and, after their discontinuance, evoke withdrawal symptoms, is not totally wrong. Those who press 400 pounds on the bench with the aid of steroids and then, after discontinuing the substance, press only 360 pounds, then 320 pounds, and after a some time only 300 pounds, can suffer problems with their ego. Many athletes simply forget that the performance cannot remain at the same level without steroid use. In the traditional sense, steroids are not habit forming.

GASTROINTESTINAL SYMPTOMS:

These are associated solely with the use of oral, 17-alpha alkylated steroids. Some athletes suffer from epigastric fullness, diarrhea, nausea or even vomiting. Other athletes cannot take steroids in tablet form, since even with the ingestion of Winstrol or Primobolan they feel ill. In some cases this problem can be resolved by taking the tablets with each meal.

BALDNESS:

Steroids can quicken the balding process in those with a genetic predisposition. The receptors of the scalp have a high affinity to dihydrotestosterone (DHT), therefore, steroids are also considered the main cause of acne since the steroids convert largely into DHT. Here also the injectable testosterone and Anadrol are in first place. Also steroids that are derivatives of DHT, e.g. Masteron or Primobolan, can promote baldness. This can result in a receding hairline or a general thinning of the hair. Females can, in rare cases, also suffer from this. One must classify these side effects as irreversible, since the chances of recurring hair growth are slim. It must, once again, be stressed that anabolic/androgenic steroids do not automatically cause baldness but can speed up this process in those with a hereditary predisposition for hair loss.

CARDIOVASCULAR DEFECTS:

Anabolic/androgenic steroids are also linked with cardiovascular defects. This theory is supported by the fact that steroids actually can elevate the cholesterol and triglyceride levels. At the same time it has been noticed that a decrease of the HDL value and an increase of the LDL value are possible. HDL (high density lipoprotein) protects the arteries by eliminating the excess, unused cholesterol which has been deposited on the arterial walls, and by transporting it to the liver where it is then metabolized. For this reason a high HDL level is desirable, whereas athletes taking steroids have a low HDL level and thus are exposed to an increased risk of cardiovascular defects and heart disease. An increase of the LDL values, on the other hand, is undesirable since LDL brings about exactly the opposite effect, by promoting the cholesterol deposits in the arterial walls. Consequently, steroids can cause an overall unfavorable situation: high cholesterol level, low HDL and high LDL values. For this reason athletes should regularly have their triglyceride and cholesterol levels checked, in order to avoid following into this high risk group. In combination with the generally used mass-buildup diet (lots of calories, lots of fat, fast food, and sweets) this possible risk is also increased. Other unfavorable factors are stress, high blood pressure, weight increase, a bad aerobe predispostition, and smoking. Here, once again, it seems that the steroid choice, the dosage, the duration of intake, and especially the constitution of the individual, play an important part in the development of defects. It has been shown that the changed values practically return to their original values within several weeks after steroid termination. Although older athletes are usually more at risk, one cannot exclude defects in younger people and females. It is still not clarified, if the increased glucose intolerance and elevated cortisone level possibly brought about by steroids, contribute to the development of cardiovascular defects.

VIRILIZATION:

This term refers to the possible masculinization that females may sustain due to the ingestion of anabolic/androgenic steroids. As in male athletes, steroids also cause a suppression of the gonad cycle in females. The hypophysial excretion of HDL and FSH is inhibited which results in a secondary amenorrhea, meaning absence or abnormal cessation of the mensis. This side effect is reversible after the steroid has been discontinued. Visible signs of a virilization can be acne vulgaris (simple acne), hirsutism (excessive bodily and facial hair), alopecia (androgen-induced loss of hair), and changes of the skin structure similar to the males'. These side effects are usually considered reversible but, depending on predisposition or with the consumption of high dosages of mostly androgenic steroids and with extended usage, there is a possibility that these changes may remain after the steroid has been discontinued. The same is to be said about a possible clitorihypertrophy. The first sign of virilization is often a slight change in the voice in form of hoarseness. A deepening of the voice is irreversible and usually remains life long. In women one must also take a possible increase in the libido into account. Some females become increasingly aggressive during steroid intake only to fall into a depressive state after steroids are discontinued. The increased aggressiveness is due to the elevated androgen level, whereas the possible depression is suggestive of an estrogen rebound which occurs after the steroid regime has been discontinued. Since the estrogen production is suppressed by the LH and FSH inhibition, a significant elevation in production can follow. If steroids are taken during pregnancy, there is the possibility of a masculinization of the female fetus. The occurrence and manifestation of these side effects depends largely on genetic factors, the dosages, the length of consumption, and the type of steroids given. In spite of all the known excellent, performance-enhancing effects of anabolic/androgenic steroids in female athletes, one must weigh the risk against the gain, since many of the potential side effects are not reversible.

GROWTH DEFICIT:

The use of anabolic/androgenic steroids can stunt the growth potential of children and adolescents. It is interesting to note that often there is a short-term accelerated growth of the bones. With continued ingestion one must count on a premature closure of the epiphysial cartilage which leads to a growth stunt and ultimately results in a decrease in the normal predicted height. Further growth is impossible making this an irreversible side effect. Young athletes who, because of their extreme ambition have decided to take steroids should, for this reason, reconsider. The only steroid that does not cause this serious problem is Oxandrolone (see also Oxandrolone), so one hopes that its producer does not remove it from the market.

PROSTATE HYPERTROPHY:

The possibility that steroids cause a prostate enlargement or prostate cancer can be neither dismissed nor affirmed. In case studies one could not find a connection between these manifestations and the ingestion of anabolic/androgenic steroids. Since prostate problems occur mainly in older males, it is advisable that athletes over forty should refrain from taking strong androgenic steroids. Most steroid manufacturers recommend "regular rectal exams of the prostate as required in physicals."

HIGH BLOOD PRESSURE:

The occurrence of high blood pressure is often noticed in athletes taking steroids. One of the major causes is probably the increased cardiovascular strain brought about by the pronounced water and salt retention. The increased body weight of many of the athletes who eat large quantities of food and work out on heavy movements such as squats or bench presses where the breath is held, can be contributing factors. The blood pressure should be measured regularly to ensure that the value is not higher than 130/90.

CARDIAC HYPERTROPHY:

The existence of a direct connection between steroid consumption and a cardio-muscular hypertrophy has not yet been established. It is true that athletes using steroids generally have an enlarged (more efficient) heart than non-athletes; however, one must not forget the fact that athletes have an enlarged (more efficient) heart to begin with due to the higher activity rate of any athlete. äOne problem that makes it difficult to determine whether steroids have an effect on the cardiac hypertrophy is the fact that the increased training already increases the heart size, thus making it difficult to decide what amount of the hypertrophy was caused by the steroids." (From: *Anabolic Steroid Side effects: Facts, Fiction and Treatment*, Dr. Mauro G. di Pasquale, p. 47).

KIDNEY DAMAGE:

The kidneys are under more strain during steroid intake. They are involved in the filtration and excretion of toxic by-products. A high blood pressure as well as variations in the water and electrolyte balance of the body can lead to long-term changes in the kidney's function. A Wilm's tumor, a fast-growing kidney tumor normally only seen in infants and children has been noticed in certain rare cases in athletes using steroids. It is doubtful if there is a direct connection between the two. It is certain though, that during steroid consumption several athletes may develop a dark-colored urine and, in extreme cases, even blood in the urine. The former Finaject and today's

Parabolan, in particular, seem to have a toxic effect on the kidney function.

Other possible side effects that may occur during the use of anabolic/androgenic steroids are a prolonged bleeding time, headaches, nausea, feeling poorly, increased risk of injuring muscles, joints and connective tissue, anaphylactic shock (life-threatening reaction), and abscesses secondary to injection.

The occurrence of side effects is different from one athlete to another. Factors such as age, gender, constitution, the respective physical and psychic condition of the individual, as well as the dosage, the length of intake, and the selection of the steroid play an important part in the development and seriousness of side effects.

THE PROBLEM WITH FAKE STEROIDS

The athlete has two options in order to obtain steroids. He takes the legal route and consults a physician who writes a prescription for the desired compounds which then can be picked up in a pharmacy. Or the athlete follows the illegal route and procures his steroids through friends, colleagues, hobby dealers, professional dealers, small dealers, large dealers—the circle of persons who are better defined by the term "black market." Since athletes do not intend to do something illegal they all consult their primary physicians and then pick up their long list of pharmaceutical products a few minutes later at the pharmacy around the corner. Correct? —Completely wrong, unfortunately, and therefore zero points for the candidate. Based on today's situation more than 95% of all athletes are FORCED to purchase steroids on the black market. The reasons for this are on hand: Rarely is a physician willing to prescribe steroids for athletes; an increasing number of steroid compounds were removed from the market by the respective manufacturers so that there are very few left to be prescribed; the few remaining steroids are expensive so that the athlete cannot afford them. All this would be no problem if a reliable, legal, and effective substitute for synthetic hormone compounds were to be available. Athletes do not take steroids because they are nicely packaged and have a great-sounding name but only for the reason of their high   performance-improving characteristics. The former Mr. America, Steve Michalik, in the book *Pumping Iron* once said that he also "would eat lubricants for one dollar an ounce" as long as they work. Since lubricants do not build up muscles athletes must come back to prescription drugs. What remains is an ever-increasing demand for steroids with few official means to procure them. There exists a huge gap which is filled by the black market.

On the black market the athlete finds a large variety of steroids from all countries and by various manufacturers which come in various sizes, forms, colors, and under different names. "Great," you will say, "happy growth for my muscles.ô Steroid dealers are trying their best to stay in touch with pharmacies and dealers. They buy direct from the manufacturer, purchase through the back door, or have direct connections to production lines and are so able to obtain tablets/ampules." (Rumor has it that at Schering AG in Germany applicants are asked during their job interviews whether they are bodybuilders. If the answer is yes this does not increase their chance of being employed.) No matter how large the numbers of original foreign steroids, the Spanish, Italian, Greek, and East European compounds, in particular, are smuggled to the U.S. to supply everyone. EVERYONE?—Not at all. Many receive drugs but the demand for the products is much higher than the supply. And this is exactly where fake steroids come into play. Fakes are clandestinely manufactured, illegal copies of original pharmaceutical steroids. This would not be much of a problem if the content of these products were equivalent to the quality of the original version or if these compounds were at least to contain the substances listed on their packaging. Not a chance since usually most fakes contain a completely different substance, are more or less strongly underdosed, or do not contain anabolic/androgenic substances at all. Another problem is the doubtful purity and sterility of these products since no offical authority is checking the conditions under which the products are manufactured and processed. This is exclusively a question of making a deal. Making a lot of money quickly is the motto so that during manufacturing and packaging only the minimum is done in order to increase the profit. Those of you who once had an abscess secondary to injection (at the point of injection) fever-related symptoms, an allergic reaction, or a very strong acne can confirm that this is almost exclusively the case with fake steroids. The manufacturers of these steroids are trying their best to design an appealing, credible, sale-promoting packaging: the label and imprint on the package are improved constantly; continuous forms of ampules are used; high-quality push-through strips, indented tablets, expiration dates and batch numbers are imprinted at a later date; package inserts are enclosed; colored tablets and burnt-in imprints on ampules appear. These are all factors which make it very difficult to tell originals from fakes and fakes often give the impression of being originals.

The problem is that most athletes have never seen the original compounds, let alone used them so that a comparison based on appearance and effect is very difficult. This makes it easy to sell fakes. So what can one do? We have tried to put together compounds which we know are not original compounds, meaning that they do not come from an official, pharmaceutical manufacturer and are not sold in pharmacies. A laboratory analysis of the various products would be very expensive and make little sense since it cannot be excluded that the following ampule or tablet of the same compound contains completely different substances or that its manufacturer decides to fill the ampule with a completely different solution. In the following we offer a checklist which helps recognize fakes. The reader will find illustrations of common and widely-used fakes which, together with the information in this chapter, will help the athlete to select the right products among the large variety of "steroids" that are available. There is one thing we would like to clarify at the beginning: We do not know exactly what these steroids contain. We have not analyzed them in a laboratory. We do not know whether they are good or bad. We do not know whether they always have the same effect. It is possible that several of these preparations contain a part of the substances indicated and are therefore "good" fakes which are better than no steroids. Among insiders the products by International Pharmaceuticals, for example, are quite well liked. We do not want to make any evaluation but only distinguish between original and fake steroids. Nevertheless we recommend that women and female competing athletes, in particular, be extremely careful when selecting steroids since it can be very irritating if a supposedly 2.5 mg Oxandrolone tablet contains 5 mg methyl-testosterone.

1.) Principally, be very skeptical toward the authenticity of all steroids available on the black market. Almost all European ampules containing more than 2 ml injection solution (with the exception of veterinary preparations) are fakes no matter whether they have a silver, red, green, or gold screw-cap or whether they are packaged in a box with a package insert. Ninety-nine point nine percent of all 10 ml, 30 ml, and 50 ml multi-injection vials are fakes. The probability of purchasing an original multi-injection vial is nonexistent. The black market is flooded with these vials because they can be imitated quite easily and are difficult to detect without a comparable original preparation. Of course there is always someone who can guarantee 100% that the drugs he offers are original compounds. The question is only who are then the ones manufacturing and distributing the fakes. Probably always someone else. Be careful!

2.) Almost all European injectable steroids contained in an ampule or a vial with brown glass are fakes. Brown glass is almost exclusively used for American steroids and in veterinary medicine. An exception, however, are the injectable Spanish steroids by Schering (Primobolan, Testoviron, etc.). Testosterone cypionate by Leo/Spain is also offered in brown glass ampules which is rather the exception for European steroids.

3.) With almost 100% probability all steroids available on the black market in the U.S. that have a U.S-American manufacturer name, are fakes. The chance that one of the very few original American preparations will be available on the black market in large quantities is almost nonexistent.

4.) Special attention must be paid to Parabolan, Deca-Durabolin, Dianabol, injectable Testosterone, and Oxandrolone and Winstrol since there are several available fakes of these compounds.

5.) Oral and injectable steroids with the following imprint/name/ form of administration are fakes:

Finajet; Finaject; Stromba; Strombaject; Boldone; Primobolan 50 mg tablets; all injectable Dianabol (with the exception of Anabolikum 2.5% Vet. Meca, Germany and Metandiabol Vet. Quimper, Mexico); Testosterone Cypionate (by Lemmon, Goldline, International Pharmaceuticals); Bolasterone; Dihydrolone; Hexalone; Nordiethylene; Quinolone; Dihydromesterone; all products by International Pharmaceuticals (although they are not the worst); Pronabol in normal push-through strips; Oxandrolone in plastic boxes; push-through strips with only the imprint Oxymetholone 50 mg; round "Anabol tablets"; all injectable stanozolol, where the substance does not separate from the injection fluid; all 2 ml Deca-Durabolin-ampules without a label; the same is true for all Sustanon 250 ampules; all 2 ml Deca-Durabolin break-off ampules; Russian Sustanon by Organon with rounded corners of the label; push-through strips which only have the imprint Methandrostenolone 5 mg; Nerobolil 50 mg ampules without a label; and all 5 mg Winstrol tablets.

6.) Take a close look at the label and packaging, in particular. This is usually your best chance to recognize a fake. Check how the expiration date and the batch number are imprinted. If they were printed together with the other writing you can be sure that it is a fake. Original steroids always have this information stamped on, punched in, burnt in, or imprinted later. The reason is that the manufacturer of the originals usually has several thousand labels and boxes printed in advance. Only later when the ampules and tablets are to be properly labelled and packaged the expiration date and the batch numbers are imprinted. Examine also the corners of the labels on the ampules and glass vials. Ninety-nine percent of the fakes come with labels that have square or rectangled corners, while the original labels mostly have rounded corners. Make sure that the label is attached in a straight line and not crooked. Make sure that the label does not show "bubbles," can be well felt, and is flat on the glass. Try to tear it off. The labels of fakes can usually be removed from the glass surface in one piece while the labels of originals can only be torn off in pieces. In addition to the expiration date and batch number of the package one must also check that they match the form of the preparation. It is especially important that the width is matching (while the height is not important). The label ends must also not overlap.

7.) Glass ampules without a label: You must make sure that the imprint on the ampule cannot be removed or smeared with your finger. (Exception: Polish Omnadren). The imprint of original drugs is often burnt into the glass and can be felt when touched with your finger. The imprint on the ampule must not be diagonal.

8.) Pay attention that the ampules offered have an identical, symmetrical form. Check that all ampules contain the exact same quantity of injection solution and are of the same color. An irregular form of the ampule tip or small bubbles in the glass of the ampule are also indicators that this is a fake. There are only a few fakes of the injection ampules at this time since their manufacturing is usually too expensive for fakers.

9.) Do not buy loose tablets or tablets contained in a plastic bag (Exception: Anabol tablets from Thailand). Avoid tablets which easily crumble and fall into pieces. Pay attention that the tablets and ampules are complete, including packaging, push-through strips, and package insert.

10.) Be skeptical if somebody tells you that he has a very large variety. Statements such as "everything you want" or "as much as you want" or "no problem; will be available tomorrow" sound great but must be looked at with caution. These are usually fakes since original steroids are not always available in sufficient quantities on the black market.

11.) Also pay attention if someone is offering you steroids at very low prices. The manufacturing of fakes costs very little and, therefore, the fakes can be sold at a relatively low price. Original Deca in a strength of 200 mg in 2 ml usually costs $20-$25 on the black market. A 10 ml vial which is offered and apparently contains 200 mg/ml (!) of substance costs $130. Thus 200 mg cost only $13, that is half of the price of the original.

12.) Still very popular is the purchase of steroids through mail order! In foreign countries such as Holland, England, Switzerland, Portugal, the former Czechoslovakia, Poland, Mexico, and Canada steroid dealers who supposedly have only original steroids, after prepayment mail them to all countries. Be careful since these people usually do not mail anything at all or if they do, these will be mostly fakes. When contacting these people, by return mail you receive a list with several available steroids. We are looking at one such price list by an English "mail order house." The prices are okay, however, their products are not. Several 10 ml, 30 ml, and 50 ml injection vials, compounds such as Finajet and Boldone show clearly that these are mostly fakes.

Finally, we would like to conclude this chapter by showing you through an actual example, the Anapolon 50 tablets by Syntex, England, how difficult it has become to distinguish the originals from the fakes.

Anapolon 50 - Fake or Original?

Those who do not have an original version available will have difficulty distinguishing between the two. You will only know for certain that you have a fake after you have swallowed the first 50 tablets and the expected progress does not occur. To allow you to make the right decisions as to purchase and intake before buying the compound we would like to list the following characteristics which will help tell the original from the fake.

1. Packaging:
The expiration date on the original package is printed on the back while on the fake it is printed on the right lateral side. There is a fake version on which the expiration date is printed in the same blue-purple color as the rest of the packaging. This makes it easy to identify the preparation as a fake. On the original and the better fakes the expiration date and charge number are punched in in black. On

the box of the fake the expiration date can be easily felt with your finger while on the box of the original it can be hardly felt. On the front and back of the fake one reads: "Oxymetholone B.P. 50mg" while on the original one reads: "Oxymetholone B P 50 mg". The two dots after the letter B and P are not present on the original box. When taking a closer look at the left side of the box one recognizes clear differences between the original and the fake. Especially eye-catching is that the one-line type denomination on the original is "PL 0286/5009" while on the fake it is four lines long (see photos left side of box). The top of the box also shows differences. On the original package the manufacturer has printed the name "Anapolon 50" in blue-purple color. On the fake the top only has the name "Anapolon" in blue-purple, the number "50", however, is printed in red. When opening the package from the top you will notice two tongue-shaped flaps made of carton. The original has the letters "SDS" on the left flap and directly under the "D" the number "3". The fake does not have this imprint on its flaps.

2. Plastic Box:
The print on the label of the original box is quite dark while the writing on the fake appears dull. This makes the letters on the original label appear larger than on the fake (see photos). The expiration date both on the fake and also on the original is in black and imprinted on the label of the plastic box. The difference: on the fake the expiration date is printed on the label (and not punched in) so that the surface is smooth when touching it. On the original the manufacturer has punched in the expiration date so that one can clearly feel that the surface is different when touching it with your finger. When closing your eyes during one of these "touch strokes" you will feel the difference one hundred percent and you will have another proof whether or not the preparation is an original. It is very important that you do not buy a preparation with the batch number (BN), date of manfucturing (DOM) and an expiration date (EXP) that reads as follows: BN 91143, DOM 4/92, EXP 4/97. Should you find these three denominations on the label and/or the packaging, the product is a fake. The last criterion on the label of the plastic box again refers to the batch number (BN), the date of manufacturing (DOM), and the expiration date (EXP). Both on the fake and the

original they are one below the other, i.e. printed in three lines. The difference is as follows: On the fake all three lines are exactly left-bounded; on the original the three lines are not aligned.

3. Content of the Plastic Box and Tablets:

When you tear off the packaging and take off the white cover of the plastic box, in both the fake and the original you will notice a small round piece of rubber foam. The rubber foam of the original is yellow-white with a diameter of 32 mm so that it must be pressed together in order to fit into the plastic box. The rubber roam of the fake is usually white and fits without being pressed together. The original tablets, like the fakes, are indented and have the number "5" on the left of the breakage line and the letter "0" on the right of the breakage line. Together they read as number "50". On the other side of the tablet both versions have the manufacturer name "SYNTEX" punched in. The fake tablets are simple and white (like chalk) whereas the original tablets have a slightly yellow/beige color. The difference in color can especially be noticed in daylight. For absolute clarity— whether you have a fake or an original— the following "suck/masticate/taste test" is suggested. Put a tablet on your tongue and start mixing it with saliva. A part of the fake, after a few seconds, will separate and mix with the saliva into a paste. When masticating the remaining tablet a soft, mucous paste will form. The original tablet will not dissolve either in part or entirely when sucked and mixed with saliva but remain intact. When then masticating the tablet no soft, mucous paste will form but rather a crystalline, bitter-tasting mixture.

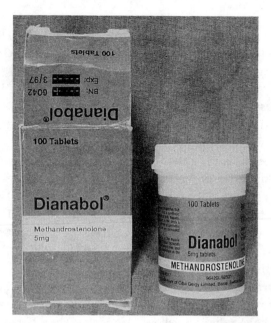

Fake D-bol by Ciba Geigy

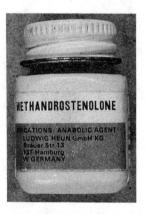

Fake D-bol by Ludwig Heun GmbH KG, a nonexisting company

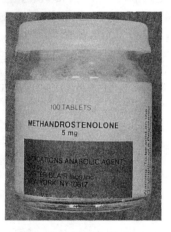

Fake D-bol by C. Blair

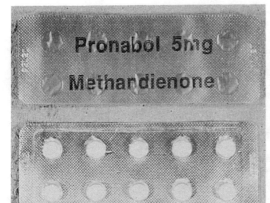

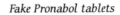
Fake Pronabol tablets

*Fake Dianabol
with blister*

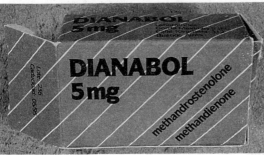

*Fake Anabol
Tablets from
Thailand,
there are 3
counterfeits
around*

*Teslosen from China! with
Stanozolol and Methyltestosteron*

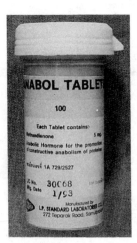

Fake Anabol tablets from Thailand, this small version is not in production!

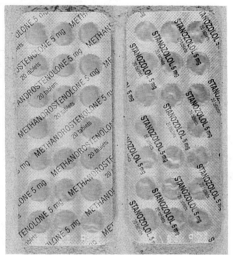

Counterfeited Methandrostenolone and Stanozolol blister

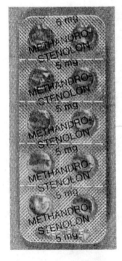

Two counterfeited Methandrostenolone blister

Fake Stanozolol

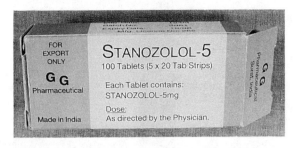

Fake Stanozolol-5 box with blister by G.G. / India

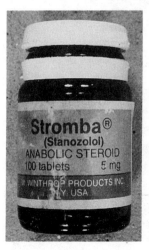

Fake Stromba by Winthrop

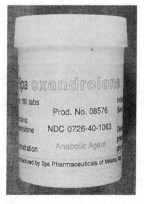

Fake Oxandrolone by SPA, the original version is always in blisters

355

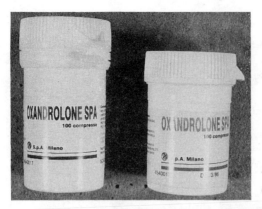

Two fake versions of Oxandrolone

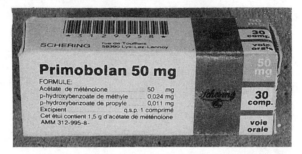

Counterfeited Primobolan 50mg box and glass container

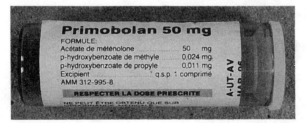

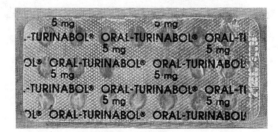

Oral-Turinabol, fake blister

*Two fake and one legitimate Anapolon 50 from a mail order company.
The real one is on the right side*

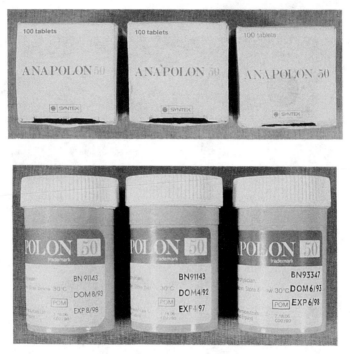

The real one is on the right side

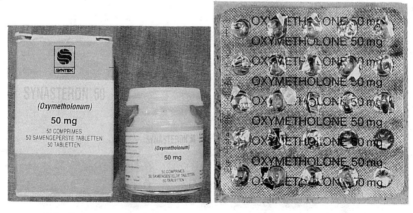

Fake Synasteron by Syntex   *Fake Oxymetholone blister*

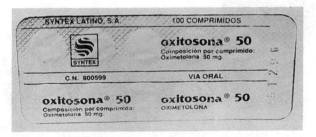

Four different Oxymetholone blisters, all fake

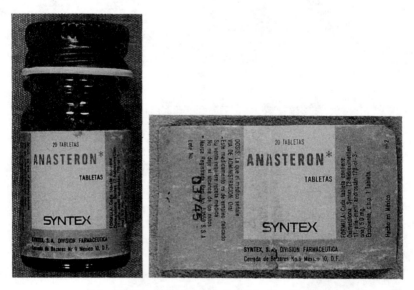

Fake Oxitosona with blister by Syntex

Anapolon 50 by Syntex
from Mexico, totally bogus

Fake Anasteron by Syntex, glass bottle with label

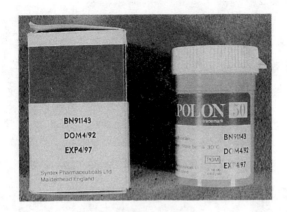

Fake or real? Take a close look

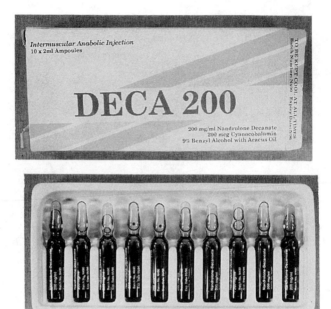

Intermuscular Anabolic Injection
10 x 2ml Ampoules

DECA 200

200 mg/ml Nandrolone Decanate
200 mcg Cyanocobalamin
9% Benzyl Alcohol with Aracus Oil

TO BE KEPT COOL AT ALL TIMES
Batch Number. Note. Expiry Date.95/96

Counterfeited Deca with vitamin B, you can find it on the black market with no problem

Nandrolone-Decanoate
200 mg/ml
Batch No. N490
Exp. Date 05/96

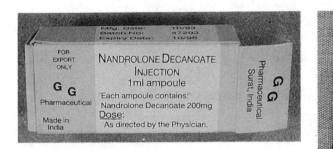

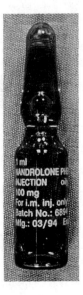

G.G. from India again, this time with a fake Deca, 200mg

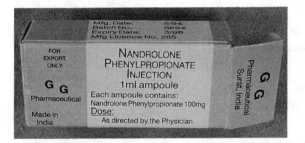

Nandrolone phenylpropionate, 100mg/1ml, G.G. again, the company that makes a lot of different solutions!

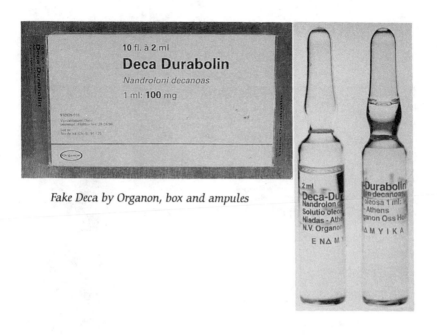

10 fl. à 2 ml

Deca Durabolin

Nandroloni decanoas

1 ml: **100 mg**

Fake Deca by Organon, box and ampules

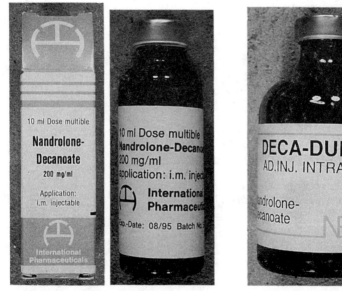

Fake Nandrolone decanoate by International Pharmaceuticals

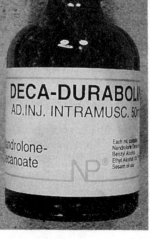

Fake Deca–Durabolin in a 50ml vial!

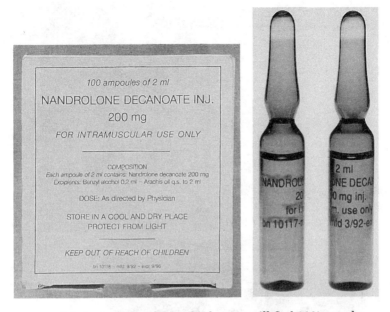

100 ampoules of 2 ml

NANDROLONE DECANOATE INJ.

200 mg

FOR INTRAMUSCULAR USE ONLY

COMPOSITION
Each ampoule of 2 ml contains: Nandrolone decanoate 200 mg
Excipients: Benzyl alcohol 0,2 ml – Arachis oil q.s. to 2 ml

DOSE: As directed by Physician

STORE IN A COOL AND DRY PLACE
PROTECT FROM LIGHT

KEEP OUT OF REACH OF CHILDREN

bn 10118 – mfd: 9/92 – exp: 9/96

Fake box and ampules, in this box you will find 100! ampules

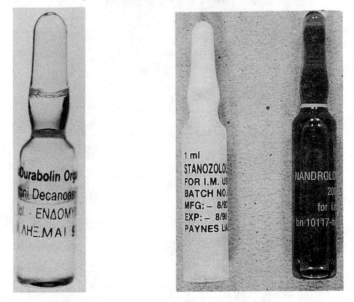

Fake Deca from Greece

*Fake Stanozolol and Nandrolone
ampules*

Different kinds of injectables by International Pharmaceuticals

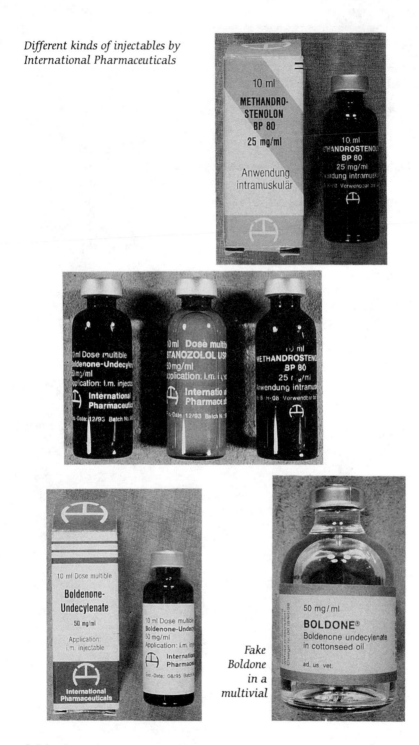

10 ml
METHANDRO-
STENOLON
BP 80
25 mg/ml

Anwendung
intramuskulär

10 ml
METHANDROSTENOL
BP 80
25 mg/ml
...dung intramusk.

10 ml Dose multible
Boldenone-Undecyle
50 mg/ml
pplication: i.m. injecta
International
Pharmaceutica
Ex-Date: 12/93 Batch No.9

10 ml Dose multib
STANOZOLOL US
50 mg/ml
application: i.m. i
Internatio
Pharmace
Ex-Date: 12/93 Batch N

10 ml
METHANDROSTENO
BP 80
25 mg/ml
Anwendung intramusk
B H-08 Verwendbar b

10 ml Dose multible

Boldenone-
Undecylenate

50 mg/ml

Application:
i.m. injectable

International
Pharmaceuticals

10 ml Dose multible
Boldenone-Undec
50 mg/ml
Application: i.m. in
International
Pharmaceu
Exc.-Date: 08/95 Batch

50 mg/ml

BOLDONE®
Boldenone undecylenate
in cottonseed oil

ad. us. vet.

*Fake
Boldone
in a
multivial*

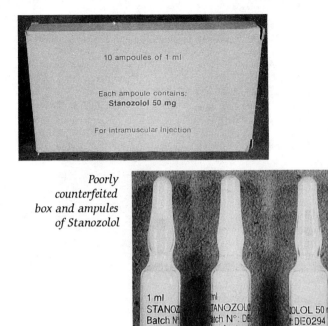

10 ampoules of 1 ml

Each ampoule contains:
Stanozolol 50 mg

For intramuscular Injection

Poorly counterfeited box and ampules of Stanozolol

1 ml
STANOZ
Batch N
Manufac
Expiry

ml
TANOZOLO
atch N°: DE
anufacture
piry

OLOL 50 m
DE0294
ture: 6/91
: 6/95

L 50 mg
9294
6/91
6/95

WINSTROL DE
Stanozolol 50 m
Agitese antes
ZAMBON,
Lote:H-28 Ca

NSTROL DEPO
anozolol 50 mg
gitese antes de
ZAMBON, S
Lote:H-28 Cad.

EPOT - 1 ml
mg - via i.m.
s de usarse
, S. A.
Cad.:11-98

PRIMOBOLAN
DEPOT
SCHERING

Fake Winstrol ampules by Zambon

Fake Primobolan by Schering

59.61
Fake Retandrol by Richter

59.62
Fake Dynabolon by ?

59.63
Fake Retabolil by Richter

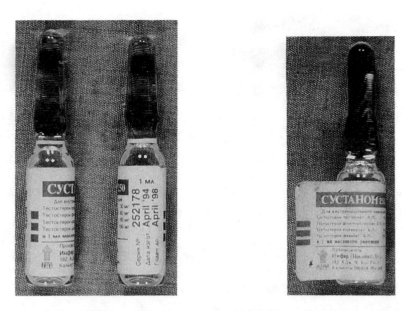

Two different faked Sustanon from Russia, the label has rounded corners and you can pull it off

Another fake Sustanon by Organon

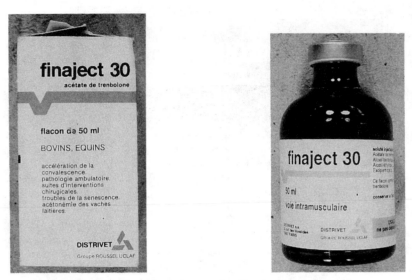

Fake Finaject, the real one is out of production since 1987

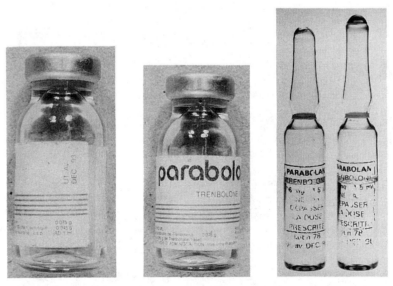

Two different kinds of faked Parabolan

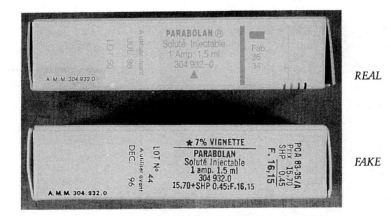

REAL

FAKE

To show you the difference

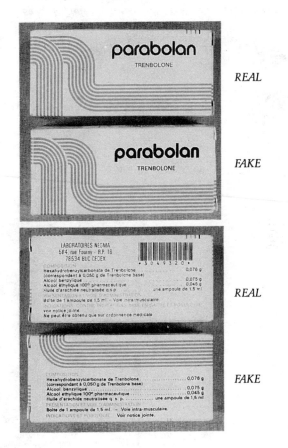

REAL

FAKE

REAL

FAKE

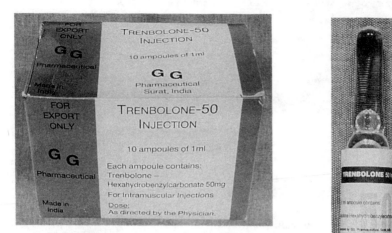

Fake Trenbolone by G.G. from India, 10 single packaged ampules will fit into the big box

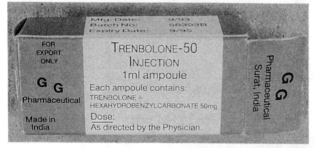

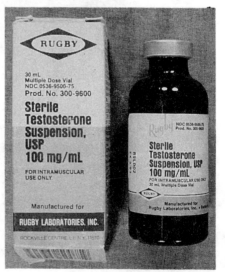

Fake Testo by Rugby, box and vial

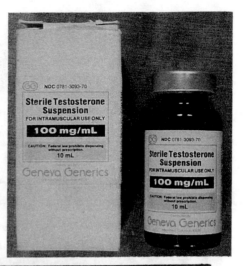

Fake Testo by Geneva Generics, box and vial

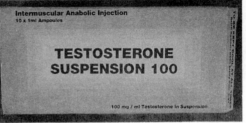

Another fake Testosterone suspension, box and ampules

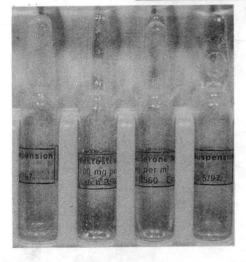

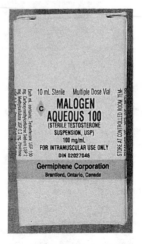

Fake Malogen from Canada

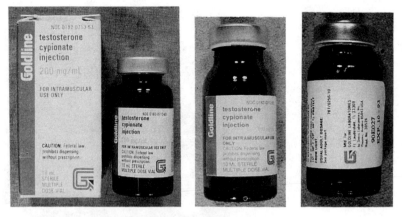

Fake Testosterone cypionate by Goldline / U.S.

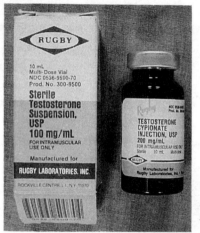

Fake Cypionate and suspension by Rugby

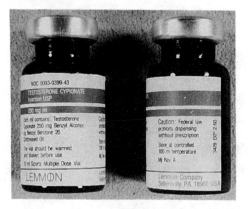

Fake Cypionate by Lemmon

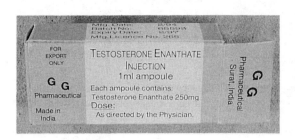

Mfg. Date 8/94
Batch No. 88504
Expiry Date 8/97
Mfg.Licence No. 266

FOR
EXPORT
ONLY

TESTOSTERONE ENANTHATE
INJECTION
1ml ampoule

Each ampoule contains:
Testosterone Enanthate 250mg
Dose:
As directed by the Physician.

G G
Pharmaceutical
Made in
India

G G
Pharmaceutical
Surat, India

Fake Enanthate by G.G. from india, box and ampule

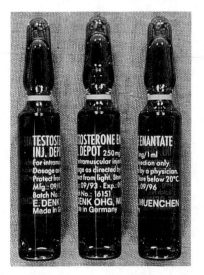

*Fake Testo ampules by Denk, a
non-existing company*

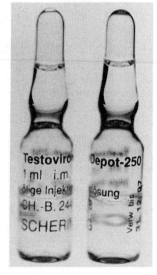

Fake Testoviron ampules

Fake Heptylate
by Theramex

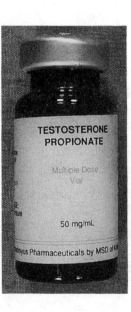

Fake Testoviron
by Schering

Fake Testo by ?

Fake Testosterone
propionate
multivial by MSD

TESTOSTERONE PROPIONATE

Multiple Dose
Vial

50 mg/mL

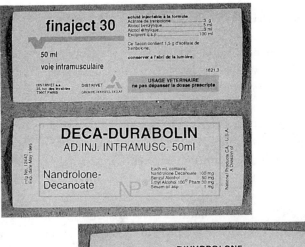

finaject 30

50 ml

voie intramusculaire

solution injectable à la formule
Acétate de trenbolone........................3 g
Alcool benzylique...............................5 ml
Alcool éthylique..................................3 ml
Excipient q.s.p...................................100 ml

Ce flacon contient 1,5 g d'acétate de trenbolone.

conserver à l'abri de la lumière.

1621.3

USAGE VETERINAIRE
ne pas dépasser la dosae prescripte

DISTRIVET s.a.
35, bd. des Invalides
75007 PARIS   DISTRIVET
                  GROUPE RHONE-POULENC AGRO

DECA-DURABOLIN
AD.INJ. INTRAMUSC. 50ml

Nandrolone-
Decanoate

Each ml contains:
Nandrolone Decanoate 100 mg
Benzyl Alcohol   50 mg
Ethyl Alcohol 100° Pharm 30 mg
Sesam oil asp   1 mg

mfg No. 12443
Exp. date May 1995

National Products CA - U.S.A.
A Division of

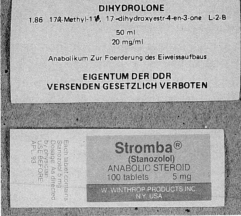

DIHYDROLONE

1.86   17ß-Methyl-11ß, 17-dihydroxyestr-4-en-3-one   L-2-B

50 ml

20 mg/ml

Anabolikum Zur Foerderung des Eiweissaufbaus

EIGENTUM DER DDR
VERSENDEN GESETZLICH VERBOTEN

Each tablet contains:
Stanozolol 5 mg
Dosage As directed
by physician
USE BEFORE:
APL 93

Stromba®
(Stanozolol)
ANABOLIC STEROID
100 tablets   5 mg

W. WINTHROP PRODUCTS INC
N.Y. USA

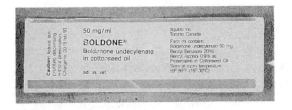

50 mg/ml

BOLDONE®
Boldenone undecylenate
in cottonseed oil

ad. us. vet.

Squibb Inc
Toronto Canada

Each ml contains:
Boldenone undecylenate 50 mg
Benzyl Benzoate 20%
Benzyl Alcohol 0.9% as
Preservative in Cottonseed Oil
Store at room temperature
59°F 86°F (15° 30°C)

Caution: federal law
prohibits dispensing
without a prescription
Charge no. 0313 Vet 93

Different faked labels

DISCONTINUANCE OF STEROIDS

"On occasion, elite bodybuilders stay on steroids for several years at a time. This is due to the fact that they must be in shape for multiple contests as well as guest appearances throughout the year. This non-stop regimen has claimed some victims. Mendenhall comes to mind. This guy had the potential to be one of the best bodybuilders in history. Yet, he admittedly burned out on steroids before he could even claim a national championship. Hill is another bodybuilder which I have recently seen suffer from the demanding, non-stop steroid regimen required at this level. After rocketing to the top, he has recently dropped out of sight. Demelo was another up and coming national competitor who burned out on steroids and never made it. I think he is trying to make a "natural" comeback - - good luck, bud. Santoriello took a serious setback after his teenage success before coming back to win the national championships. I heard that he was messed up by steroids. Some don't think he can make it as a professional because of the amount of drugs he has to take to stay in shape. (Oh, I mean the amount of Cybergenic Kits — give me a break!). Numerous pro bodybuilders and active top level national competitors find themselves in similar situations. Their contest schedule is just too busy for off cycle periods. Since their success is so heavily dependent on being in top shape, steroids become an absolute must for their program all year long".

(From: Anabolic Reference Guide, 6th Issue, 1991, by W. Nathaniel Phillips, partial excerpt of an interview with a former bodybuilder pro who participated at IFBB championships for several years.)

The reasons why athletes voluntarily or willy-nilly discontinue steroids are various. One of the main reasons which speak for an interruption of the steroid regime are, as the above example has shown, certain possible health risks. Some discontinue steroids simply out of habit because one has heard that after a maximum of 12 weeks a suspension of the same period is suggested. Some discontinue because of limited financial resources or in view of a championship with doping tests. Often, also, the decreasing effect of the administered steroids and the smaller gains which manifest themselves after several weeks are a determining factor. Something almost all athletes have in common with this scenario: One is looking forward to the following weeks with mixed feelings since one does not know what to expect and those who already have some experience (mostly negative) know only too well what lies ahead. Possible apprehensions are, by all means, justified since most athletes experience the classic interruption symptoms such as weight loss, less body strength, muscular atrophy (loss of muscle tissue) and increased fat deposits. Some experience depressions, aversion to training, lethargy, and a lack of discipline. How is this possible? Very simply, the athlete experiences a catabolic phase. The athlete now has to deal with two major problems which will burden him during the following weeks and which make several athletes go "back to the stuff" after interrupting their steroid regime for only a very short time. First, it is very likely that the body's own testosterone production will be reduced since most steroids have an inhibiting effect on the hypothalamohypopyhsial testicular axis, resulting in a reduced testosterone production in the testes by the Leydig's cells. The extent of the reduction depends on the duration of the steroid intake and especially on the strength of the steroids taken. The more androgenic a steroid the more distinct its inhibiting effect on the endogenous testosterone production. In first place are certainly the various testosterone compounds Dianabol and Anadrol, exactly what works so well. When taking the more moderate steroids including Deca-Durabolin, Primobolan, Winstrol, the extent of a possible endogenous testosterone suppression is not only lower but also much slower and more even. Studies of Dianabol, for example, have shown that a conservative dosage of 20 mg/day after only 10 days leads to a 30% to 40% suppression. Since the body's own hormone production cannot be elevated from one day to the next, the athlete experiences a critical over bridging phase. The effect of the exogenous hormones is nonexistent and the body's own testosterone level helps only little to improve the situation. Thus it is important to increase the endogenous testosterone production as quickly as possible. How this is possible we will describe in the following section.

The second problem is the clearly more relevant and probably the more decisive factor for the potentially considerable performance loss of the athletes. As we know, steroids have a highly anticatabolic effect by reducing the catabolic effect of the body's own hormone, cortisone. When taking steroids, the steroid molecules block the cortisone receptors so that the cortisone produced by the adrenal gland cannot attach to the receptors, thus remaining for the most part deactivated. The body reacts by producing additional cortisone receptors so that, in the meantime, the unusually high amount of cortisone receptors in the blood can finally do their job. This again is not very serious as long as the athlete continues to take the steroids as planned. However, when the steroid regime is terminated the cortisone receptors are suddenly freed and the large quantity of free cortisone molecules in the blood now know exactly what to do. They rush to the cortisone receptors to form a molecule/receptor complex and transmit to the muscle cell the following message which is so unpleasant for the athlete: break down amino acids. These leave the muscle cell and enter the blood where they are transformed into glucose or blood sugar. The consequence of this process has already been described in another chapter. The athlete's second problem, in addition to increasing the endogenous testosterone production, is to lower the cortisone level to an acceptable level. As the reader knows, this goal is achievable to a high extent. In the following we will describe a sensible, step-by-step approach to interrupt the steroid regime, and the time after. Particular attention will be paid to the two problematic factors described in detail. We want to, however, explicitly emphasize that this information is no guarantee to protect the athlete from a loss of performance.

1.) It is important that the athlete predetermines the time when he will stop the intake so that he can sufficiently prepare himself for it. This especially means to procure the necessary supportive preparations and to find the right mental attitude.

2.) Prepare for day X slowly and steadily. The athlete should stop taking the strongly androgenic steroids approximately four weeks before interrupting the steroid regime. When tablets such as Dianabol or Anadrol are taken, these are to be reduced slowly and evenly within fourteen days so that exactly two weeks before day X the oral intake of predominantly androgenic steroids is terminated. Those who take injectable, androgenic steroids such as Testosterone or Parabolan reduce these to zero within four weeks so that their intake will end on day X. The milder, oral steroids such as Primobolan S, Winstrol, Oxandrolone, Oral-Turinabol, etc. are slowly and evenly reduced fourteen days before day X so that after two weeks they are no longer taken. It is sufficient when the dosage of the "weaker" injectable steroids such as Deca-Durabolin, Primobolan Depot, Winstrol Depot is reduced to half of their intake about one week before termination.

3.) Avoid an abrupt discontinuance of all steroids at the same time because the body would enter an immediate catabolic phase. The cortisone receptors will be free and in combination with the low testosterone and androgen levels a considerable loss of strength and mass, and an increase of fat and water, and often gynecomastia will occur. Gynecomastia is possible because the suddenly low androgen level shifts the relationship in favor of the estrogens which suddenly become the domineering hormone. Especially eye-catching is also the extreme listlessness to training or sex and a generally weak state of mind of several athletes. If not forced because of medical reasons never discontinue steroids "cold turkey."

4.) If the athlete does not yet take antiestrogens he should begin their intake during the last weeks before ending the steroid regime. Athletes who already take antiestrogens the weeks before should continue to do so over the described interval. A daily combination of 20 mg Nolvadex and 25 mg Proviron is usually sufficient for this purpose. This avoids an estrogen surplus, an important factor, which also must be considered when in the following testosterone stimulants such as HCG are taken since HCG often also increases the estrogen level. Since the androgenic effect of Proviron also promotes the increase of the androgen level the androgen/estrogen ratio is further shifted in favor of the androgens. The possibility of a rebound effect after the discontinuance of the antiestrogen combination is considerably reduced by Proviron.

5.) In order to increase the body's own testosterone production the athlete, on one hand, takes HCG which directly and quickly stimulates the Leydig's cells in the testes and, on the other hand, takes Clomid which promotes the complete hypothalamohypophysial testicular axis, however, it needs a longer start-up phase. The administration of HCG begins during the last week of discontinuance. The athlete injects three times 5000 i.u. in a three-day interval. Following, three more injections of 5000 i.u. are injected every five days. After the third HCG injection the intake of Clomid begins since its gonadotropin-stimulating effect in the event of an already activated increased testicular activity is more effective. Clomid is now taken over two weeks, two tablets of 50 mg each per day in the first week and 50 mg tablets per day in the second week. Point 5 obviously does not apply to women.

6.) All this, however, helps only if the athlete is able to mostly block out the catabolic effect of the increased cortisone level. A compound which, because of its distinct anticatabolic effect, fulfills this requirement is the beta-2 sympathomimetic, Clenbuterol. Clenbuterol successfully blocks the cortisone receptors so that the athlete is usually able to maintain a large portion of the strength and muscle mass built up by the steroids. The intake of Clenbuterol begins directly at the end of the steroid therapy and continues over 8-10 weeks (see also Clenbuterol). Another compound of the group of sympaticomimetics which also has an anticatabolic effect (but less pronounced than Clenbuterol) is Ephedrine. Probably the most suitable drug in this situation is a preparation which in school medicine is used in the treatment of the Cushing's syndrome, a hyperfunction of the adrenal glands which causes the body to produce too much cortisone. Those who have read this book carefully will know which drug is meant: Cytadren. Since it reduces the cortisone level extremely well athletes usually take it directly after completion of a steroid treatment (see also Cytadren). Several athletes take thyroid hormones in this phase since they have an anabolic effect when taken in small dosages and for not excessively long intake intervals. Their effect can be clearly increased by the anticatabolic effect of Clenbuterol which explains why this combination is used during the phase of discontinuance. The use of growth hormone also makes sense since it has a strong anticatabolic/anabolic effect. You can forget Ornithin and Arginin which supposedly increase the realising of

GH, because they are ineffective. Distance yourself from the thought that pharmaceutically improved muscle mass can be maintained with "natural methods."

7.) Adjust your nutrition according to the new situation. After discontinuance of the steroid intake the metabolism will go back to normal. This means that the athlete should reduce his daily caloric intake over the course of several days by 25-30%. The protein supply, however, should still be relatively high at 1-1.5 g of protein per pound of bodyweight per day.

8.) Reduce your workout schedule. Avoid maintaining the same workout program as during steroid regime since this would only magnify the catabolic effect. The athlete should not come up with the crazy idea of compensating a possible loss of performance by increasing the extent and intensity of his workout since such an action would have a negative effect. Limit yourself to your basic exercises, train every muscle once a week, and try to maintain your strength as much as possible. Do not train more than four times a week and limit the workout sessions to 60 minutes. Several so-called "experts" are of the opinion that the athlete after a steroid regime should avoid the heavy basic movements for some time and suggest that exercises are carried out more frequently with lower weights. Dear Reader, try it. Those who used to make 8 repetitions of squats with 400 pounds and now switch to leg extensions or leg presses with 12-15 repetitions will wonder how fast an upper thigh can lose size.

Reality has shown that with the necessary knowledge, discipline, ambition, and willpower a considerable amount of the strength and muscle mass built up by the steroids can be maintained. Apart from the year-round steroid intake, a successful over bridging interval between the various treatments is the only way to achieve continuous improvements. Certainly, often it is necessary to go one step back in order to make two steps forward. This is absolutely normal and nothing is said against it. What many, however, do is go two steps back and move two steps forward so that their performance is stagnant. Almost everyone knows how to build up with steroids but only very few are able to maintain the results. Correctly interrupting the steroid regime in combination with a sensible interval of over bridging helps maintain results and creates the basis for a further, successful steroid regime.

SENSIBLE TRAINING PROGRAM

When you go to just any GYM and take a close look at the members working out, then come back a year later, you will notice that most of them still use the same weights as during your first visit. Why? Because most bodybuilders waste their time with their usual training programs. If the buildup of mass and muscle mass was actually connected with the general common amount of training there would be many more massive bodybuilders. Since this, however, as reality has shown, is apparently not the case a few things seem to be wrong with the typical bodybuilding program. Since most people unnecessarily create their own obstacles they tremendously complicate achieving their goals (strength and muscle buildup). The majority of them, at least those who are interested in the subject of this book, call them hardcore bodybuilders. Hardcore, however, does not mean training six times a week for three hours and copying Lee Haney's training for a competition, but something completely different. To create a sensible training plan and carry it out without compromise over a prolonged period of time is what makes a true hardcore bodybuilder because only he has the necessary willpower, discipline, ambition and perseverence that is needed. Forget endless long training routines, Mr. Olympia Superstar programs, deceicive ads such as 30 pounds of muscles in four weeks, and think of the basics without which a strong and massive body cannot exist.

You should take the following factors to heart since they are absolutely necessary for a successful training. What role does the use of anabolic/androgenic steroids play? Very simple: athletes who take steroids will make clearly faster, better, and greater progress than their natural colleagues. They will also obtain a much higher development stage than would have ever been possible without taking pharmaceutical compounds. Such stupid statements that one will achieve the same mass as a bodybuilder without taking steroids —it only takes longer— is nothing but a completely absurd publicity by the authorities who in their own interest conceal the truth. Read the following lines with an open-minded attitude and try to adapt this information for your own needs.

1. High-intensity training: The human organism vehemently refuses any unnecessary change since it feels best in a constant condition, a homeostasis. In order to lure it out of its passivity, several efforts and exertions must be made. The signal that the body needs in order to build up strength and muscle mass is triggered by heavy, hard, and intense training routines. These should consist of relatively few sets. Five to eight sets for large muscle groups and three to four sets for small muscle groups are completely sufficient when every set is carried out until muscle failure.

2. Training with relatively low repetitions: The body has two different types of muscle fibers: Since the muscle hypertrophy almost completely occurs in the fast-twitch white muscle fibers of type 2, a sensible bodybuilding workout must be developed in a way that these are sufficiently stimulated. For this purpose relatively few, heavy reps in the range of 6-10 are suitable.

3. Training with progressively heavier weights: In order to build up massive muscles they must be challenged and exposed to regular progressively-higher resistances. This can be achieved when the athlete continuously increases the weight during exercises. The stronger the muscles the larger their appearance. There is no mass without power. The basic exercises such as squats, bench presses, presses behind the neck, rows, barbell curls, dips, etc. are the most suitable.

4. Sufficient rest periods: The muscles are stimulated through training but only grow during their rest phase. The higher the intensity, the higher the damage of the muscle cell and the longer the resting phase. When you train with adequate intensity you simply cannot train each and every day nor should you attack a muscle twice a week. Learn to accept rest and recovery as important factors of your

training success. Every day you train in the GYM should be followed by a complete off day. Bodybuilders who are interested in an optimal strength and muscle gain should train every muscle once very intensely every 7-8 days.

5. Plateau and phase training: The body can be put under maximum stress only for a limited time. If this time is exceeded, development comes to a stop and if continued the performance will regress. For this reason the intensity and extent of the training program should be changed every 12-14 weeks. The athlete should enjoy several days off training and then change to a several-week long maintenance training (plateau training).

The following training program considers all essential factors which are necessary for a quick buildup of strength and muscle mass. In combination with the nutrition tips included in this book its effectiveness can be considerably increased. Based on the high intensity it is not suitable for natural bodybuilders over a long time. This training schedule is obviously only intended as a suggestion and can be changed by every athlete to meet his individual needs, as long as the discussed principles are met.

Eight-Day Training Cycle:
One day training, one day rest
(One day on, one day off)

Day 1: Chest, biceps

Bench presses	3 sets	6- 8 reps
Incline bench presses	2 sets	6- 8 reps
Dips with added weights	2 sets	8-10 reps
Barbell curls	3 sets	6-10 reps
Dumbbell curls	2 sets	6-10 reps

Day 3: Thighs

Squats	3 sets	6-10 reps
Leg presses	2 sets	8-10 reps
Leg curls	2 sets	8-10 reps

Day 5: Shoulder, triceps

Presses behind neck	3 sets	6- 8 reps
Upright row	2 sets	8-10 reps
Side laterals	2 sets	8-10 reps
Lying triceps presses	3 sets	6-10 reps
Triceps pulley pushdown	2 sets	8-10 reps

Day 7: Back, calves:

Chins with added weight	3 sets	8-10 reps
Lat pull to neck	2 sets	8-10 reps
Barbell bent-over row	2 sets	6-10 reps
Seated cable row	2 sets	6-10 reps
Standing calf raise	3 sets	8-12 reps
Seated calf raise	2 sets	8-12 reps

Note: Training is only on uneven days, i.e. every 2nd, 4th, 6th, and 8th day is a complete rest day. The intervals between the various sets should be 3-4 minutes. The athlete should pay attention that the exercises —as much as possible— are carried out with free weights and not on machines. Every muscle is directly trained only once every eight days. It is important that every set is carried out until muscle failure meaning that the athlete is unable to do another repetition on itÆs own. Only in this case are the relatively few sets and especially long rest periods justified. The muscle cell must be brought in a strongly catabolic condition since only then the distinct anticatabolic effect of anabolic/androgenic steroids develops fully. The required intensity of training, however, can only be achieved when you start (after a short warmup) with the heaviest weight possible and then decrease the weight in every following set because of the losing body strength so that the desired repetitions can still be obtained. In order to avoid any misunderstandings we would like to quickly explain this principle on an example. Our athlete is able to carry out a maximum of six repetitions with 300 pounds on bench presses.

1st warmup set:	10 reps with	140 pounds
2nd warmup set:	2 reps with	200 pounds
3rd warmup set:	2 reps with	240 pounds
1st working set:	6 reps with	300 pounds
2nd working set:	7 reps with	280 pounds
3rd working set:	7 reps with	260 pounds

The first warmup set serves to bring blood to the muscles and joints. The second and third warmup set are an approach to the weight of the first working set. The interplay between the muscle and nerve is stimulated, meaning the athlete gets a feeling for the heavy weights without wasting strength and energy at the same time. During the following chest exercises the warmup sets are completely omitted which means that they are only necessary for the first excercise of the muscle to be trained. Do not forget, however, that during every exercise or set you should try to squeeze out an additional one or two repetitions than during the previous training in order to increase training weights in the following week. This continuous tiresome struggle to increase repetitions and weight is the only way to a massive body. Always remember: HEAVY WEIGHTS BUILD BIG MUSCLES.

THE SIGNIFICANCE OF NUTRITION

An insufficient nutrition is often the reason why the athlete does not make any progress. What is the use of the best training, the intake of steroids, and sufficiently long rest periods if the body does not have the right nutrients in a sufficient amount? Eberhard Schneider in his book Krafttraining für Kung-Fu und Karate said it to the point: "Just as a skycraper cannot be built of loam it is impossible to develop a strong muscle system on a diet of beer and pizza." Intensively training bodybuilders have a distinctly higher need of nutrients which increases even further when simultaneously taking steroids. The right nutrition tremendously increases the effect of every steroid regime because steroids develop their full effect only when adequate calories and nutrients are supplied. A nutrition program suitable for this purpose must meet four basic requirements:

1.) Sufficient intake of high-quality protein: The protein intake is the decisive factor when gaining weight since protein is the building block for the muscle tissue. Of special importance is the combination of the supplied protein. Animal protein is in first place because of its high biological value and a high content of essential amino acids. The protein absorbed by the body through food is broken down into amino acids and transported through the blood to the muscle cell. The goal is to obtain a positive nitrogen balance in the muscle cell which means that it assimilates more protein than it releases. Best sources are meat, fish, poultry, eggs, and milk products. The required daily amount depends on the body weight. A supply of 1-1.5 grams of protein per pound of body weight/day is usually effective. A bodybuilder weighing 200 pounds thus needs 250 g of protein per day. Since one gram of protein has an energy value of 4.1 kcal the athlete consumes 1,000 kcal per day in form of protein.

2.) Sufficient supply of complex carbohydrates: The importance of complex carbohydrates in the nutrition schedule of a bodybuilder cannot be emphasized often enough. They provide a continuous energy supply which is very important to maintain the blood sugar level at a constant level, prevent that protein is transformed into energy, and are an important factor during the burning of fat. Preferred sources are rice, oats, whole wheat bread, noodles, and vegetables. The total daily amount of carbohydrates should be around 800-900 g, which corresponds to an energy value of 4.1 kcal per gram of a daily calorie-intake of 3,200 to 3,600 only for carbohydrates. 85% are best taken in form of complex carbohydrates, the remaining 15% as simply carbohydrates, mostly fruit.

3.) Sufficient supply of calories: Bodybilder who work out daily and eat only 2,000 to 3,000 kcal per day should not wonder when they do not obtain any sizable gains. If you have ever watched a massive bodybuilder taking steroids during his buildup phase you will know that eating a pound of steak, 4 large potatoes, and a bowl of salad together with a protein drink is nothing unusual "To get big, you have to eat big" is a favorite slogan among massive body-builders. Those who are healthy, have a normal metabolism, follow a hard and heavy training schedule, want to build up mass, and take steroids, will usually come closer to their goal when eating approx. 5,000 calories per day.

4.) Eat according to the clock: This point is most often neglected because it requires a high degree of discipline, motivation, and long-range planning.The human being is a "creature of habit" and the body loves regular schedules. It is highly recommended to put together a nutrition plan which fits your daily schedule and to follow through without compromise. Eat several meals a day, possibly 5-6 and always at the same time. No matter whether or not you are hungry, traveling, at work or with friends, at five o clock you should know that it is time for your fifth meal, so EAT. Regular meals in short intervals induce the body to continuously release insulin. This is extremely important since insulin transports amino acids to the muscle cell and the body is in an anabolic state. Irregular meals, skipping a meal, fewer large meals are totally counterproductive.

In the following we give you an example of a daily schedule which meets the abovementioned requirements. This nutrition program is obviously only intended as a guideline and can be changed by athletes in every way to meet his individual needs, as long as the discussed requirements are met.

	P	CH	F	kcal
First meal, 7 am:				
8 oz. oatmeal	25	155	18	880
0.6 l skim milk, 0.3% fat	21	29	2	240
0.2 l orange juice	—	18	—	80
3 oz. grapes	1	17	—	70
	47	**219**	**20**	**1270**

Second meal, 10.30 am:				
10 oz. whole wheat bread	18	120	6	600
4 oz. cheese, 12% fat	22	5	10	200
0.5 l kefir milk	20	20	4	200
1 banana	1	35	—	150
	61	**180**	**20**	**1150**

Third meal, 2.00 pm:				
8 oz. brown rice	22	170	6	850
10 oz. turkey	60	—	5	300
5 oz. vegetables	1	7	—	30
	83	**177**	**11**	**1180**

Fourth meal, 5.30 pm				
5 whole eggs	30	—	30	400
16 oz. baked potatoes	10	100	5	430
Mixed salad	1	10	—	50
	41	**110**	**35**	**880**

Fifth meal, 9.00 pm:				
7 oz. cottage cheese	25	5	4	200
7 oz. whole wheat bread	12	80	4	400
1 oz. peanut butter	6	3	10	120
1 apple, approx. 4 oz.	—	14	—	60
0.2 l orange juice	—	18	—	80
	43	**120**	**18**	**860**
Total:	**27**	**806**	**104**	**5340**

Note: Since meal number two and three are taken at work we recommend that you prepare them the night before, keep them in a cooler, and take them to work.

The effectiveness of this nutrition program and the indicated guidelines are based on two necessary basic requirements: MOTIVATION AND DISCIPLINE. This really shows how strong your desire really is to build strength and muscle mass and how much you are willing to do to achieve this goal. You must simply be convinced that in combination with a consequent, right nutrition optimal and quickest progress can be made. Get enthusiastic about a high-quality and often monotonous nutrition: If the spark and willpower are not there, the program is often carried out for two to three weeks and in the following the athlete goes back to his old comfortable eating habits. Bodybuilders with a clear goal before their eyes, an enormous willpower, a strong psyche, a great deal of enthusiam, and a small tendency to masochism continue this schedule over months and even years. Always keep in mind: Your results are the mirror image of your hard work.

COMMON MISTAKES

If you ask ten athletes how steroids are best used you will get ten different answers. If you ask for a reason such as why or how come you will get replies such as the following: "The other guys in the GYM do it just the same way;" "I have heard that a certain pro is taking the same compound;" "I read in the book that with this one can obtain fantastic results;" and many more can be heard. These statements only reflect what unfortunately is not reality: hardly a athlete knows how steroids should best be used. What shall be taken in what dosage for how long? Is it better when I try this combination or should I rather try another? If I could only know whether my preparations are really originals? Despite the fact that steroids have been used to improve sports performances for more than thirty years most athletes are still uncertain. Thus they can be easily manipulated and influenced. The so-urgently needed information is missing since there are no useful published scientific exams, helpful physicians who are familiar with this subject are few, special magazines conceal the problem, and top athletes deny that they ever used steroids. Consequently, many mistakes are made which, if at all, result in unsatisfying results and the often unnecessary side effects. Although the range of mistakes made is very far-reaching, some stand out since athletes keep repeating them. Everyone taking steroids or considering taking them should read this chapter carefully in order to be sure that he will not be one of the several thousand athletes who keeps making just these mistakes.

1. The use of excessive dosages: Bodybuilders like extremes more than any other athlete. One acts according to the classic incorrect assumption that "more is better." If five tablets work well, then ten

must double the effect. With such an attitude the door is open to potential side effects, and it is not even justified by a clearly improved effect. The effectiveness of almost all steroids is dosage-dependent up to a certain degree and is achieved when the bonding potential of steroid molecules and steroid receptors is exhausted. When the receptors of the muscle cell are saturated the remaining steroid molecules begin looking for another target. Liver dysfunctions, kidney dysfunctions, hair loss, acne, high estrogen levels, reduced production of the body's own hormones, and aggressiveness often have their origin in dosages which are too high. So-called megadoses do not result in a distinctly higher strength and mass gain. Those who believe that 50 Dianabol and 1000 mg testosterone per day is the only way to an "ideal body" have, to put it mildly, the wrong information.

2. Duration of intake is too long: The non-stop use of steroids is not recommended for most athletes for two reasons. First, when high dosages are taken over a long time, the risk of potential side effects increases considerable. The chances of organ damage are especially high when oral 17-alpha alkylated steroids are continuously taken. Second, such a behavior is very dubious since the effect of the administered steroids weakens after a certain time which, with a higher dosage or a different preparation, can only be stopped briefly. Everyone should know that the stronger the steroid the faster its effect decreases so that the use over a long period of time is even more foolish. With Anadrol the gain increase usually is reduced after only 3-4 weeks while with Deca-Durabolin, for example, often continuous progress can be obtained over 10-12 weeks.

3. The use of the wrong steroid preparations: not all steroids are the same. One must make a clear distinction between highly androgenic, potentially-toxic steroids such as Anadrol, Methyltestosterone, Dianabol, Holotestin, etc. and the weaker androgenic, predominantly anabolic and less toxic preparations, such as, B. Primobolan, Deca-Durabolin, Oxandrolone, Andriol, and Winstrol. Since, above all, the first-mentioned drugs are the ones which cause the severe side effects it makes sense to reduce their intake to a maximum of 6-8 weeks. Especially women, young adults, and older athletes should

be very cautious when selecting steroid preparations. It would also be desirable that the general public and the media consider this distinction in their future negative general opinions and articles.

4. The selection of an unfavorable intake schedule: The effectiveness of every steroid program can be considerably increased by a clever combination of steroids since they have a synergetic effect. This means that with a low total dosage one can obtain better results. Since various receptors are attacked it is possible to delay the receptor saturation so that the steroid combination will remain effective over al longer period of time. At the same time potential side effects can be minimized. Instead of, for example, taking 50 mg Dianabol per day, the athlete should take 20 mg Dianabol/day and 200 mg Deca-Durabolin/week. Generally one can say that best results can be obtained by combining an oral with an injectable steroid. The combination of two oral preparations such as Dianabol with Anadrol or Oxandrolone with Methyltestosterone makes less sense. Since the protein-building and nitrogen-retaining effect of most steroids decreases after a few weeks one should begin with a low dosage which is increased slowly and evenly during the intake interval. Athletes whose steroid cycle is longer than 6-8 weeks should usually switch to a completely different combination. Another frequently-made mistake is the sudden interruption of the steroid regime. Many side effects, a possible rebound effect, and strength and weight loss can be minimized if the dosages are decreased slowly and evenly. This also includes that at the end of the intake interval not the highly effective steroids such as Anadrol and testosterone are taken but that the athlete switches to milder preparations and includes these during discontinuance.

5. The use of fakes: To correct this problem is very difficult for most athletes since the black market with its overwhelming preponderance of faked steroids represents the only source of supply. Unsatisfying results, often no positive results at all, and an unusual number of side effects are unfortunately common and caused by the use of fakes. Many faked steroids are impure, do not contain the alleged substances, are often considerably underdosed or contain something completely different as specified on the label.

6. Disinterest in periodical exams by a physician: Every athlete who takes steroids should have a physician periodically check his blood, urine, ph value, liver values, and the blood pressure. As important as the preliminary implementation of these tests is the right timing. It is important that the first exam is carried out before the regime. Thus it can be determined whether the athlete has the physical condition to use steroids or, based on certain factors should avoid certain preparations. This also helps obtain reference and comparison data so that in a later exam possible changes in results can be easily determined. The second exam is recommended 5-6 weeks after the steroid intake. Further administration of steroids should depend on the result of the exams. If the results are acceptable, four weeks after termination of the steroid program another test should be made to check whether or not possible smaller deviations were normalized. Have your physician give you a written copy of your blood results and check the various values together with your physician.

7. Negligence of external factors: The use of steroids alone does not guarantee impressive results. Their effect strongly depends on four individual factors which together have a synergetic effect and are therefore called the magic rectangle: Training, nutrition, rest, and attitude. Especially when steroids are taken many athletes have a tendency to neglect these important requirements.

BIBLIOGRAPHY

American Drug Index - 1994, N.F. Billups, R.PH., M.S., Ph.D., S.M. Billups, R.N., L.P.C., M.Ed.

Anabolic Alternative Handbook, Fahey-Fritz

Anabolic-androgenic Steroids, Ch. Kochakian

Anabolic-androgenic Steroids toward the year 2000, H. Kopera

Anabolic Reference Guide (5th Issue) 1990, W.N. Phillips

Anabolic Reference Guide (6th Issue) 1991, W.N. Phillips

Anabolic Reference Update no. 1-27, W.N. Phillips

Anabolic Steroids, Datafax, Christina Dye

Anabolic Steroids-A Review of Current Literature & Research, Do It Now Foundation

Anabolic Steroids: A review of the literature, MD. H.A. Haupt, MD. G.D. Rovere

Anabolic Steroids: Altered States, Wright

Anabolic Steroids: What Kind and How Many, Dr. Frederick C. Hatfield

Anabolic Steroids and Athletic Performance, D.R. Lamb

Anabolic Steroids and Bodybuilding, L&S Research, Scott Chinery

Anabolic Steroids and the Athlete, Dr. William N. Taylor

Anabolic Steroids and Sports, Vol. 1, 2, Wright

Anabolic Steroids in Sport and Exercise, Charles E. Yesalis

Anabolic Steroid Side Effects: Facts, Fiction and Treatment, Dr. Mauro G. Di Pasquale

Anabolic Steroid News, Vol. 1 - 28, Belle International

Anabolic, Training and Nutrition Handguide, C. Whitford

Anabolika im Leistungssport, Leistungssport Vol. 7, 1977, A. Mader

Anabolika und muskuläre Systeme, H.J. Appel

Anabolika und Sportschäden an Sehnen, H. Michna

Androgene / Anabolika in Klinik und Praxis, H.K. Kley, R. Schlaghecke

Androgenic Disorders, Geoffrey P. Redmond

Arzneimittelgesetz 1995, Dr. Hermann Josef Pabel

Arzneimittelspezialitätenkunde 1991, 92, 93, 94, Dr. Rolf Bausch

'Ask the Guru', Daniel Duchaine

Beyond Anabolic Steroids, Dr. Mauro G. Di Pasquale

Bodybuilding, Eiweiß - Anabolika, Andeas Bredenkamp

Clenbuterol, Leistungssport 9/1993

Clenbuterol: Ein Anabolikum?, PZ, No 33, 1992

Clenbuterol-Das Mittel der Zukunft, Manfred Bachmann

Death in the Lockerroom Vol.1, Dr. Bob Goldman
Death in the Lockerroom Vol.2, Dr. Bob Goldman
Delta Index, Delta Liste – Das Wirkstoffverzeichnis der Tierarzneimittel,
Delta medizinische Verlagsgesellschaft mbh.
Deutsche Zeitschrift für Sportmedizin, Sonderheft 1988,
Deutscher Ärzte – Verlag GmbH
Die Hormontherapie, Prof. Dr. Dr. med. Johannes Huber
Doping, Doping und kein Ende, Klaus Huhn
Doping im Leistungssport, Karl H. Bette
Doping im Sport, Heinz Lünsch
Doping is cheating, International Amateur Athletic Federation 1994
Doping – verbotene Arzneimittel im Sport, Dirk Clasing,
Manfred Donike u.a.
Dopingkontrollen, M. Donike, S. Rauth
Doping: Von der Forschung zum Betrug, Brigitte Berendonk
Drogen im Bodybuilding, Dr. J. Gothelf, Mark Davis
Drogen im Sport, Sehling, Pollert, Hackfort
Drug Facts and Comparisons, JB Lippincott Co.
Drug Testing... So What! How to Beat the Test, Anthony Fitton
Drug Use and Detection in Amateur Sports, Updates 1-5, Dr. Mauro
G. Di Pasquale
Drugs in Sports – Newsletter Vol. 1-9, Pasquale
Einfluß von Anabolika und Training auf Körper und Organgewichte,
R. Aigner
Erhöht Tamoxifen das Risiko für ein Endometriumkarzinom?,
DAZ 12/95, Dr. P. Jungmayr
European Drug Index – Third Edition 1994, N.F. Müller, R.P. Dessing
External Symptoms from the use of Anabolic Steroids, IFBB Special
Report
Fortschritte in der Wachstumshormontherapie 1993, Prof. Dr. med.
M.B. Ranke
Genentech 1993 Annual Report, Genentech Inc. USA
Hormone Manipulation, William N. Taylor, M.D.
Hormonelle Regulation und psychophysische Belastung im Leistungssport,
R. Häcker, H.De Marees
Hypothyroidism and your health, Boots Pharmaceuticals Inc.
Hypothyroidism in women, Boots Pharmaceuticals Inc.
Ich bin clean, Deutscher Leichtathletik – Verband
Index Nominum – International Drug Directory 92/93, Swiss
Pharmaceutical Society

In Quest of Size - Anabolics and other ergogenic aids, L&S Research,
S. Chinery
Leistungsfähigkeit und Schädigungsmöglichkeit bei Einnahme
von Anabolika, J. Keul, W. Kindermann
Lexikon der Tierarzneimittel, Delta medizinische Verlagsgesell-
schaft mbH.
Mechanismen und Grenzen des Muskelwachstums, H.-J. Appel
Medical, Pharmaceutical & Surgical Supply Catalog, Henry Schein Inc.
Muscle Media 2 000 No. 28-43, Bill Phillips
Muskeln durch Drogen?, Vitamine - Anabolika, Dr. D. Zittlau, J. Strzeletz
Optimum Sports Nutrition - Your Competitive Edge, Dr. Michael Colgan
Palliative Therapie des Prostatakarzinoms, H.W. Bauer, J.E. Altwein
Pharmakologie der Hormone 4., M. Tausk, J.H.H. Thijssen,
T.B. van W. Greidanus
Pharmakologische Beeinflussung der Fertilität beim Mann, DAZ 2/95,
H. Neye
Rekorde durch Doping? Melvin H. Williams
Rote Liste 1993, 1994, 1995, Bundesverband der Pharmazeutischen
Industrie e.V.
Somatropin-Mangel immer ausgleichen, Christine Vetter, PZ,
No. 23, 1995
Spektrum androgene und anabole Steroide, H.Schmidt
Spiropent-Fachinformation 1991, Dr. Karl Thomae GmbH
Sterbliche Maschinen, J. Hobermann
Steroidhormone. Biosynthese, Stoffwechsel, Wirkung, L.Träger
Steroids 1993 - The Laymans Guide, Mick Hart
Steroids - The Facts, Zef Eisenberg
Steroid Myths: The responsible use of anabolic Steroids, Phil J. Embleton,
Gerard J. Thorne
Steroid Protection: The Facts, Cambridge Ergogenic Institute
Substitution aus biochemischer Sicht, Leistungssport 2/95, M. Donike
Tamoxifen und Blutlipide, W. Kämmerer, PZ, No 44, 1992
Testosteron - der Männlichkeitsfaktor, Robert Bahr
The Battle Against Steroids Goes on, International Federation of
Bodybuilders, I.F.B.B.
The Hardgainer, Vol. 1-33, Stuart McRobert
The History of Synthetic Testosterone, Scientific American,
J.M. Hoberman, C.E. Yesalis
The Practical Use of Anabolic Steroids With Athletes, Dr. Robert Kerr
The Secret of Clenbuterol, W.N. Phillips

The Steroid Bible, Vol. 1,2,3, Steve Gallaway
The Steroid Supermen, Jeff Everson
Ultimate Dieting Handbook, Daniel Duchaine
Ultimate Muscle Mass, Daniel Duchaine
Underground Steroid Handbook, Daniel Duchaine
Underground Steroid Handbook, Updates 1-10, Daniel Duchaine
Underground Steroid Handbook 2, Daniel Duchaine
Underground Steroid Handbook Update 1992, Daniel Duchaine
Untersuchung zum Nachweis von Testosteron, J. Zimmermann
Ultimate Steroid Manual, Cambridge Ergogenic Institute
Wirkungen und Risiken bei der Anwendung von Anabolika,
Pharmazeutsiche Zeitung Nr. 3, 139. Jahrgang, 1994,
Friedmund Neumann
Zum Gebrauch von Dopingmitteln, B. Askevild
Zur Frage des Dopings, Wolfgang Wolf
Zur Problematik, der Anwendung sexualhormonwirksamer Anabolika beim landwirtschaftlichen Nutztier, B. Hoffmann, P. Evers, LR. Höveler
Zur Wirkung von Testosteron und Training auf Funktionsstrukturen des vegetativen Nervensystems, Georg Hartmann

This book offers the following:

— Extensive and comprehensive information on more than 100 various steroids that athletes use today.

— The most complete summary ever published on originals and fakes. More than 520 photos that help you recognize dangerous black market preparations.

— The truth about the effect of anabolic steroids; why almost everyone uses them incorrectly; and what role steroids play in the development of top athletes.

— Everything about possible side effects, growth hormones, the importance of nutrition and a sensible training program.